Perspectives in Law, Business and Innovation

Series Editor

Toshiyuki Kono, Faculty of Law, Kyushu University, Fukuoka, Japan

Over the last three decades, interconnected processes of globalization and rapid technological change—particularly, the emergence of networked technologies—have profoundly disrupted traditional models of business organization. This economic transformation has created multiple new opportunities for the emergence of alternate business forms, and disruptive innovation has become one of the major driving forces in the contemporary economy. Moreover, in the context of globalization, the innovation space increasingly takes on a global character. The main stakeholders—innovators, entrepreneurs and investors—now have an unprecedented degree of mobility in pursuing economic opportunities wherever they arise. As such, frictionless movement of goods, workers, services, and capital is becoming the "new normal".

This new economic and social reality has created multiple regulatory challenges for policymakers as they struggle to come to terms with the rapid pace of these social and economic changes. Moreover, these challenges impact across multiple fields of both public and private law. Nevertheless, existing approaches within legal science often struggle to deal with innovation and its effects.

Paralleling this shift in the economy, we can, therefore, see a similar process of disruption occurring within contemporary academia, as traditional approaches and disciplinary boundaries—both within and between disciplines—are being re-configured. Conventional notions of legal science are becoming increasingly obsolete or, at least, there is a need to develop alternative perspectives on the various regulatory challenges that are currently being created by the new innovation-driven global economy.

The aim of this series is to provide a forum for the publication of cutting-edge research in the fields of innovation and the law from a Japanese and Asian perspective. The series will cut across the traditional sub-disciplines of legal studies but will be tied together by a focus on contemporary developments in an innovation-driven economy and will deepen our understanding of the various regulatory responses to these economic and social changes.

The series editor and editorial board carefully assess each book proposal and sample chapters in terms of their relevance to law, business, and innovative technological change. Each proposal is evaluated on the basis of its academic value and distinctive contribution to the fast-moving debate in these fields.

All books and chapters in the Perspectives in Law, Business and Innovation book series are indexed in Scopus.

More information about this series at http://www.springer.com/series/15440

Mark Fenwick · Steven Van Uytsel ·
Bi Ying
Editors

Regulating FinTech in Asia

Global Context, Local Perspectives

Springer

Editors
Mark Fenwick
Graduate School of Law
Kyushu University
Fukuoka, Japan

Steven Van Uytsel
Graduate School of Law
Kyushu University
Fukuoka, Japan

Bi Ying
Zhejiang University
Hangzhou City, China

ISSN 2520-1875 ISSN 2520-1883 (electronic)
Perspectives in Law, Business and Innovation
ISBN 978-981-15-5818-4 ISBN 978-981-15-5819-1 (eBook)
https://doi.org/10.1007/978-981-15-5819-1

This Springer imprint is published by the registered company Springer Nature Singapore Pte Ltd.
The registered company address is: 152 Beach Road, #21-01/04 Gateway East, Singapore 189721, Singapore

Preface

This edited collection aims to bring together scholars working in fintech regulation in an Asian context. Our aim in developing this collection was to connect local developments—specifically regulatory developments in Asia, broadly defined—with broader economic and technological trends.

This volume is based on ideas explored at a symposium, 'Regulating Fintech in Asia: Global Contexts, Local Perspectives,' held in Kyushu University, Fukuoka, Japan, on 3 December 2018.

Steven Van Uytsel would like to thank Kyushu University's 'Progress 100: Research Hub for the Humanities, Social Sciences, and Interdisciplinary Knowledge' (RINK). The grant for the project 'Regulating Algorithms: Multi-Disciplinary Perspectives on New Technology & the Law' helped in supporting the symposium.

The editors also owe a word of gratitude to Mrs. Y. Matsumura, whose help was instrumental in organizing the symposium.

Fukuoka, Japan — Mark Fenwick
Fukuoka, Japan — Steven Van Uytsel
Zheijinga, China — Bi Ying

Contents

Editors and Contributors

About the Editors

Mark Fenwick is Professor of International Business Law at the Faculty of Law, Kyushu University, Fukuoka, Japan. His primary research interests are in the field of transnational business regulation in a digital age. Recent publications include New Technology, Big Data and the Law (Springer, 2017), The Shifting Meaning of Legal Certainty in Comparative and Transnational Law (Hart, 2017) and International Business Law: Emerging Fields of Regulation (Hart, 2018). He has a master's degree and a Ph.D. from the Faculty of Law, University of Cambridge. He has been a visiting professor at Chulalongkorn University, Duke University, the University of Hong Kong, Shanghai University of Finance and Economics, the National University of Singapore, Tilburg University and Vietnam National University and has conducted research for the EU, OECD and World Bank.

Steven Van Uytsel is Associate Professor in the Faculty of Law at Kyushu University, Fukuoka, Japan. He received his legal education at the University of Antwerp. During his studies at the University of Antwerp, he spent half a year at Uppsala University in the framework of the European ERASMUS Exchange program. He then went on to complete his LL.M. & LL.D. at Kyushu University and his Master of Arts (Japanese Studies) at the Mercator Hogeschool. Steven specializes in competition law, with a particular interest in enforcement issues, price fixing and competition law in Asia. Steven has received various grants from the Japanese Society for the Promotion of Science for research on competition law issues, including leniency programs and algorithmic collusion. Kyushu University has awarded Steven with grants to do research on algorithms (Progress 100–RINK Grant) and the law and autonomous vehicles (Tsubasa Grant). His most recent book on competition law is Research Handbook on Asian Competition Law (Edward Elgar, 2020).

Bi Ying is an Associate Professor of law at Zhejiang University in Hangzhou, China. She holds an LL.B. and LL.M. from Tsinghua University in Beijing, China, and LL.D. from Kyushu University in Japan. She previously worked for the Japanese law firm Soga Uryu & Itoga in Tokyo and researched at Waseda University, Japan as a visiting scholar. Her major research interest covers trade and competition, regional economic integration, Belt and Road Initiative and global governance on SOEs.

Contributors

Christopher Chen School of Law, Singapore Management University, Singapore, Singapore

David C. Donald Faculty of Law, The Chinese University of Hong Kong, Shatin, Hong Kong

Mark Fenwick Faculty of Law, Kyushu University, Fukuoka, Japan

Pawee Jenweeranon Faculty of Law, Thammasat University, Bangkok, Thailand

Sunseop Jung School of Law, Seoul National University, Seoul, Gwanak-Gu, Korea

Fan Liao Institute of International Law, CASS, Beijing, China

Hai Yen Nguyen Hanoi Law University, Hanoi, Vietnam

Akira Tokutsu Department of Law, Tohoku University, Sendai, Japan

Steven Van Uytsel Faculty of Law, Kyushu University, Fukuoka, Japan

Erik P. M. Vermeulen Tilburg Law School, Tilburg, The Netherlands;
Senior Legal Counsel Corporate Structure, Signify (formerly known as Philips Lighting), Eindhoven, The Netherlands

Ren Yatsunami Faculty of Law, Kyushu University, Fukuoka, Japan

Bi Ying Zhejiang University, Guanghua Law School, Hangzhou, People's Republic of China

Regulating Fintech in Asia: An Introduction

Mark Fenwick, Steven Van Uytsel, and Bi Ying

Abstract In the context of a fast-developing, technology-driven economy, policy-makers increasingly regard regulation as an essential element in gaining a competitive edge and establishing themselves as a regional hub for technology-focused businesses. In the context, of fintech, for example, a number of Asian jurisdictions have recently introduced regulatory reforms that aim at filling gaps in existing legislation or resolving uncertainties. Such legal reforms are motivated by the desire to encourage the development of fintech, while also ensuring that vital public interests are adequately protected. This book is a preliminary attempt to map some of these legal developments in an Asian context via a series of case studies focused on key jurisdictions. Here, by way of introduction to the substantive chapters that follow, we briefly review the disruption of incumbents and the new opportunities that have been triggered by the emergence of fintech and summarize the chapters and regulatory reforms that different jurisdictions have introduced. Common themes across all chapters are a recognition of the importance of fintech in the future development of financial services and the importance of more flexible regulatory forms that provide the freedom for all stakeholders to bring new financial technologies to the market.

Keywords Banking law · Crypto-assets · Fintech · Payments · Regulatory sandbox

Over the last decade, 'fintech'—broadly understood as the use of new information technologies to compete in the marketplace of financial institutions and intermediaries—has disrupted the financial services sector. And like other 21st century technological developments such as artificial intelligence, fintech is a global event that

M. Fenwick (✉) · S. Van Uytsel (✉)
Faculty of Law, Kyushu University, Motooka, Nishi-Ku, Fukuoka, Fukuoka, Japan
e-mail: mdf0911@gmail.com

S. Van Uytsel
e-mail: uytsel@law.kyushu-u.ac.jp

B. Ying
Zhejiang University, Guanghua Law School, Hangzhou, People's Republic of China
e-mail: biying@zju.edu.cn

M. Fenwick et al. (eds.), *Regulating FinTech in Asia*, Perspectives in Law, Business and Innovation, https://doi.org/10.1007/978-981-15-5819-1_1

plays out in local economic, political, and legal contexts. This dynamic interplay between global trends and local circumstances has created a complex and rapidly evolving landscape.

Diverse stakeholders in the fintech ecosystem (most obviously incumbent financial service providers and tech start-ups) all pursue a competitive edge against a background of profound uncertainty about the future direction and uncertain effects of multiple emerging technologies. Compounding these business and economic difficulties are uncertainties surrounding the regulatory environment. Most obviously, there is uncertainty regarding the degree to which existing regulatory frameworks can accommodate new products and services, or whether new actors can gain the necessary 'license to operate.'

Policymakers and regulators also struggle to identify an appropriate regulatory response. On the one hand, they see enormous opportunities in fintech and regard regulation as an essential element in gaining a competitive edge and establishing themselves as a regional hub for innovative financial services. On the other hand, there are inevitable concerns about protecting individuals and the economy, more generally.

The result? Enormous challenges and uncertainties for *all* the different actors in the fintech space—both private actors looking to develop and deliver new products and services, and the public actors responsible for regulating them and guaranteeing the public interest.

A number of Asian jurisdictions have recently introduced regulatory reforms that respond to this challenge by looking to fill gaps in existing legislative regimes. Such legal changes are motivated by the desire to encourage the development of fintech while ensuring that public interests are also protected. This book aims to offer a preliminary attempt to map these developments in an Asian context via a series of case studies outlining these developments on a country-specific basis. Here, by way of an introduction to the substantive chapters that follow, we first review the disruption of incumbents and the new opportunities that have been triggered by the emergence of fintech and then briefly summarize the chapters and the regulatory reforms that are discussed.

1 Global Trends

Broadly speaking, fintech has disrupted existing financial service providers in at least three different ways.[1] First, emerging technologies have facilitated incumbent financial service providers in providing a range of new and innovative services that remove intermediaries and make transactions more efficient and less susceptible to inaccuracy.[2] In this way, financial services are made more 'decentralized' and 'flatter.' The most obvious example here, for instance, is the growth of mobile banking, i.e.,

---

[1]Chishti and Barberis (2016), King (2018), McMillan (2014), Sironi (2016).

[2]On 'disintermediation,' see Haycock and Richmond (2015).

banking that allows customers to perform different transactions online.[3] Networked access to financial services facilitates better access to all manner of transactions from an examination of one's financial status, making payments, to withdrawing or transferring funds.

The 'back office' activities of financial institutions are similarly disrupted. In part, this disruption involves the use of Big Data to deliver more efficient services. Still, such data also allows firms to use technology to manage legal risk more effectively than previously.[4] The fallout from the 2008 financial crisis, for example, resulted in a lot of new banking regulations that incumbents had to navigate.[5] One consequence of this has been the use of technology to help banks comply with increasingly complex regulatory requirements and associated legal risk.[6]

Second, fintech has facilitated the emergence of start-ups and other 'non-financial' companies that offer an alternative source of financial services. In particular, 'app-based' companies are emerging all over the world.[7] These start-ups challenge and disrupt incumbents, such as traditional banks, by supporting a wide range of financial services, including marketplace lending platforms, equity crowdfunding platforms, insurance services, algorithm-driven 'Robo-advisors' offering smarter, more personalized financial advice, and blockchain-based crypto-currency and payment systems.[8] Crypto-assets have been particularly widespread in an Asian context, for example.

Large technology companies are similarly moving into the financial services sector. Tech companies (Chinese tech companies, in particular, provide a good illustration of this trend) show how quickly these large businesses can leverage their economic power and expand into new areas.[9] Think of ridesharing companies that become fintech companies that become insurance companies that become healthcare companies (Uber). Similar moves into financial services have been made by Amazon, Apple, Facebook, Google, Microsoft, Samsung, and Tencent, to give some high profile (and prominent) examples.[10]

The life cycle of companies is becoming shorter, and companies are under greater business pressure to move into new sectors of the economy. In this context, the challenge for incumbent banks posed by the digital transformation is particularly pressing. Whereas industries were relatively closed in the 20th century—they were dominated by large corporate-style organizations—digital technologies have made market-entry and expansion into new sectors much less costly. The fact that banks are disrupted by 'Techfin' (companies that started in a different industry, but (often

[3]See Krishnan (2014).

[4]On recent developments in Big Data in banking, see Fernandez Naveira et al. (2018).

[5]See International Bar Association (2010), Sironi (2018), p. 103.

[6]See Arner et al. (2017), Enriques (2017), Zetzsche et al. (2019), p. 35.

[7]For an overview of such apps, see Pratskevich (2019).

[8]See Sironi (2016).

[9]For example, on Alibaba's move into financial services, see Weihuan et al. (2015).

[10]See Parker et al. (2016), Moazed and Johnson (2016).

accidentally) expanded to the financial sector) is one example of the fast-changing economic context that incumbent service providers now face.[11]

Finally, fintech leverages technology to improve the quality of and access to financial services for individuals or social groups that have traditionally been excluded from such opportunities, particularly in emerging economies.[12]

Driving this change is the global proliferation of smartphones. Smartphone penetration is expanding rapidly all over the world, with approximately 6.1 billion smartphones in use in 2020.[13] Several start-ups are already leveraging this new reach and providing access to credit in markets in Africa, South America, and South-East Asia. The range of such services is expanding. Example use cases include providing an easier way to maintain land rights data, which can then serve as collateral for accessing credit or verifying identities. This is often a challenging requirement for individuals looking to access financial and non-financial services.[14]

The emergence of large successful platforms offering multiple functions, including financial services in Indonesia (GoJek), illustrates the possibilities in terms of financial inclusion. The rise (and success) of such firms shows how economies might employ digital technologies as a means of 'leapfrogging' an earlier (industrial) phase of economic development and 'jump' directly into the digital age. At least, that is what many national governments, as well as regional and international organizations, now seem to believe. They are acting accordingly to promote and implement such a strategy.[15]

The takeaway of these trends? Despite the multiple uncertainties and risks, diverse actors—incumbent financial service providers, policymakers, and entrepreneurs—have recognized the potential opportunities and benefits of fintech. This claim is borne out by the investment data. Since 2010, more and more investments have been made in the fintech sector. Moreover, even though there is some evidence that activity has slowed somewhat recently, there is little reason to believe that the growth of fintech is likely to falter or collapse in the short- to medium-term.[16]

Nevertheless, significant uncertainties remain. Since the 2008 financial crisis, banks have found themselves confronted with an unprecedented combination of new business pressures. These include (1) developing more customer-friendly services to attract more customers and maintain relationships with existing customers in order to retain them in the face of more competition; (2) rethinking distribution models and internal organization; (3) responding to disruptive competition from new entrants to the market (both start-ups but also corporations from other sectors, most obviously the technology sector, as mentioned above); and (4) rebuilding trust

[11]On the emergence of Techfin and its regulatory implications, see Zetzsche et al. (2017).

[12]See Blakstad (2018), Buckley and Webster (2016), Realini and Mehta (2015).

[13]IHS Markit (2020).

[14]For some real-world applications and case studies, see Green Invest (2017).

[15]The World Bank, for example, organised a Disrupting Development event on this theme in Bali in October 2018. See World Bank Live (2018). See Mohieldin (2018).

[16]On decline in Fintech investments in Q1 and Q2 2019, see Accenture (2019).

with all stakeholders, especially customers, after the reputational hit financial service providers undoubtedly took for their perceived role in causing the 2008 crisis.[17]

The crucial point here is that all of these challenges require engagement with disruptive new technologies, either directly or indirectly. Technology both facilitates the delivery of better performance and is a crucial infrastructure for managing costs and risks in the provision of financial services.

In this volume, however, we are mainly concerned with a different category of uncertainty, namely the legal risks created when disruptive innovation ‘meets’ a complex regulatory environment. Post-2008, there has been a significant expansion in regulatory requirements, and navigating this new environment has created high compliance costs. Moreover, the emergence of new technologies reveals significant gaps in existing legislation. This combination of a regulatory ‘thicket’ and legislative ‘gaps’ is particularly acute in the context of fintech, and it has driven the need for regulatory action that we aim to describe in the various case-studies collected here.

2 Local Contexts

After the UK launched the first regulatory sandbox regime in 2016, the approach was quickly transplanted to numerous other countries as a means of promoting innovation, improving competition, and enhancing financial inclusion. However, it remains unclear whether the approach can effectively achieve the relevant policy goals and thus justify the differential regulatory treatment that defines a sandbox. Christopher Chen provides an introduction to the regulatory sandbox regime adopted in Singapore and examines its potential benefits and problems. The chapter provides some empirical evidence analyzing the sandboxes awarded in the UK and Singapore between 2016 and 2018 to identify what kind of business model the businesses awarded the sandboxes are doing, the services they provide, and their current regulatory status. The evidence provides a basis on which to assess the effectiveness of the regulatory sandbox approach and provide useful feedback for regulators on the effectiveness of such a scheme.

David C. Donald examines the rise of fintech in Hong Kong, its regulation, and the particular challenges these present for an international financial center, specifically a commercial center with limited economic breadth. Fintech offers automation opportunities for financial institutions, and such automation will, in most cases, make banks more competitive and lower their labor costs. The Hong Kong government has actively embraced fintech to ensure competitiveness, and its regulation tracks leading international positions on ICOs, cryptocurrency, and electronic payment.

However, Hong Kong regulators have not facilitated fintech activities that would stimulate the local economy, such as equity crowdfunding. Automation will generally translate into a reduction of human labor, particularly in mid-level jobs. In a vast and varied economy, persons laid off from jobs at banks can seek engagement elsewhere.

[17] For an overview, see PwC (2014), p. 3.

This is not necessarily true in a financial center with a less diversified economy. Hong Kong presents the highly unusual case of persons in a small IFC who have access to a large and diverse economy in mainland China yet may refuse to seek new positions in the broader workplace for cultural or political reasons. The chapter argues that the Hong Kong government has followed a 'market leads, government facilitates' philosophy of laissez-faire for decades and thus also has failed to prepare for the social costs of fintech. While such preparation would indeed constitute social planning, an activity generally discouraged in Hong Kong, circumstances dictate that the HKSAR government begin to act socially, rather than merely facilitate the largest businesses.

Sunseop Jung explores developments in Korea. After reviewing the financial regulatory system and market structure in Korea, this chapter examines the recent growth of fintech in the area of banking, capital markets, and payment services. In the banking sector, the main focus is on the development of internet-only banking. Under the strict regulations on the separation of financial capital and industrial capital, technological companies' entry into the banking business causes serious banking law debates. In capital markets, the application of the fintech model in capital markets such as equity and debt-based crowdfunding and 'robo-advisors' are discussed. Easy payment & remittance and crypto-assets emerged as a concern for both legal practitioners and the business sector. The legal character and function of crypto-assets is also a significant issue in Korea. Institutional efforts to introduce new financial products and services in accordance with the combination of technology and finance have been developed in various fields such as banking and securities. Particularly noteworthy is the introduction of new means of payment. The regulatory sandbox, newly introduced by Korea, aims to have a potentially significant impact on the Korean financial regulatory system, which has traditionally been very conservative.

The contribution of Fan Liao focuses on the suitability of the sandbox to China. A regulatory sandbox is generally understood as a safe space in which businesses can test innovative products, services, business models and delivery mechanisms without immediately incurring all the normal regulatory consequences of engaging in the activity in question. The fundamental purpose of the regulatory sandbox is to facilitate the development of fintech, especially the 'disruptive innovation' activities of the start-up enterprises. In nature, the regulatory sandbox is conditional, limited, and controlled deregulation. From this perspective, it can be seen as a reaction to the somehow overly burdensome regulatory requirements post-2008 and aims to create a 'lifeline' for financial innovation and, in particular, fintech.

In contrast, the chapter suggests that the situation is somewhat different in China, where the major problem for the most important manifestation of fintech, namely internet finance, is not over-regulation but under-regulation. With a vast territory, diversified areas, and numerous institutions, China does not have a highly developed or highly concentrated financial market like that of the UK, Singapore, or Hong Kong. The chapter argues that although the regulatory sandbox is a remarkable policy innovation, with its specific background, exterior conditions, and intrinsic limitations, it is by no means an inevitable choice or universal model for the regulation of fintech. Based on the actual circumstances, the chapter argues that a sandbox is not appropriate for China, at least for the time being.

In recent years, Thai policymakers have adopted laws aimed at keeping pace with technological developments, and this provides the context for the developments described by Pawee Jenweeranon. This can be seen from several legislative measures regulating innovative products and services that cannot be effectively dealt with under existing laws and regulations, including those related to financial services. More specifically, the so-called Thailand 4.0 project has been presented by the government as a policy to transform Thailand into a more innovation- or technology-driven economy.

Following the policy, there is a plan to develop a technology cluster and future industries which are related to digital, Internet of Things, artificial intelligence, and embedded technology. The aim is to use digital tools and the IoT as a platform to enhance productivity, quality, and innovation across multiple sectors of the economy. This can be considered an essential step in Thailand in responding to the rapid development of innovation and technology in various areas. This chapter reviews these efforts, with a particular emphasis on fintech, as well as considering supplemental initiatives that might be useful to develop further the fintech ecosystem in Thailand. Finally, the chapter describes government efforts to intervene to strengthen industry associations as an example of developing 'soft law' mechanisms.

Yen Hai Nguyen focuses on Vietnam. The chapter argues that Vietnam has been considered as a potential market for fintech because of its young and 'tech-savvy' population, high mobile phone and internet penetration rates, and relatively low financial inclusion rates. Although the fintech market in Vietnam is still at a fledgling stage, more than 150-plus companies have joined with increasing transaction volumes and high growth rates. As such, they have provided customers with financial and banking services such as digital payment, crowdfunding, peer-to-peer lending, remittance, blockchain, personal finance management, and information comparison with modern technologies, lower costs, and more straightforward procedures. Also, the government has been making efforts to spur the development of fintech companies by setting up a fintech steering committee, preparing a national financial inclusion strategy, and cautiously seeking to identify the best approach to regulating fintech. This chapter examines the potential of fintech to facilitate socio-economic development in Vietnam. It considers what kind of regulatory framework for fintech might provide the best mechanism to achieve such a goal.

Akira Tokutsu describes the situation in Japan. Fintech became a 'buzzword' in Japan in 2015. The fintech business model in Japan is similar to other countries, involving crowdfunding, cryptocurrency, blockchain, AI, Big Data, and cashless payments. The chapter suggests that although fintech seems to require a change in the financial regulation framework, there is not a need for wholesale reform and that a focused adjustment may be preferable to more radical change. In Japan, traditional financial regulation has adopted a piecemeal or 'trident' approach, with a separate legislative framework for banking, insurance, and securities. This framework is not unreasonable because it is designed to respond to different risks. Of course, some other new financial businesses appeared before fintech, and regulation responded to the new risk.

From this perspective, fintech is not an entirely new business model but rather involves the 'unbundling' of current financial businesses. In particular, payments have become more independent from banking, as a result of the rise of fintech. Therefore, regulation for payment is necessary. Currently, the Japanese Financial Services Agency is planning to create a new category of regulation for such payments. It seems fintech requires the change of the framework of financial law. But both in practice and in theory, a pure payment service has attracted attention before fintech. Therefore, fintech, as with other technological innovations, does not always require a complete change of regulation but a clarification of specific fields of current law.

Ren Yatsunami also discusses the Japanese situation focusing on how transactions on virtual currencies were introduced when revisions to the Payment Service Act and changes to the Act on Prevention of Transfer of Criminal Proceeds came into effect in April 2017. As a result of recent hacking incidents and social problems on crypto-assets, the Financial Services Agency in Japan established a 'Research Group on Virtual Currency Exchange Business, etc.' in March 2018, to review how the law was operating. Legislative efforts mainly based on the report by the Research Group resulted in the revisions of the Payment Services Act, etc. On March 15, 2019, the 'Bill to Revise the Payment Services Act, etc. in Response to Diversification of Financial Transactions Associated with the Development of Information Communication Technology' was approved at a Cabinet meeting. On the same day, a bill was submitted to the Diet by the Financial Services Agency. Through the proceedings of the Diet, the Act to revise the Payment Services Act, etc. was enacted on May 31, 2019, and promulgated on June 7, 2019. As a result of this legislation, which entered into force in 2020, revisions to the Payment Services Act, changes to the Financial Instruments and Exchange Act, and amendments to the Act on Sales, etc. of Financial Instruments, significant efforts have been made to develop regulation for crypto-asset transactions.

Steven Van Uytsel's contribution goes beyond a specific country and focuses on investments in the fintech sector in Asia. Starting from the observation that 'ridesharing' firms, such as Grab and Go-Jek, are driving the turn to fintech in Asia, Van Uytsel illustrates that the funding for the shift to fintech services is drawn from institutional investors. These institutional investors do not hesitate to finance competitors. These competitors could be both other fintech orienting ridesharing firms or firms that find their origin in the fintech sector, the so-called fintech firms *pur sang*. This evolution towards support from institutional investors is characterizing more and more sectors in the economy. It is, therefore, unsurprising that several competition law scholars started to pay attention to this evolution, which is often referred to as horizontal shareholding. However, scholars have not yet reached an agreement on this trend. There is uncertainty on whether anticompetitive effects are generated by horizontal shareholding and on which competition law provisions should be applied if there are anticompetitive effects. Despite the uncertainty, there is a call to research what could go wrong if this horizontal shareholding continuously advances. Van

Uytsel argues that, for the fintech sector in Asia, vigilance is needed for market division. Such an effect may be triggered when moves the fintech sector moves towards more concentration, for example, through a merger. If a merger would manifest itself, horizontal shareholding should be taken seriously by the Asian enforcement authorities.

Mark Fenwick and Erik P. M. Vermeulen don't offer a country-specific account but instead explore the thought that the historical significance of fintech derives from the leveraging of the unique properties of digital technologies by non-traditional actors to offer consumers a better—and different—user experience of banking and other financial services. The chapter identifies a 'friction-free' user experience as the core feature driving many recent developments in a fintech context, in Asia and elsewhere. It explores the implications for incumbent financial institutions and regulators of such an account.

From the perspective of incumbents, any re-design of the consumer experience requires banks and other financial institutions to organize-for-innovation. There needs to be a shift in mindset to meet the new challenge of digital technologies. Two effective strategies to achieve this goal are outlined. Firstly, adopting more decentralized forms of organization and governance—what they refer to as 'decentralized ecosystems.' A defining feature of such ecosystems is that engagement with consumers is given much higher priority. Secondly, adopting a more strategic approach to venturing, i.e., purchasing start-ups from the fintech sector and integrating their innovations into incumbent operations.

From a regulatory perspective, this requires a greater willingness on the part of regulators and other policymakers to foster responsible experimentation in financial services. As such, the goal of regulation needs to shift away from a traditional focus on managing systemic risk and consumer protection. Instead, we need more dynamic, multi-dimensional models that seek to facilitate responsible innovation by working together with incumbents and start-ups in the decentralized financial service ecosystems of the future. The regulatory sandboxes and legal reforms described in the country-specific case studies suggest that there was an awareness of this need for regulatory innovation. The chapter concludes by asking whether policymakers, in Asia or elsewhere, have gone far enough and whether the full benefits of the fintech revolution have been realized.

References

Accenture (2019) Global fintech fundraising fell in first half of 2019, with decline in China offsetting gains in the US and Europe (Accenture Analysis Finds). https://newsroom.accenture.com/news/global-fintech-fundraising-fell-in-first-half-of-2019-with-decline-in-china-offsetting-gains-in-the-us-and-europe-accenture-analysis-finds.htm. Accessed 31 March 2020

Arner DW et al. (2017) Fintech and regtech: enabling innovation while preserving financial stability. Georgetown J Int Affairs 18(3): 47–58

Blakstad S (2018) Fintech revolution: universal inclusion in the new financial ecosystem. Palgrave Macmillan, Cham

Buckley RP, Webster S (2016) FinTech in developing countries: charting new customer journeys. J Financ Transform 44:151–159

Chishti S, Barberis J (2016) The fintech book: the financial technology handbook for investors, entrepreneurs and visionaries. Wiley, Chichester

Enriques L (2017) Financial supervisors and regtech: four roles and four challenges. Revue Trimestrielle de Droit Financier 53. https://ssrn.com/abstract=3087292. Accessed 31 March 2020

Fernandez Naveira C et al (2018) Smarter analytics for banks. https://www.mckinsey.com/industries/financial-services/our-insights/smarter-analytics-for-banks. Accessed 31 March 2020

Green Invest (2017) Fintech, green finance & developing countries (United Nations Environment Program). http://unepinquiry.org/wp-content/uploads/2017/06/Fintech_Green_Finance_and_Developing_Countries-input-paper.pdf. Accessed 31 March 2020

Haycock J, Richmond S (2015) Bye bye banks? How retail banks are being displaced, diminished and disintermediated by tech start-ups – and what they can do to survive. Wunderkammer, London

International Bar Association's Task Force on the Financial Crisis (2010) A survey of current regulatory trends. https://www.ibanet.org/Article/NewDetail.aspx?ArticleUid=2C72F588–7222-47C9-83E4-7DB0A0A8BF1C. Accessed 31 March 2020 [International Bar Association (2010)]

IHS Markit (2020) More than six billion smartphones by 2020. https://news.ihsmarkit.com/press-release/technology/more-six-billion-smartphones-2020-ihs-markit-says. Accessed 31 March 2020

King B (2018) Bank 4.0: banking everywhere, never at a bank. Wiley, Chichester

Krishnan S (2014) The power of mobile banking: how to profit from the revolution in retail financial services. Wiley, Hoboken

McMillan J (2014) The end of banking: money, credit, and the digital revolution. Zero/One Economics, Zurich

Moazed A, Johnson NL (2016) Modern monopolies: what it takes to dominate the 21st century economy. St. Martin's Press, New York

Mohieldin M (2018) Leveraging technology to achieve the Sustainable Development Goals (Voices, World Bank Blogs). https://blogs.worldbank.org/voices/leveraging-technology-achieve-sustainable-development-goals. Accessed 31 March 2020

Parker GG, Van Alstyne MW, Choudary SP (2016) Platform revolution: how networked markets are transforming the economy and how to make them work for you. W W Norton & Company, New York

Pratskevich A (2019) New! 2019 financial apps report. https://liftoff.io/blog/finance-apps-2019/. Accessed 31 March 2020

PwC (2014) Retail banking 2020: evolution or revolution. https://www.pwc.com/gx/en/banking-capital-markets/banking-2020/assets/pwc-retail-banking-2020-evolution-or-revolution.pdf. Accessed 31 March 2020

Realini C, Mehta K (2015) Financial inclusion at the bottom of the pyramid. Friesen Press, Victoria

Sironi P (2016) FinTech innovation: from robo-advisors to goal based investing and gamification. Wiley, Chichester

Sironi A (2018) The evolution of banking regulation since the financial crisis: a critical assessment (BAFFI CAREFIN Centre). https://ssrn.com/abstract=3304672. Accessed 31 March 2020

Weihuan Z, Arner DW, Buckley R (2015) Regulation of digital financial services in China: last mover advantage? Tsinghua China Law Review 8:25–62

World Bank Live (2018) Disrupting development: digital platforms and innovation. https://live.worldbank.org/disrupting-development. Accessed 31 March 2020

Zetzsche DA et al. (2017) From fintech to techfin: the regulatory challenges of data-driven finance (6 European Banking Institute Working Paper Series). https://ssrn.com/abstract=2959925. Accessed 31 March 2020

Zetzsche DA et al (2019) The future of data-driven finance and regtech: lessons from EU Big Bang II (35 European Banking Institute Working Paper Series). https://ssrn.com/abstract=3359399. Accessed 31 March 2020

Rethinking the Regulatory Sandbox for Financial Innovation: An Assessment of the UK and Singapore

Christopher Chen

Abstract After the UK launched the first regulatory sandbox regime in 2016, the approach was quickly transplanted to numerous other countries as a means of promoting innovation, improving competition and enhancing financial inclusion. However, it remains unclear whether the approach can effectively achieve the relevant policy goals and thus justify the differential regulatory treatment. This chapter provides a broad overview of the regulatory sandbox regime and examines its potential benefits and problems. The chapter then provides some empirical evidence by analyzing the sandboxes awarded in the UK and Singapore between 2016 and 2018 with the aim of identifying what the businesses awarded the sandboxes are doing, the services they provide and their current regulatory status against the backdrop of the financial technology revolution. These cases provide a basis on which to assess the effectiveness of the regulatory sandbox approach in its infancy stage and provide some reflections for regulators.

Keywords Financial technology · Fintech · Regulatory sandbox · Financial innovation · Financial regulation

1 Introduction

This chapter examines the use of regulatory sandboxes as a tool for promoting a variety of policy objectives, such as increased innovation and greater financial inclusion, amid the rise of fintech in a sector marked by intensive regulation. In addition, we examine whether the regulatory sandbox approach has effectively achieved the relevant policy goals. In other words, can the sandbox regime justifiably provide temporary regulatory exemptions for the sake of promoting new technological applications in the financial services sector? The chapter seeks to provide an early assessment of the sandbox approach by examining the sandboxes awarded in the UK and Singapore between 2016 and 2018.

C. Chen (✉)
School of Law, Singapore Management University, Singapore, Singapore
e-mail: chchen@smu.edu.sg

M. Fenwick et al. (eds.), *Regulating FinTech in Asia*, Perspectives in Law, Business and Innovation, https://doi.org/10.1007/978-981-15-5819-1_2

Fintech is a catchword that refers to the use of new technology in the financial industry to complement and potentially address any deficiencies in firms' existing financial services (e.g., peer-to-peer lending/borrowing for individuals who might not have a good credit score). The phenomenon appears in all corners of the financial market ranging from banking-related services (e.g., peer-to-peer lending and cross-border payments) and insurance (e.g., insurance services with smart contract and automated payment features) to fundraising (e.g., crowdfunding and initial coin offerings), capital market operations (e.g., robot financial advice) and even back-office operations (e.g., the use of blockchain in post-trade settlements and clearing). Although the use of technology is not new in the financial sector (e.g., automatic teller machines),[1] the rapid growth in computing power and the rise of the internet and Big Data have transformed the traditional financial models. In this regard, the use of fintech has helped to revamp many of the traditional financial services (e.g., peer-to-peer lending bypassing traditional commercial banks), provide more convenience (e.g., payment via mobile phones), and improve the level of financial inclusion, especially in developing markets and sectors.[2] Some markets have also embraced fintech to maintain or increase the level of competition in the financial sector.

However, the fintech phenomenon has also generated some regulatory concerns and legal risk. Given that a breach of financial regulations will often lead to criminal penalties[3] and/or sometimes result in a firm leaving the market[4] and that the existing regulations already place a heavy burden on financial institutions, there is also a need to balance the needs of the regulated and unregulated entities.[5] First, new financial technologies do not necessarily change the nature of finance and the same old problems may persist. For example, in recent years, many Chinese peer-to-peer lending platforms have been plagued by fraud.[6] Similarly, financial advice based on algorithms may not be immune from human manipulation and money laundering remains an issue as long as firms handle their own cash flows. Thus, regulators certainly have an interest in regulating the use of fintech by licensed financial institutions and the new technology firms that are venturing into financial services.

Second, aside from the issue of whether regulators should regulate fintech, the threshold question remains as to whether a fintech service or product falls within the ambit of the financial regulations in a given market. For example, a practical issue may be whether an issuance of crypto-coins should be deemed as 'securities' in that a prospectus may be required in principle or as a kind of currency or commodity. In these cases, the interpretation and application of the existing regulations may generate some uncertainties for the market participants. A regulator may also be

---

[1] See Arner, Barberis and Buckley (2017), pp. 378 *et seq.*

[2] Jenik and Lauer (2017).

[3] E.g., Banking Act Sect. 4 (Singapore); Banking Ordinance Sect. 11 (Hong Kong).

[4] Some countries might grant regulators the power to liquidate a firm for conducting illegal financial services. E.g., *Digital Satellite Warranty Cover Ltd v Financial Services Authority* [2013] UKSC 7.

[5] Zetzsche et al. (2018), pp. 31–32.

[6] Feng (2018).

reluctant to issue a clear guidance before understanding the nature of a new fintech service.

These issues have given rise to the idea of the regulatory sandbox. As explained in Sect. 2 below, by some offering short-term exemptions, the sandbox approach can buy some time for regulators, incumbent financial institutions and new technology firms to try out new services with minimal legal risk. This legal certainty can allow firms to apply new innovative technologies and services that might benefit the market and the general public in the long run. However, the fundamental question remains as to whether the sandbox approach has achieved its policy objectives and whether the approach has been over-used. If the latter is true, it is arguable whether the regulatory sandbox approach is still justifiable.

Although it is apparent that the long-term effects of the regulatory sandbox approach and the fintech phenomenon may take some time to emerge, this chapter examines some preliminary empirical evidence on the sandboxes awarded in the UK and Singapore between 2016 and 2018 to provide some early insights into the workings of the regulatory sandbox regime in the fintech era. Rather than revealing whether the sandbox approach is sustainable, our analysis of the existing sandboxes aims to provide insights into the early practical applications of the regulatory sandbox approach.

The remainder of this chapter is organized as follows. In Sect. 2, we provide a general discussion of the regulatory sandbox approach and its pros and cons. Section 3 offers some empirical evidence based on the sandboxes awarded in the UK and Singapore between 2016 and the end of 2018. Based on this empirical evidence, the chapter offers some policy reflections on the implementation of the regulatory sandbox approach. Section 4 concludes the chapter.

2 The Rise of the Regulatory Sandbox

2.1 Regulatory Sandbox in a Nutshell

In general, a regulatory sandbox is a 'framework set up by a financial sector regulator to allow small scale, live testing of innovations by private firms in a controlled environment (operating under a special exemption, allowance, or other limited, time-bound exception) under the regulator's supervision.'[7] The sandbox provides 'regulated and unregulated entities with the opportunities to test, pursuant to a testing plan agreed and monitored by a dedicated function of the relevant [regulator], innovative products or services, business models, or delivery mechanisms, related to the carrying

[7] Jenik and Lauer (2017), p. 1.

out of financial services.'[8] The idea refers to 'a regulatory 'safe space' for experimentation with new approaches involving the application of technology to finance.'[9] A regulatory sandbox can create an environment in which businesses can test products with less risk of being punished by the regulator for non-compliance. In addition, the regulators may require applicants to incorporate appropriate safeguards to insulate the market from the risks associated with their innovative business.[10] In this regard, the regulatory sandbox approach represents a kind of 'structured experimentalism' and is one of the four main approaches for dealing with fintech and innovation.[11] Therefore, a 'key tenet in the new regulatory initiatives is regulatory suspension in the test environment.'[12]

The objectives of the regulatory sandbox regime vary depending on the country. A common goal is to promote competitive innovation, market competition and more efficiency in the market.[13] In emerging markets, a major motive may be to promote financial inclusion[14] because sandboxes can 'enable innovations that are likely to benefit excluded and underserved customers.'[15] On the macro level, the sandbox regime is expected to contribute to economic growth[16] or serve to maintain the competitiveness of a market as a financial center.[17] According to a joint report issued by three European regulatory authorities, the objectives of a regulatory sandbox may also include enhancing firms' understanding of the expectations and application of the existing regulatory framework to innovative business models and to increase the regulatory authorities' knowledge of financial innovation.[18]

The sandbox regime was first launched in the UK in December 2015. Since then, the approach has been quickly adopted around the world. One report notes that '[r]egulatory sandboxes have been widely adopted as an innovative regulatory initiative.'[19] This is perhaps the quickest transplantation of a regulatory regime in history. For example, in the Asia Pacific, Singapore, Malaysia, Australia and Thailand all issued their first versions of the regulatory rules regarding regulatory sandboxes

[8]ESMA, EBA and EIOPA (2018).

[9]Zetzsche et al. (2018), p. 45.

[10]Zetzsche et al. (2018), p. 64.

[11]Zetzsche et al. (2018), p. 35.

[12]Chiu (2017), p. 747.

[13]Zetzsche et al. (2018), p. 45 and 68; Jenik and Lauer (2017), p. 1.

[14]UNSGSA FinTech Working Group and CCAF (2019), pp. 28–30.

[15]Jenik and Lauer (2017), p. 2.

[16]Zetzsche et al. (2018), p. 68.

[17]E.g., Singapore aims to be a smart financial centre. Monetary Authority of Singapore, Fintech Regulatory Sandbox (Consultation Paper P005-2016) 1.1.

[18]ESMA, EBA and EIOPA (2018), pp. 18–19.

[19]UNSGSA FinTech Working Group and CCAF (2019), p. 7.

in 2016.[20] In Northeast Asia, Taiwan and South Korea[21] both passed laws allowing regulatory sandboxes in 2018, after Japan's financial regulator launched the 'FinTech Proof-of-Concept Hub' in 2017.[22] In Hong Kong, the three financial regulators each have their own regulatory sandbox regime, with the Hong Kong Monetary Authority first adopting the policy in September 2016,[23] followed by the securities and insurance regulators in September 2017.[24] Regulatory sandboxes have also been introduced in a variety of European countries, including Spain, France, Germany, Austria, Belgium, Bulgaria, Cyprus and Estonia.[25]

In addition, regulatory sandboxes have been extended to the international level, i.e., as cross-border regulatory sandboxes. For example, the UK's FCA proposed the Global Financial Innovation Network (GFIN) and Global Sandbox in August 2018.[26] The GFIN was launched in January 2019 with 25 members at the time of writing.[27] The Monetary Authority of Singapore promoted the ASEAN Financial Innovation Network (AFIN)[28] for Southeast Asia with other stakeholders including the International Finance Corporation (under the World Bank Group), ASEAN Bankers Association and Japan.[29]

Although the regulatory sandbox regimes around the world share some similar features, there are some variations. First, in some countries anyone can apply for a sandbox (e.g., Singapore and the UK), whereas in other countries they are limited to existing financial firms. For example, the Hong Kong Monetary Authority's Fintech Supervisory Sandbox is limited to licensed banks (although they may collaborate with technology firms).[30] Second, in terms of timing, some countries (e.g., Singapore) accept applications on a rolling basis, while others (e.g., the UK) accept and review

[20]For Malaysia, see Bank Negara Malaysia (2016); For Australia, see Australian Securities & Investment Commission (2017). For Thailand, see Bank of Thailand (2016), pp. 30 and 63.

[21]See the Financial Technology Development and Innovative Experimentation Act (Taiwan), promulgated on 31 January 2018, and the Special Act on Promotion and Vitalization of Convergence of Information and Communications Technology (South Korea), passed on 20 September 2018.

[22]Gehrke (2018).

[23]Hong Kong Monetary Authority on the Fintech Supervisory Sandbox. Available at: https://www.hkma.gov.hk/eng/key-functions/international-financial-centre/fintech-supervisory-sandbox.shtml. Accessed 31 March 2020.

[24]Hong Kong Securities and Futures Commission on the SFC Regulatory Sandbox. Available at: https://www.sfc.hk/web/EN/sfc-fintech-contact-point/sfc-regulatory-sandbox.html. Accessed 31 March 2020; Hong Kong Insurance Authority on the Insurtech Corner. Available at: https://www.ia.org.hk/en/aboutus/insurtech_corner.html. Accessed 31 March 2020.

[25]ESMA, EBA and EIOPA (2018), pp. 40–41.

[26]See FCA website. Available at: https://www.fca.org.uk/publications/consultation-papers/global-financial-innovation-network. Accessed 31 March 2020.

[27]See FCA website. Available at: https://www.fca.org.uk/firms/global-financial-innovation-network. Accessed 31 March 2020.

[28]See AFIN website. Available at: https://afin.tech/. Accessed 31 March 2020.

[29]See AFIN website. Available at: https://afin.tech/index.php/2017/11/02/afin-partners/. Accessed 31 March 2020.

[30]See Hong Kong Monetary Authority website. Available at: https://www.hkma.gov.hk/eng/key-functions/international-financial-centre/fintech-supervisory-sandbox.shtml. Accessed 31 March 2020.

applications in batches. Third, in terms of the legal foundations, some markets (e.g., Taiwan and South Korea) require the legislative body to pass a law, whereas other markets allow sandboxes to be created based on the existing regulatory guidelines or rules (e.g., Malaysia and Australia). Fourth, the sandbox approach implies that some regulatory standards can be relaxed at least on a temporary basis. However, while some markets clearly lay out the bottom-lines to which the regulator will not yield, others are not clear on this issue. For example, in Singapore, certain rules clearly have to be followed by the sandbox applicant in any event, including the confidentiality of customer information, fit and proper criteria regarding honesty and integrity, the handling of customers' money and assets by intermediaries and the prevention of money laundering and the financing of terrorism.[31] Fifth, in addition to a one-size-fits-all standard application process, a regulator may provide a fast-track process for certain applicants. For example, Singapore introduced the 'sandbox express' in late 2018 to facilitate sandbox applications for certain types of services (e.g., insurance brokerage or remittance) that the regulator deemed to be relatively low risk or as having known risks that can be easily contained.[32]

Another difference is the availability of other forms of exemptions other than a regulatory sandbox. For example, in the UK, other than a regulatory sandbox, a firm may apply for restricted authorization before full authorization. In other words, firms can apply for a limited license to offer financial services. At the end of experiment period, a firm may apply to have the restrictions lifted and acquire full authorization to offer full financial services under the supervision of the FCA. In addition, the FCA may issue a waiver or no action letter to a firm to provide some certainty to fintech firms if the regulator agrees not to pursue the firm for offering financial services illegally within the confines of the waiver or letter.

Similarly, the Australian Securities and Investments Commission (ASIC) has implemented a three-pronged approach for fintech. First, a technology firm can apply to work with an existing financial institution, which will act as the principal facing the clients.[33] Second, ASIC can offer more specific fintech licensing exemptions,[34] which appear to be limited to existing financial firms, for small-scale experiments with regard to limited types of services. [35] Third, ASIC may provide some relief on a case-by-case basis, such as standard applications (following published ASIC policies), minor and technical applications (involving the application of existing policies to new situations) and new policy applications (which require a form review by ASIC).[36] In contrast, in Singapore, the guidelines for regulatory sandboxes do not

[31] Monetary Authority of Singapore (2016) Annex A.

[32] Monetary Authority of Singapore (2018), pp. 4–5.

[33] Australian Securities & Investment Commission (2017), RG257.26 to 28.

[34] ASIC Corporations (Concept Validation Licensing Exemption) Instrument 2016/1175, Sect. 4.

[35] ASIC Corporations (Concept Validation Licensing Exemption) Instrument 2016/1175, Sects. 5–6; Australian Securities and Investment Commission (2017), RG257. 18–19.

[36] Australian Securities & Investment Commission (2009), RG51.6.

clearly mention other alternatives such as waivers, no action letters or other exemptions, even though technically the financial regulator may provide some exemptions or waivers whenever the legislation allows.[37]

With respect to procedure, regulators can implement a combination of legal tools. For example, in the UK, the FCA may issue participants in the sandbox regime with no-action letters with regard to an agreed scope of activities, usually in regard to regulatory compliance rather than consumer safeguards.[38] In contrast, in some places, the regulators may issue temporary or conditional licences to facilitate sandboxes.[39] Nevertheless, the conditions attached to a sandbox are usually not made public.

2.2 *Benefits and Concerns of the Regulatory Sandbox Approach*

The regulatory sandbox approach seems to have been well received by the industry and can provide a number of benefits. First, it might help to improve the interaction between the financial regulator and the industry, especially for firms within the technology sphere. As has been noted, '[a] sandbox may potentially change the nature of the relationship between regulators and financial services providers toward a more open and active dialogue.'[40] In this way, the regulatory sandbox approach allows 'regulators to proactively seek new firms or *pre-regulates*, moving away from the previous position of being passive and reactive.'[41] Thus, the experimental period can enable regulators to gain a greater understanding of particular fintech applications and assess the innovation and risks of such applications[42] before determining the appropriate regulatory actions or strategies, instead of implementing a one-size-fits-all approach.

Second, by controlling the regulatory risk and liability, the sandbox approach can promote more financial innovation and competition in the market, and incentivize financial firms to accelerate their digital transformation.[43] Moreover, the sandbox approach provides 'pre-defined entry (and exit) criteria [that may] provide greater transparency and replicability than prior approaches' (e.g., doing nothing or partial exemption).[44] Thus, the approach may be more flexible for the regulators and market participants.

---

[37]E.g., Banking Act Sect. 15D (Singapore).

[38]Chiu (2017), p. 748.

[39]Zetzsche et al. (2018), pp. 58–59.

[40]Jenik and Lauer (2017), p. 1; Zetzsche et al. (2018), p. 78.

[41]Chiu (2017), p. 747.

[42]Zetzsche et al. (2018), p. 79; ESMA, EBA and EIOPA (2018), p. 16.

[43]Zetzsche et al. (2018), p. 78.

[44]Zetzsche et al. (2018), p. 64.

However, the sandbox regime also raises some concerns. First, the sandbox approach may send a negative signal to the market and potential users[45] when it is clear that the sandbox firms are not fully regulated and the end-users may not be fully protected. Depending on the scale, a sandbox does not change the fact that the service providers are experimenting with real customers, who may still suffer losses or be subject to misconduct. The customers may also perceive a sandbox as a kind of endorsement by the regulators.[46] Moreover, if the conduct requirements are unclear for a particular firm in a sandbox, there may be little protection for financial consumers.[47] In some countries (e.g., Singapore) the regulators clearly state that the customers of sandbox firms cannot rely on the financial consumer protection dispute resolution regimes (although this is usually disclosed to customers).[48]

Second, there are some concerns relating to the lack of standardization and its impact on cost reduction,[49] given that sandboxes are often awarded separately with different conditions, which may also lead to a lack of transparency in how sandboxes are awarded.[50] In addition, at the macro level, the use of regulatory sandboxes might create an imbalance between the existing financial firms and unregulated technology firms[51] because the sandbox approach provides some leeway for fintech firms (at least temporarily) to operate while the traditional financial institutions are still subject to the full regulations. This imbalance may also raise some fairness concerns.

Third, the sandbox approach does not resolve the underlying challenges and dilemmas in dealing with the junction between finance and technology. In particular, the question remains as to what comes under the scope of the financial regulator and what happen after the end of a sandbox? An underlying assumption of the regulatory sandbox approach is that new services might fall wholly or only partly within the scope of the existing regulatory framework, which may not be the case. In addition, although sandboxes are not meant to last forever (at least at this moment), it is unclear what will happen after the completion of a sandbox.

Thus, the question remains as to whether the benefits will materialize or whether some of the abovementioned concerns will decide the future of the regulatory sandbox approach. To make the approach effective, it has been suggested that 'sandboxes need to be made smarter and equipped to self-monitor activity within them, as opposed to just being a process-driven application method for entry, typically for a limited time, to a regulatory safe space, as they are currently.'[52] Furthermore, Professor Chiu argues

---

[45]Zetzsche et al. (2018), p. 79.

[46]ESMA, EBA and EIOPA (2018), p. 35.

[47]ESMA, EBA and EIOPA (2018), pp. 35–36.

[48]The Monetary Authority of Singapore's website for experimenting in the sandbox. Available at: http://www.mas.gov.sg/Singapore-Financial-Centre/Smart-Financial-Centre/FinTech-Regulatory-Sandbox/Experimenting-in-the-sandbox.aspx. Accessed 31 March 2020.

[49]Zetzsche et al. (2018), p. 79.

[50]Zetzsche et al. (2018), p. 80.

[51]Zetzsche et al. (2018), p. 80.

[52]Zetzsche et al. (2018), p. 46.

that the 'sandbox regimes should focus on governance rather than promoting innovation,'[53] because promoting innovation might affect the objectivity (i.e., desire to service new firms, rather than to regulate) and rationality of the regulator in designing new regulatory policies.[54]

3 Early Assessment of Cases in the UK and Singapore

In this Section, we present some empirical evidence on the sandboxes awarded in the UK and Singapore and offer some preliminary assessments of the early implementation of the regulatory sandbox regime. The UK and Singapore are leading international financial centers and both markets are keen to attract fintech businesses. In addition, as illustrated below, despite the hype, the two markets also show some contrasts in the practices related to sandboxes.

Before presenting the data, it is important to understand the limitations of this chapter. First, the publicly available information does not cover the conditions applicable to each sandbox. Thus, it is difficult to determine the rules or conditions that the regulators were willing to relax to give the fintech firms more room to experiment. Hence, we can only speculate from the information available on the internet. Second, because it may take some time before the longer-term effects of the regulatory sandbox approach become clear, we can only provide some early assessments based on known data. Thus, the future implications of the sandbox approach will require a longer-term study.

In the following sections, we first describe the respective regulatory sandbox regimes in the UK and Singapore. In addition to briefly outlining the general legal requirements, we present some empirical evidence on the sandboxes awarded thus far. We then evaluate the current state of the regulatory sandbox approach based on the evidence from the two markets.

3.1 United Kingdom

In October 2014, the FCA initiated Project Innovate to encourage innovation in the interests of consumers and promote competition through disruptive innovation. The project aimed to help new fintech firms to meet the FCA's eligibility criteria and to better understand the regulatory policies and strategies. The idea of a regulatory sandbox was subsequently introduced in December 2015.

To evaluate whether a fintech firm should be granted a sandbox, the FCA considers a number of factors. For example, the applicant must have some consumer protection mechanism (e.g., limiting its services to some customers or enabling customers to

---

[53]Chiu (2017), p.765.

[54]Chiu (2017), p. 745.

Table 1 Numbers of applications and awarded sandboxes in the UK

Cohort	Number of applications	Number of awards	%
Cohort 1	69	14	20.29
Cohort 2	77	31	40.26
Cohort 3	61	18	58.65
Cohort 4	69	29	42.03
Total	276	92	33.33

Source Available at https://www.fca.org.uk/firms/regulatory-sandbox. Accessed 31 March 2020

complain to the Financial Ombudsman Services). The FCA also considers whether an applicant is ready to conduct testing, secure outsource partners and have a significant UK presence.[55] The FCA requires an applicant to have a UK bank account,[56] which is likely to help UK customers to seek compensation (if there are sufficient funds in the account). Each sandbox is then assigned a dedicated case officer to 'help firms understand how their innovative business models fit within the regulatory framework.'[57]

Between the launch of the sandbox regime in 2015 and the end of 2018, there were four cohorts of applicants (about every half year per cohort). Table 1 shows the numbers of applications and cases accepted in the first four cohorts.

Table 1 shows that the UK attracted quite a number of applications (compared with Singapore and most other countries). The acceptance rate varies by cohort, ranging from as low as 20% (in Cohort 1) to as high as 42% (Cohort 4). The overall acceptance rate after four cohorts is 33.33%. Of the 92 cases awarded a sandbox, 87 cases have started testing and we can draw some information from the FCA's website about how those firms' intended to use technology.

We can analyze the 87 cases that were tested or are still testing from several angles. First, in terms of the technology applied, only 8 (9.2%) of the sandboxes in the UK clearly indicated using artificial intelligence, whereas 34 (39.08%) claimed to apply distributed ledger technology, notably in the fields of payment services and capital markets.[58] Because we can only observe what has been disclosed by the FCA or on the firms' websites, the actual rates of adoption of artificial intelligence and blockchain technology could be higher. The use of blockchain could include helping customers to pay money to another entity (e.g., Billon or Epiphyte), the issuance or transfer of shares or securities (e.g., Nivaura or Otonomous), assisting firms in conducing compliance or the know-your-customer process (e.g., Tradle) and personal data management (e.g., Nuggets). In contrast, far fewer sandbox winners clearly indicated they would be using artificial intelligence. In these cases, the applications

[55]Financial Conduct Authority (2017–2020).

[56]Financial Conduct Authority (2017–2020).

[57]Financial Conduct Authority (2017), par. 2.4.

[58]The FCA also noted in 2017 that distributed ledger technology was the most popular technology used across the first two cohorts. Financial Conduct Authority (2017), par. 3.8.

mainly focus on asset management (e.g., Beekin) and analyzing financial actions or behaviors (e.g., nViso or Moneyhub Enterprises).

Second, in terms of the identity of the applicant, at least 9 of the 87 (10.34%) applications were from existing financial firms (usually banks) with the rest being start-ups or technology companies. Interestingly, applications were also received from non-profit organizations (e.g., Citizens Advice UK).[59] Thus, the bulk of the sandboxes in the UK were issued to new entrants, although a number of banks did participate in the sandbox regime.

Third, we may fit those sandboxes into different sectors in the financial market. The financial market is traditionally divided into three main pillars: banking, insurance and the capital markets. However, there could be some challenges in designating a sector for fintech firms because in some cases, the firms appear to straddle two or more traditional fields. In addition, payment services may be difficult to categorize because, although traditionally dominated by the banking sector, in recent years, we have seen a flurry of third-party payment service providers that operate independently of commercial banks.

Thus, this chapter divides the sandboxes into five broad categories:

(1) services related to the provision of credit, deposit-taking, trade finance and money exchanges or otherwise those involving traditional banking services (but excluding domestic or cross-border payment and remittance);
(2) services related to the capital markets, including the primary market and the issuance of securities, the secondary market and trading, investment/asset management (which may include some private banking business), financial advisory services and derivatives;
(3) insurance-related services, including the provision of insurance, insurance intermediaries or aggregators, claim processing and other auxiliary services;
(4) payment-related services, including third-party payment solutions and remittance (but excluding crypto-currencies); and
(5) other services that cannot be classified into any of the above.

This classification largely follows the traditional demarcation of the banking, capital market and insurance sectors, except that we isolate payment services (from banking) as a separate class to highlight the widespread use of fintech in payment services.

Based on this classification, we can observe the distribution of the regulatory sandboxes in the UK after the first four cohorts. The distribution of the sandboxes by sectoral lines is shown in Fig. 1 below.

Figure 1 above clearly shows that the majority of the sandboxes (31 out of 87, 35.63%) were for capital market-related services, followed by payment services and insurance. There is also a considerable number of cases relating to other services. In contrast, only eight cases clearly concern traditional banking services if we take out payment services.

---

[59]Our result is consistent with the FCA's assessment after the first two cohorts. Financial Conduct Authority (2017), par. 3.5.

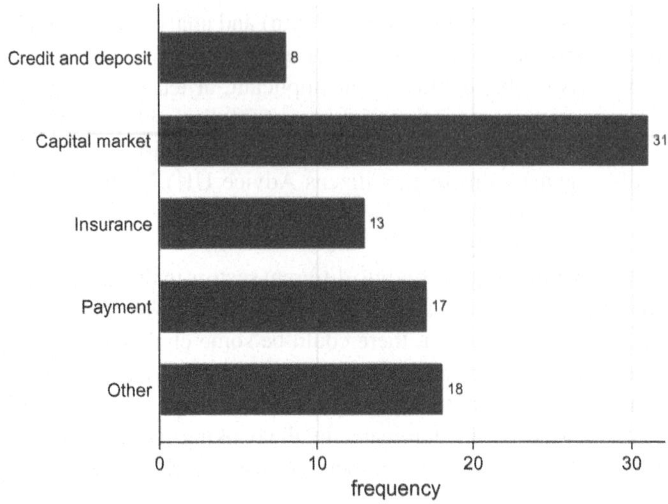

Fig. 1 Distribution of sandboxes by sector

Except for two cases, the traditional banking service sandboxes are mostly related to loans or savings. However, only two of the six banking service providers clearly provide loans (e.g., Nextday Property and Salary Finance) with the rest focusing on savings management, mortgage eligibility and the application of credit lines. The two cases that are not related to lending or savings involve the use of digital identity tokens for applying for bank accounts (Communist First Credit Union) and a governance model with distributed ledger technology to develop decentralized applications (NatWest, a bank).

Of the 31 sandboxes focusing on capital market-related services, 11 (35.48%) involve raising finance by issuing securities with another three cases (9.68%) concerning the trading of securities. Most of the applications in the primary and secondary markets (11 of 14 cases) clearly indicate using distributed ledger technology. Of the other applications, seven cases (22.58%) concern asset or investment management and nine cases (29.03%) concern financial advisory services in addition to a sole case concerning hedging and derivatives. Among the advisory and asset management service providers, artificial intelligence (5 out of 11 cases) is the most prominent type of technology deployed.

Most of the insurance-related sandboxes (8 out of 13, 61.54%) are related to the provision of insurance protection with two cases (15.38%) offering intermediary services and three cases (23.08%) involving other auxiliary services (e.g., tracking a customer's driving behavior or helping clients to transfer their pensions). Some of the fintech-based insurers combine automation with smart contracts (e.g., FloodFlash or Etherisc), while some adapt the traditional model to provide customers with more benefits (e.g., savings premiums).

In addition to classifying the sandboxes along the traditional sectoral lines, we regroup them by function. For this purpose, regardless of the financial sector, we identify three major functions: raising funds (by loans, offering securities or other methods), managing financial conditions and financial advisory services. Of the 87 sandboxes in the UK, only 13 (14.94%) clearly focus on helping customers to raise funds, 18 (20.69%) concern some form of financial management and 11 (12.64%) provide financial advice, which largely reflects that nearly 20% of the cases concern payment services and another 20% concern other services. Thus, only a minor proportion of the sandboxes in the UK actually focus on 'finance,' with most of the sandboxes concerning other finance-related or support services.

In a paper published in 2017, the FCA stated that '[t]he first year of operation provides an early indication that the sandbox has been successful in meeting its overall objective.'[60] The FCA's self-assessment showed that 75% of firms accepted into the first cohort (77% for second cohort) had successfully completed testing and that around 90% of the firms that completed testing in the first cohort continued to develop wider markets.[61] The FCA noted that testing in the sandbox helped firms to raise finance from potential investors due to the higher degree of legal certainty.[62] The FCA also recognized that the sandboxes allowed the regulator to work with innovators to build appropriate consumer protection safeguards for the new products and services.[63] In Section C below, we provide some early reflections based on the data from the first two years of the regulatory sandbox regime.

3.2 *Singapore*

Similar to the UK, Singapore has been actively pursuing fintech to maintain Singapore's position as an international financial (and financial technology) center. The Monetary Authority of Singapore (MAS) started evaluating the sandbox regime after the UK launched the concept. Eventually, in November 2016, the MAS published the Fintech Regulatory Sandbox Guidelines,[64] which state that the MAS will provide support to increase efficiency, manage risks better, create new opportunities and improve people's lives.[65] The guidelines state that licensed financial institutions and other interested firms can apply for a sandbox.[66] However, the MAS also makes it clear that sandboxes are not suitable for firms that propose to implement services that are similar to those already offered, unless the applicants can demonstrate some differences. In this case, the MAS will only consider the application if the firm has

[60] Financial Conduct Authority (2017), par. 2.7.

[61] Financial Conduct Authority (2017), par. 2.9.

[62] Financial Conduct Authority (2017), paras. 2.10 and 2.11.

[63] Financial Conduct Authority (2017), paras. 2.17 and 2.18.

[64] Monetary Authority of Singapore (2016).

[65] Monetary Authority of Singapore (2016), par. 5.2.

[66] Monetary Authority of Singapore (2016), par. 2.2.

conducted due diligence to understand the environment and ensure that the proposed service has a reasonable chance of surviving.[67]

The MAS does not predetermine the industry sectors or areas in which fintech services may be applied. When reviewing a sandbox application, the MAS considers whether the application includes new technology or uses existing tools in an innovative way, whether the application addresses a problem or offers benefits to the customer/industry, whether the applicant intends to deploy the service in Singapore on a broader scale after the sandbox (or otherwise contribute to Singapore in other ways), whether the test outcome or boundary conditions are clearly defined and reported to the MAS, whether significant risk has to be addressed and whether the applicant has acceptable exit and transition strategies.[68] After the sandbox period expires, the applicant is expected to continue providing the services on a broader scale if the MAS is satisfied with the outcome and the firm is able to comply with the legal and regulatory requirements.

Nonetheless, the MAS was rather cautious in awarding sandboxes. In contrast with the UK, the MAS had only awarded six sandboxes by the end of 2018. In terms of sectors, three of the six sandboxes (50%) are related to insurance (PolicyPal, Inzsure and MetLife), one concerns digital advisory services (Krystal Advisors), one is about money changing (Thin Margin) and one focuses on cross-border remittance (TransferFriend). The limited sample suggests that the MAS awarded sandboxes to certain targeted industries and thus it could be argued that each sandbox represents a separate service sector (or type of service).

Furthermore, in a consultation paper on the sandbox express regime published in November 2018,[69] the MAS stated that it wished to create 'a set of predefined sandboxes, to complement the existing customized sandboxes.'[70] The objective is to provide faster options for firms to bring innovative ideas to the market for testing and to reduce the time and resources required to make an application.[71] For this purpose, the MAS proposed three main areas for pre-defined sandboxes, namely, insurance broking, recognized markets and remittances.[72] If a service falls under one of these pre-defined sandboxes, the MAS will only review essential factors such as whether the applicant's stakeholders are fit and proper and whether the proposed service or product is sufficiently technologically innovative.[73] A pre-defined sandbox usually implies a small scale operation and full disclosure of its status to customers.[74] For example, for a pre-defined sandbox for insurance broking, no more than 1,000 transactions can be made within the stated period,[75] a maximum volume of S$5

---

[67]Monetary Authority of Singapore (2016), par. 5.5.

[68]Monetary Authority of Singapore (2016), par. 6.2.

[69]Monetary Authority of Singapore (2018).

[70]Monetary Authority of Singapore (2018), par. 2.2.

[71]Monetary Authority of Singapore (2018), par.2.3.

[72]Monetary Authority of Singapore (2018), par. 3.1.

[73]Monetary Authority of Singapore (2018), par. 3.4.

[74]Monetary Authority of Singapore (2018), par. 3.6.

[75]Monetary Authority of Singapore (2018), par. 4.2.

billion (about US$3.8 billion) is set for market operators (e.g., an exchange)[76] or a maximum of S$100,000 (about US$77,000) for remittance services.[77] However, at the time of writing, the 'sandbox express' regime had not yet come into effect.

3.3 Evaluation of the Sandbox Approach

Because the approach is still in its infancy, it would not be prudent to make any early predictions of how the sandbox regime can accommodate fintech innovation. However, we can make some preliminary judgments based on the experiences in the UK and Singapore. Comparing the two countries, it is clear that the UK has attracted a larger pool of applications for sandboxes and has a higher award rate. In contrast, Singapore's approach is rather cautious, and it remains to be seen how the newly proposed regulatory sandbox express will progress. However, it is too early to determine whether the UK regime is too easy or the Singapore system is too difficult.

It is evident that the longer-term effects of the sandbox regimes in enhancing innovation and boosting the economy will need more time to surface. One report has indicated that the early sandboxes in some markets were neither necessary nor sufficient to promote financial inclusion.[78] In addition, there is a danger that the regulators might divert more resources to 'prioritize resource-intensive sandbox programs over more comprehensive innovation policies, market engagement strategies, or financial inclusion programs.'[79]

This chapter provides some early reflections on the nature of the sandboxes awarded in the UK and Singapore between 2016 and 2018. First, it is unclear whether the sandbox approach has attracted technology firms (especially those that do not seem to be concerned about financial regulations in the first place) to volunteer to be regulated. By inviting certain firms to apply for sandboxes, the regulators appear to assume that particular services fall within their regulatory scope. However, whether specific services definitely fall within the scope of the regulatory authorities is a legal question that requires careful analysis. Although the sandbox regime may have simply deferred the question, the issue will not disappear and still has to be addressed on a firm-by-firm basis.

Judging by the number of sandbox applications, it appears that there is still ample room to attract more fintech firms. Although the UK accounts for the lion's share of the sandbox applications, the FCA still issued fewer sandboxes than the number of fintech firms in the market. For example, a report published by the accounting firm Ernest and Young in 2016 lists 138 fintech firms operating in the capital market

76 Monetary Authority of Singapore (2018), par. 5.2.

77 Monetary Authority of Singapore (2018), par. 6.2.

78 UNSGSA FinTech Working Group and CCAF (2019), pp. 30–31.

79 UNSGSA FinTech Working Group and CCAF (2019), p. 30.

(broadly defined).[80] This figure is considerably larger than the total number of sandboxes awarded in the UK and Singapore combined and does not take into account other fintech firms in the banking, insurance and payment services sectors.

There should be no doubt that the sandbox regime will help regulators to develop a greater understanding of the application of technology in the financial services sector. However, it is possible that a number of fintech firms will remain outside the existing regulatory framework until the threshold question (i.e., whether a service is a regulated activity) is clarified. Again, it will remain to be seen whether the sandbox regime can provide a means to incorporate technological advancement in the regulatory framework.

Second, do sandboxes help firms to raise finance? We do not possess the firm-level data needed to address this question. Moreover, at a more macro level, due to the limited sample of countries, we cannot determine whether regulatory sandboxes help fintech firms to attract finance. According to a report published by the accountancy firm KPMG, Singapore attracted significant amounts of investment (including venture capital, private equity and merger and acquisitions) between 2016 and early 2018. However, perhaps due to the shorter time-frame, there is no perceivable pattern in terms of the amount of finance invested per quarter. For example, nearly US$100 million was invested in the third and fourth quarters of 2016, before dropping to as low as $20 million in the first quarter of 2017 and then rising to over $120 million in the third quarter of 2017.[81] The 2018 data also show a wide swing from as low as US$10 million in the first quarter to over $60 million in the second quarter.[82]

Similarly, the KPMG report does not appear to show that the regulatory sandbox regime in the UK had any impact on financing activities. For example, between the first quarter of 2016 and the second quarter of 2017, the amount invested in fintech (including venture capital, private equity and merger and acquisitions) in the UK did not exceed US$0.4 million per quarter (even less than 2015), although the figures rebounded later in 2017, rising to $1.7 million in the fourth quarter of 2017, $13.1 million in the first quarter of 2018 and $3 million in the second quarter.[83] Therefore, in the two years following the launch of the regulatory sandbox regimes in the UK and Singapore, there is no convincing evidence that the sandboxes helped fintech firms to raise finance.

Third, the evidence from the UK and Singapore raises the question of whether the firms that were awarded sandboxes were sufficiently innovative to justify differential legal treatment. Although some sandboxes clearly applied technology to areas not covered by the existing financial firms, there are a number of potential counter-examples that suggest the regulatory sandboxes were not necessarily awarded based on the innovativeness of their technology. For example, Lloyd's Banking Group was awarded a sandbox by the FCA for 'an approach that aims to improve the experience

---

[80] Ernst & Young (2016).

[81] KPMG (2018), p. 51.

[82] KPMG (2018).

[83] KPMG (2018), p. 38.

for branch customers aligned with the online and over the phone experience.'[84] Barclays Bank was awarded a sandbox for a 'RegTech proposition which tracks updates to regulations within the FCA Handbook and aligns their implementation to Barclays' internal policies.'[85] However, it is unclear what regulatory requirements or legal risks apply to improving customers' branch experiences or developing a regtech tool to track the UK's financial regulations. It is not that those services have no merit or do not involve technology. Rather, if the purpose of a sandbox is to reduce the legal risk and promote innovation, it is unclear from the short description provided by the FCA why those services might need a sandbox. In other words, because a bank can arguably improve the branch experiences of its customers and/or develop a regtech tool without regulatory implications, a sandbox appears unnecessary. Accordingly, on a general level, the regulators should provide more publicly accessible information on the types of technology involved and the reasons for awarding sandboxes. Otherwise, the regulatory sandbox regime could be used for bragging purposes rather than real merit, especially in places that award large numbers of sandboxes.

Fourth, another yardstick is what happens after the end of the sandbox period. In Singapore, of the six sandboxes awarded by the end of 2018, most succeeded in acquiring regulatory licences after the completion of the sandbox experiment. One is operated by a licensed insurance company (MetLife), while another three firms continued to be licensed after the expiration of the sandbox (PolicyPal, Krystal Advisors and Thin Margin). However, one firm (TransferFriend) ceased to be licensed after the end of sandbox. Another firm (Inzsure) is still completing the sandbox experiment and thus it is unclear whether it will continue to be licensed.

In the UK, of the 87 sandboxes awarded before the end 2018, 45 firms are included in the Financial Services Register maintained by the FCA.[86] Although the FCA claims that 'the majority of sandbox firms have required authorization in order to conduct testing,'[87] a search of the register revealed that this is not necessarily the case. While Cohort 4 is still ongoing at the time of writing, six firms in the cohort (of 27 sandboxes) are already licensed firms in the UK. With the previous cohorts, 15 of the 18 firms in Cohort 1 (83.33%), 16 of the 24 firms in Cohort 2 (66.67%) and eight of the 18 firms in Cohort 3 (22.22%) continue to be licensed *post* sandbox.[88] Although the regime has not been operating long enough to produce reliable data, the rate seems to be dropping. Although we could not find any information on the other 42 firms in the FCA's register, these firms may be licensed in other countries or may have changed their business names. Of the 44 firms for which we could obtain licensing information in the UK, at least 24 are licensed as agencies and/or insurance

[84]FCA website. Available at: https://www.fca.org.uk/firms/regulatory-sandbox/cohort-1. Accessed 31 March 2020.

[85]FCA website. Available at: https://www.fca.org.uk/firms/regulatory-sandbox/cohort-3. Accessed 31 March 2020.

[86]See FCA website. Available at: https://www.fca.org.uk/firms/financial-services-register. Accessed 31 March 2020.

[87]Financial Conduct Authority (2017), par. 2.5.

[88]This is in line with the FCA's self assessment in 2017. See Financial Conduct Authority (2017), par.2.9.

distributors and 16 are licensed for payment or money services. This is in line with the distribution of the sandboxes according to the financial sector.

4 Conclusion

In conclusion, in this chapter, we examine the sandboxes awarded in the UK and Singapore to provide a preliminary assessment of the sandbox regimes in the two markets. We find that the UK, which pioneered the concept in the financial sphere, has attracted numerous sandbox applications and the FCA seems to be willing to award a relatively high proportion of sandboxes. In contrast, Singapore has adopted a more cautious approach by targeting specific sectors. However, there are signs that the MAS might be willing to award more sandboxes in certain sectors in the future with the proposed regulatory sandbox express regime.

Overall, the long-term effects of the regulatory sandbox approach remain to be seen, as any effects in promoting financial innovation, improving financial inclusion or maintaining market competitiveness should take some years to surface. The early applications between 2016 and 2018 suggest that most of the sandboxes awarded in the UK were for capital market or payment services, with blockchain being a popular technology. In contrast, the insurance and traditional banking sectors account for a relatively small proportion of the sandboxes, especially with respect to the size of the banking and insurance markets. In contrast, Singapore initially implemented a more cautious approach by targeting the insurance and foreign exchange and remittance services markets (with three and two sandboxes, respectively, of the six sandboxes awarded). However, other than the one case for digital advisory services, it is unclear whether the MAS will grant more sandboxes for capital market and traditional banking-related services. Moreover, in both markets, most of the sandboxes were not directly concerned about raising finance. Thus, because most of the sandboxes were awarded to finance-related firms the regime may help to improve the provision of financial services. Whether these finance-related firms should to continue to receive temporary exemptions through regulatory sandboxes is a question that the regulators will need to consider in the future.

The early evidence from the UK and Singapore suggests that there are some concerns that may require the attention of the regulators. First, it is unclear whether the sandboxes have successfully attracted technology firms (or existing financial institutions) to experiment with the use of new technologies in the provision of financial services. In addition, although it is difficult to measure how innovative a service is based on simple descriptions, there are signs that some sandboxes are not necessarily awarded based on factors other than the innovativeness of the technology, which could increase the likelihood of the sandbox regime being abused by some market participants. If this is the case, it may imply that the regulators are awarding sandboxes for the sake of having sandboxes rather than serving real policy goals in some situations.

Furthermore, there is no clear evidence thus far that the regulatory sandbox regime has helped firms raise more finance due to the higher legal certainty. Although many firms continue to be licensed after completing the regulatory sandbox, there are some warning signs that more and more firms may be dropping off the radar. If this is the case, this might in turn challenge the validity of the regulatory sandbox regime and the award process.

Overall, regulators should provide more transparency on the sandbox application process and the content of the successful applications. The additional information would help potential customers to ascertain what they are dealing with and may help other market participants to pick up the pace without having to over-spend on research and development. Moreover, releasing more information to the public would help improve the credibility of the regulators' decisions in awarding short-term legal exemptions and support the long-term future of the sandbox regime.

References

Arner DW, Barberis J, Buckley RP (2017) Fintech, regtech, and the reconceptualization of financial regulation. Northwestern Journal of International Law & Business 37:371–413

Australian Securities & Investment Commission (2017) Regulatory guide 257: Testing fintech products and services without holding an AFS or credit licence. https://download.asic.gov.au/media/4420907/rg257-published-23-August-2017.pdf. Accessed 31 March 2020

Australian Securities & Investment Commission (2009) Regulatory guide 51: applications for relief. https://download.asic.gov.au/media/1238972/rg51.pdf. Accessed 31 March 2020

Bank Negara Malaysia (2016) Financial technology regulatory sandbox framework. https://www.bnm.gov.my/index.php?ch=57&pg=137&ac=533&bb=file. Accessed 31 March 2020

Bank of Thailand (2016) Annual Report 2016. https://www.bot.or.th/English/ResearchAndPublications/Report/DocLib_AnnualEconReport/BOTAnnualReport_2016.pdf. Accessed 31 March 2020

Chiu IHY (2017) A Rational Regulatory Strategy for Governing Financial Innovation. European Journal of Risk Regulation 8:743–765

Ernst & Young (2016) Capital markets: innovation and the fintech landscape. https://www.ey.com/Publication/vwLUAssetsPI/EY-capital-markets-innovation-and-the-finTech-landscape/%24FILE/EY-capital-markets-innovation-and-the-finTech-landscape.pdf. Accessed 31 March 2020

Feng E (2018) Chinese government faces peer-to-peer lending scandals dilemma. Financial Times (12 November). https://www.ft.com/content/c71cca4a-c198-11e8-84cd-9e601db069b8. Accessed 31 March 2020

Financial Conduct Authority (2017) Regulatory sandbox lessons learned report. https://www.fca.org.uk/publications/research/regulatory-sandbox-lessons-learned-report. Accessed 31 March 2020

Financial Conduct Authority (2017–2020) Applying to the regulatory sandbox. https://www.fca.org.uk/firms/regulatory-sandbox/prepare-application. Accessed 31 March 2020

Gehrke N (2018) The Japan FSA regulatory sandbox. https://medium.com/tokyo-fintech/the-japan-fsa-regulatory-sandbox-b7e9f38e962e. Accessed 31 March 2020

Jenik I, Lauer K (2017) Regulatory Sandboxes and Financial Inclusion. https://www.cgap.org/research/publication/regulatory-sandboxes-and-financial-inclusion. Accessed 31 March 2020

KPMG (2018) The pulse of fintech 2018. https://assets.kpmg/content/dam/kpmg/xx/pdf/2018/07/h1-2018-pulse-of-fintech.pdf. Accessed 31 March 2020

Monetary Authority of Singapore (2018) Consultation paper P015–2018: sandbox express. https://www.mas.gov.sg/-/media/MAS/News-and-Publications/Consultation-Papers/2018-Nov-Sandbox-Express/Consultation-Paper-on-Sandbox-Express.pdf. Accessed 31 March 2020

Monetary Authority of Singapore (2016) Fintech regulatory sandbox guidelines. http://www.mas.gov.sg/~/media/Smart%20Financial%20Centre/Sandbox/FinTech%20Regulatory%20Sandbox%20Guidelines%2019Feb2018.pdf. Accessed 31 March 2020

UNSGSA FinTech Working Group and CCAF (2019) Early lessons on regulatory innovations to enable inclusive fintech: innovative offices, regulatory sandboxes, and regtech. https://www.unsgsa.org/files/3515/5007/5518/UNSGSA_Report_2019_Final-compressed.pdf. Accessed 31 March 2020

Zetzsche DA et al. (2018) Regulating a revolution: from regulatory sandboxes to smart regulation. Fordham Journal of Corporate and Financial Law 23:31–103

Hong Kong's Fintech Automation: Economic Benefits and Social Risks

David C. Donald

Abstract This chapter examines the rise of fintech, its regulation, and the particular challenges these present for an international financial center (IFC), specifically an IFC with limited economic breadth. Fintech offers automation opportunities for financial institutions, and such automation will in most cases make banks more competitive and lower their labor needs. The Hong Kong government has actively embraced fintech to ensure competitiveness, and its regulation tracks leading international positions on ICOs, cryptocurrency and electronic payment. However, Hong Kong regulators have not facilitated fintech activities that would stimulate the local economy, such as equity crowdfunding. Automation will generally translate into a reduction of human labor, particularly in mid-level jobs. In a large and varied economy, persons laid off from jobs at banks can seek engagement elsewhere. This is not necessarily true in an IFC with a less diversified economy. Hong Kong presents the highly unusual case of persons in a small IFC who have access to a large and diverse economy in mainland China yet may refuse to seek new positions in the larger workplace for cultural or political reasons. The Hong Kong government has blithely followed a 'market leads, government facilitates' philosophy of laissez-faire for decades and thus also has failed to prepare for the social costs of fintech. While such preparation would indeed constitute social planning, an activity generally discouraged in Hong Kong, circumstances dictate that the HKSAR government begin to act socially, rather than merely facilitate the largest businesses.

Keywords Automation · Fintech · Hong Kong · Financial regulation

D. C. Donald (✉)
Faculty of Law, The Chinese University of Hong Kong, Shatin, Hong Kong
e-mail: dcdonald@cuhk.edu.hk

M. Fenwick et al. (eds.), *Regulating FinTech in Asia*, Perspectives in Law, Business and Innovation, https://doi.org/10.1007/978-981-15-5819-1_3

1 Introduction

The Hong Kong Special Administrative Region (HKSAR) presents an excellent test area for examining the development, regulation and implementation of fintech, as well as measuring its potential competitive benefits and social risks. As an international financial center (IFC) that has ranked within the top five in financial and regulatory competitiveness during the last decade,[1] Hong Kong has great interest in establishing an environment that encourages development and use of the best fintech applications. Regulation in an IFC can tend to be outward-looking, meeting the needs of the major global institutions connecting the IFC to the world rather than focusing on stimulating activity in its small, local economy. This has been true for the HKSAR, and its regulation has not sought to create a hospitable environment for small companies seeking innovation, although it has encouraged activity important to the major institutions of international finance. A contradiction is thus present between general policies to lead in fintech development and a specific failure to nurture those aspects of fintech which could support innovation in the local economy. But this is not the only difficulty faced by an IFC lacking a large local economy.

While fintech will create opportunities for entrepreneurs and jobs for the technical staff they hire, the attraction and profitability of all fintech firms lies in automation. Fintech automation ranges from the processing of loan application data and investment firms' need to 'know your customer' (KYC) achieved through data analytics, to faster processing of payment transactions and use of 'chatbots' to advise customers.[2] Automation means 'the use of machines and computers that can operate without needing human control,'[3] and thus in the workplace it means replacing human work hours with those of machines. While it is occasionally asserted that such automation is undertaken to improve the job satisfaction of employees by shifting boring or repetitive tasks from human to machine,[4] it would be the rare bank or investment firm in today's shareholder value market that would make this kind of large infrastructural investment to better the lives of employees and without seeking a return through reducing labor costs. Effective fintech automation can simultaneously reduce costs and increase revenue by allowing an increase in productivity despite a decrease in staff.[5] Unemployment is the universally expected externality of automation and there is no concrete reason why fintech automation should be different.

In most economies, the primary question arising from automation displacing workers is whether they can transition to new employment, and the obviously recommended policy measures are education and training programs for displaced workers. However, in tiny Hong Kong, with an economy split quite evenly between finance (and associated services), logistics, and tourism, it is difficult to guess where displaced, mid-level bankers will find a position compatible with their skillset broadly

[1] Z/Yen Group (2007) through (2019) and World Economic Forum (2014) through (2019).

[2] CCAF (2019), pp. 15–16.

[3] Cambridge Dictionary (2019), 'automation'.

[4] Snyder (2019).

[5] KPMG (2017), p. 6.

understood, including after acquiring any available retraining. The logistics industry, in particular, is highly data-intensive and is experiencing automation faster than is finance (aside from the actual driving of trucks or flying of planes).[6] Tourism, moreover, has in recent decades focused primarily on visitors from mainland China, and this source of revenue is drying up, as discussed in Sect. 5. The lack of employment mobility for displaced financial industry staff could materially exacerbate the existing social problems in Hong Kong by adding another large group of people to those already distrustful of the way in which their city/region is being governed. Unemployed Hongkongers have the option of seeking employment in China's large and diverse economy, but may be unwilling to do so because of cultural or political preferences. Fintech in this way presents special and especially serious risks for Hong Kong.

Fintech adoption is nevertheless inevitable for Hong Kong and financial economies globally. Most of the 'back office' functions in financial service providers can already be performed more effectively by robotic process automation (RPA)—a combination of data collection, data analytics, and data processing replicating an existing human activity and improving upon human performance. As noted above, fintech innovations are bringing RPA and its latest augmentation, cognitive robotic process automation (CRPA), to the 'front office' of client relations in the form of KYC and chatbots. Given the nature of competitive behavior in the financial industry, the fact that finance is essentially data management, and the fact that an IFC like Hong Kong is competing closely with financial centers around the world, it would be nearly impossible for banks operating in Hong Kong to opt out of increasing automation.

This is especially true because mainland China is a global leader in fintech, and Singapore is one of the world's most active jurisdictions for fintech research and development. Hong Hong's strongest competition is found in these markets, in particular, Shanghai, Shenzhen and Singapore. Faced with this competition, Hong Kong would have to cease any aspiration to be a leading IFC if it were to place a Luddite moratorium on automation in order to protect jobs and social order. Economic consequences would follow. A response to such dilemmas occasionally heard is that of Leibniz's theodicy 'that everything always occurs for the best,'[7] so that some predict an unforeseen technology will arise in the nick of time to create good jobs currently not imagined today.[8] This did not prove true in the last wave of automation during the 1960s, which contributed to increased economic inequality in the US,[9] and there is no reason to expect an eleventh-hour miracle technology to arise in Hong Kong. The dilemma for Hong Kong thus remains. It should be addressed by the HKSAR's government—which at last declaration embraced fintech enthusiastically without making preparations in any way for its social consequences.

---

[6] 'McKinsey Global Institute estimates that the transportation-and-warehousing industry has the third-highest automation potential of any sector.' Dekhne (2019).

[7] '[T]he evil that occurs is an inevitable result of the best…. To permit the evil, as God permits it, is the greatest goodness.' Leibniz (1710), p. 195.

[8] Malito (2018).

[9] Ford (2015), pp. 32–38.

This chapter will address the economic benefits and social risks of Hong Kong's fintech automation with the following organization. Section 2 will define fintech and describe applications of fintech currently in existence and expected. Section 3 will review the regulation of fintech in Hong Kong, in particular distinguishing between tools for the international and local economies, and explaining the manner in which this body of regulation can be expected to channel fintech development. Section 4 will examine the estimated impact of automation in the workplace, with a particular focus on employment. Section 5 will study the possible solutions available for the HKSAR, particularly for displaced financial sector employees in Hong Kong. Section 6 will conclude.

2 The Nature and Application of Fintech

Google Trends shows worldwide searches for the term 'fintech' lingering near an insignificant level of public interest, judged by web search, from 2004 until 2013, when it begins to take off, working its way steadily toward peak popularity in November 2019 and (although temporarily dipping in December) remains near that peak at time of writing in February 2020.[10] By contrast, the number of searches for the word 'blockchain'–one of the technologies used in fintech, particularly in cryptocurrency—departed from the frequency of searches for fintech in early 2017, reached a high peak late that year, and has since descended rapidly to the comparable level of searches.[11] That is to say that in comparison to the 'blockchain' fad, 'fintech' does not seem to enjoy any particular favor in market sentiment, but rather appears as a steadily growing reality within the financial industry. In 2019, the Cambridge Centre for Alternative Finance (CCAF) found in a study of ASEAN countries the following financial activities and technologies to be those undertaken and employed by fintech firms (the activities and technologies do not necessarily correspond horizontally in the following table) [12]:

Top five financial activities	Top five technologies used
Lending	Predictive analytics
Payments	Machine learning
Capital raising	Robotic process automation (RPA)
Improving enterprise operations	Image recognition
Big Data, for e.g., credit scoring	Blockchain

The CCAF also uses respondent data to link each of the technologies listed above with the type of activity it has been found to support. The industry mainly uses

[10] See https://trends.google.com/trends/explore?date=all&q=fintech. Accessed 25 February 2020.

[11] See https://trends.google.com/trends/explore?date=now%204-H&q=blockchain. Accessed 25 February 2020.

[12] CCAF 2019, pp. 15–18.

predictive analytics to support Big Data activities such as credit assessment, digital lending and chatbots; machine learning is used to support Big Data and enterprise operations such as KYC and transaction processing; RPA is used to support digital lending, Big Data and enterprise operations; image recognition is used to support Big Data and enterprise operations, and blockchain is used to support enterprise operations and crowdfunding.[13] The main technologies adopted in fintech are thus aimed almost solely at labor-intensive data-oriented activities within the financial institution or between that institution and customers, such as internal enterprise operations, customer logging through KYC and credit assessment, and customer advice in the form of a chatbot. The way the transition is undertaken from a human performing a task to the same task undertaken by machine can be found in the following practical guidance offered by a consultancy to firms adopting RPA:

Start with rule-based, standardized processes that cross multiple systems, which need a nonintrusive approach to automation. Evaluate RPA opportunities where you have people acting as 'swivel chair integration'—rekeying data between systems—and where work is being performed by humans that involves structured, digitalized data processed by predefined rules. This analysis forms the basis for your enterprise automation roadmap.[14]

Ernst and Young argues that RPA can reduce costs by '50–70% for high-frequency tasks,' although they project that the short- to mid-term focus on RPA will eventually plateau and wane as new, 'game-changing technologies are introduced that eliminate the need for specific operational activities.'[15] It has been argued that one of those 'game-changers' is CRPA, which instead of imitating human activity can train itself on data and develop its own processes ad hoc.[16] This application of machine learning and self-training is a less sophisticated version of what Google's Alphago used to defeat a grandmaster of the game Go, and then what Alphazero used to teach itself chess in a few hours and badly to beat a computer named Stockfish that held in memory every known strategy and technique humans have devised over hundreds of years for the game of chess, and could process these options 1000 times faster than could Alphazero.[17] During the 100 games in which Alphazero beat or tied Stockfish, the former's technique was described as playing chess 'intuitively and beautifully, with a romantic, attacking style. It played gambits and took risks…. Grandmasters had never seen anything like it…. humankind's first glimpse of an awesome new kind of intelligence.'[18]

RPA is already present in Hong Kong. Large financial institutions have of course rationalized much of their transaction activity for efficient processing by administrative staff and all such activity is 'low-hanging fruit' for automation. One of the city/region's largest employers, HSBC, famously exemplified RPA in 2018

[13]Soriano et al., p. 23.

[14]Gartner 2018.

[15]Ernst and Young (2016), p. 24.

[16]Davenport 2019.

[17]Strogatz (2018).

[18]Strogatz (2018).

by converting the processing of letters of credit (LoC) into an automated process containing a 'smart contract' at its core.[19] Smart contracts are sequences of encoded behavior, or 'programmatically executable transactions,'[20] that allow legal performance to be triggered automatically in reaction to the behavior of a counterparty that follows the agreed terms of a contract encoded in the mechanism, usually on a distributed ledger. LoCs are a means of reducing risk in paying for internationally shipped goods, and the legal structure of a LoC has been so reliably formalized that it merely requires clerical staff within a bank to perform a few standardized steps in order to ensure proper payment. The rule-based uniformity and simplicity of the transaction makes LoC processing ripe for RPA. A second step we could potentially see in the longer term with the application of CRPA would involve the reconceptualization of the LoC process itself, cutting the ties to the previous, human limitations.

3 Hong Kong's Regulation of Fintech

The Hong Kong Special Administrative Region (HKSAR) regularly ranks at the top of the various league tables for the quality of its law and the efficiency of its market regulation.[21] Law is often benchmarked against that of the UK and the content and tenor of Hong Kong's regulatory model follows the UK more than the US, with principle and relationship generally outweighing rule-based enforcement. Since the founding of its Securities and Futures Commission (SFC) in 1989, Hong Kong has played a 'bonding' role for investment in the mainland Chinese economy, particularly through hosting the listing of its large, state owned enterprises (SOEs), which it assisted to become globally active companies.[22] It follows from this that the regulatory style of the HKSAR has generally been more cautious and less open to free experimentation than has been the case in mainland China. Moreover, when mainland China has clearly prohibited a fintech activity,[23] such as initial coin offerings (ICOs), the HKSAR was careful not to create too liberal an offshore haven for the same, which would thwart the mainland regulatory aims.

Nevertheless, the HKSAR must remain competitive in areas deemed to be truly innovative in substance. As an international financial center, Hong Kong has at least since 2016 declared a strong policy stance in favour of Fintech.[24] Policy addresses

[19] Browne (2018).

[20] Rauchs et al. (2018), p. 67

[21] For example, the World Bank's Doing Business Report 2019 ranked Hong Kong 4th out of 190 jurisdictions examined, World Bank (2019) p. 5, and Hong Kong has ranked in first place on the 'Index of Economic Freedom' for a quarter-century. Heritage Foundation (1995) through (2019).

[22] See Donald (2015), pp. 192–193.

[23] Chen and Lee 2017.

[24] HKSAR (2016), p. 6.

by the Chief Executive have stressed the importance of financial technology development and substantially increased funding has been allocated to projects such as the Hong Kong Science Park, an environment designed to encourage and support new technology start-ups.[25] While each of Hong Kong's three financial regulators have actively addressed new fintech products, they have also entered into MoUs with their counterparts in mainland China and other financial centers around the world to develop a framework which is not only complementary with China but attractive to globally active financial institutions.[26] Hong Kong supervisors have consistently been more circumspect of the IFC's place in the global market than the impact of their regulation on the Hong Kong local economy, and that can be seen in the individual regulatory actions.

3.1 Equity-Based Crowdfunding

The nonlocal focus of HKSAR when regulating fintech is exemplified by its treatment of equity-based crowdfunding, which is a form of alternative finance for small and medium-sized enterprises (SMEs) and has little or no interest for international financial services firms. Equity crowdfunding employs platform communication to facilitate offers to the public to purchase shares issued by a start-up company and investors' acceptance of such offers. This activity potentially triggers two types of regulation: public offerings of securities and the operation of a platform for dealing in such securities. However, it tries to avoid the—cumbersome and expensive—traditional regulation of both.

When some local firms and branches of foreign firms advertised crowdfunding in Hong Kong, the SFC responded by issuing a public warning that absent proper licensing and compliance with the regulations that may well apply, crowdfunding could run afoul of existing investor protection and market supervision provisions.[27] Offers of securities to the public normally require publication of a prospectus meeting all legal requirements,[28] and approval of the same by the SFC.[29] However, exemptions for offerings of securities have existed in the Companies Ordinance for decades. These exemptions track international usage and exempt (i) offers made to qualified investors, (ii) offers that are for small amounts and (iii) offers that are made to a small group of people. In Hong Kong, qualified investors are 'professional investors' such

[25]Lam (2018), p. 46

[26]Memoranda of understanding have been signed with XXX

[27]SFC (2014).

[28]Sec. 38D Companies (Winding Up and Miscellaneous Provisions) Ordinance (CWUMPO), CAP 32.

[29]Secs. 2 and 103(1) Securities and Futures Ordinance (SFO), CAP 571.

as banks, insurance companies, investment schemes and other financial intermediaries, plus any group that the SFC names in regulations issued for this purpose.[30] Offerings for a small monetary amount must have total consideration payable for the shares not exceeding HK$5.0 million (roughly $637,000).[31] Offerings exempted because made to small groups of persons must not exceed 50 offerees in total.[32]

In early 2016, the Hong Kong Financial Services Development Council, an advisory body of private market participants, recommended that the Region regularize crowdfunding with either legislative amendment or regulatory action in order to facilitate SME finance in the HKSAR.[33] The SFC chose not to respond to the request, and no action was ultimately taken.[34] As a result, any offering of securities must either be accompanied by a prospectus meeting all legal requirements or meet the conditions of one of the exemptions referred to above. In 2019, the SFC nevertheless began to follow the practice that had been embraced in Singapore for some time, which is to refer to offerings of securities made under the traditional exemptions as 'crowdfunding'.[35] This crowdfunding 'without the crowd' does facilitate private dealings between financial institutions, but is of much less use for local SME financing.

3.2 *Microfinance and Internet Lending*

Both as a colony and in its current state as SAR, Hong Kong has suffered from significant inequality of wealth (both income and assets), which placed a large portion of its population on the edge of poverty.[36] To the Hong Kong residents

---

[30]Sec. 2(1) CWUMPO in connection with Schedule 17, pt. 1, sec. 1 CWUMPO, in connection with Schedule 1, pt. 1, sec. 1 SFO, in connection with sec.397 SFO.

[31]Sec. 2(1) CWUMPO in connection with Schedule 17, pt. 1, sec. 3 and pt. 2 CWUMPO, in connection with Schedule 1, pt. 1, sec. 1 SFO.

[32]Sec. 2(1) CWUMPO in connection with Schedule 17, pt. 1, sec. 2 CWUMPO, in connection with Schedule 18,pt. 3 CWUMPO. Other exemptions limiting the total proceeds raised and setting a floor for the minimum consideration collected from each investor are less well adapted to the needs of crowdfunding.

[33]FSDC (2016).

[34]An additional problem was raised that crowdfunding platforms may violate the monopoly of registered stock exchanges under sec 19 SFO. Under this provision, only a recognized exchange company may operate a stock market, which includes 'a place at which facilities are provided for bringing together sellers and purchasers of securities.' SFO sec 19(1) in connection with Schedule1, Part 1, s 1.

[35]MAS (2015).

[36]'According to the Hong Kong Census Reports, Hong Kong's Gini coefficient based on original monthly household income rose from 0.533 in 2006 to 0.539 in 2016… In May 2018, the total net worth of the wealthiest 21 mega-tycoons in Hong Kong amounted to HK$1.83 trillion.' Oxfam Hong Kong (2018), p. 1. The net worth of those 21 billionaires thus constituted about 64% of the Hong Kong GDP for the seven million residents of Hong Kong in 2018 (which was about HK$2.84 trillion).

living hand to mouth, consumer credit can become a necessity of life,[37] and Hong Kong has traditionally provided such credit through a number of channels: banks and non-bank money lenders, as well as pawnbrokers. Banks licensed by the Hong Kong Monetary Authority (HKMA) receive the requisite permissions in connection with their general authorization. Pawnbrokers receive authorization from Commissioner of Police pursuant to the Pawnbrokers Ordinance.[38] Fintech has seen expansion, however, mainly under the Hong Kong Money Lenders Ordinance (MLO), which provides that any 'person whose business …is that of making loans' must be licensed.[39] Such licensing is administered by the Registrar of Companies, not the HKMA.

Licensing requirements for the MLO focus on whether the operations and management of the licensee are fit and proper for the activity, and the MLO also requires that 'any of the premises to which the application relates … [be] suitable for the carrying on of the business of money-lending.'[40] The reference to the word 'premises' in the MLO has not prevented the Registrar from licensing virtual platforms for lending. Of the roughly 2500 persons declared by the Registrar as licensed for money lending at December 2019, a handful of these are virtual lenders, including the local Hong Kong start-ups, WeLend, MoneyMonkey and Moneysq.

The larger lenders in Hong Kong are generally licensed as banks, rather than under the MLO, and the HKSAR has made significant efforts to ensure that its regulatory environment for banking does not fall behind other IFCs. In 2018 the HKMA issued a guideline on virtual banking to update regulations originally issued in 2000 to clarify that banks may conduct all operations virtually.[41] Regulatory requirements for capital, governance and risk management are the same as for their brick-and-mortar counterparts, but virtual banks are expressly required to maintain 'a physical presence in Hong Kong, which will be its principal place of business,' and they must also provide expert certification that their 'security and technology-related controls' are "fit for purpose', i.e., appropriate to the type of transactions which the virtual bank intends to carry out.'[42] Virtual banks are also expressly permitted to outsource their IT facilities. The HKMA has also issued guidance regarding virtual 'on-boarding' of clients, under the general principle that 'technology solutions …for remote on-boarding … be at least as robust as those performed when the customer is in front of the staff.'[43] Early virtual bank licensees were units of four large mainland Chinese firms: Ant SME Services (controlled by Alibaba), Ping An OneConnect

[37]Piketty describes this phenomenon in turn-of-the-century US: 'one consequence of increasing inequality was virtual stagnation of the purchasing power of the lower and middle classes in the United States, which inevitably made it more likely that modest households would take on debt.' Piketty (2011), p. 297.

[38]Sec. 5 Pawnbrokers Ordinance, CAP 166.

[39]Secs. 2 and 7, Money Lenders Ordinance, CAP 163.

[40]Sec. 11(5) MLO.

[41]HKMA (2018).

[42]HKMA (2018), pars 12, 14.

[43]HKMA, 'Remote on-boarding of individual customers' (1 February 2019).

Company Limited (controlled by the insurance giant Ping An Insurance), Infinium Limited (now Fusion Bank, controlled by Tencent), and Insight Fintech HK Limited (controlled by Xiaomi).

3.3 E-Payment

Efficient cash transfer is at the heart of every IFC, and Hong Kong is well equipped with a legacy real time gross settlement (RTGS) cash payment systems in HK dollars, US dollars, Euro and Renminbi to serve its traditional function as an international transaction hub. With the advent of fintech, however, innovation in retail payment has received much attention internationally, as nonbanking firms like Alibaba and Apple become prominent in a field that has been joined by companies as diverse as Facebook and JPMorgan, which recently have announced plans to create payment systems with their own digital currency. It thus makes good sense for an IFC like Hong Kong to foster such innovation. Hong Kong does have a stored value payment system called the 'Octopus Card', used in connection its Mass Transit Railway Corporation (MTR) and popular in the Region for making small-value payments (under HK$1000) at convenience and grocery stores, although it is relatively old, established in 1997. It is unusual that such a popular payment method that was clearly ahead of its time was not developed further in a way that would have assisted the local economy.

In 2016, a number of new licensees—including Alipay and PayPal—joined Octopus to operate stored value e-wallet systems in Hong Kong. In 2018, Hong Kong competed a broad set of measures gathered under the rubric 'Faster Payment System' (FPS) and designed to facilitate person to person (P2P) and person to merchant (P2M) payments.[44] These include:

- full connectivity between banks and e-wallets as well as among different e-wallets;
- retail registration for payments and fund transfers with a mobile phone number or email address;
- real-time settlement in Hong Kong dollar and renminbi 24 h a day, seven days a week across all banks via banks' accounts with the HKMA; and
- Free of charge for small-value fund transfers or payments between personal customers.

The HKMA also worked with local banks to create a unified payment method through a QR code that 'can combine multiple QR codes from different payment service providers into a single, combined QR code,' so as to facilitate smaller merchants' acceptance of e-payment systems.[45] This is one initiative that could help small businesses in the local Hong Kong economy compete more effectively.

---

[44] Chan (2018b).

[45] Ibid.

3.4 *Cryptocurrency and ICOs*

Cryptocurrency in its first wave served mainly as a medium of speculation, and was treated with caution by the large, international banks.[46] The Hong Kong SFC thus has played a wait-and-see strategy similar to many other jurisdictions, such as the US,[47] by initially stating that regulation of cryptocurrency and ICOs would hinge on whether the assets traded constituted 'securities' under Hong Kong law.[48] The HKMA Chief Executive has flatly stated that cryptocurrency cannot be defined as money because it is not generally accepted as a medium of exchange, does not have a reasonably stable value and for these reasons cannot be a unit of account.[49] The concept of 'money' is key to the HKMA's jurisdiction.[50]

In early 2018, the SFC took 'regulatory action against a number of cryptocurrency exchanges,' and 'sent letters to seven cryptocurrency exchanges in Hong Kong or with connections to Hong Kong warning them that they should not trade cryptocurrencies which are 'securities' as defined in the' SFO.[51] It also sent warnings to seven ICO issuers, stating that 'ICOs are essentially crowdfunding by blockchain start-ups.'[52] This again shows the tack taken by the Hong Kong regulators, to meet international expectations—particularly by providing a safe and well-ordered market—while focusing much less attention on the financing needs of the local economy.

3.5 *Regulatory Sandboxes*

The regulatory sandbox is one of the most visible regulatory innovations appearing since the global financial crisis. Similar to pharmaceutical licensing, the regulator using sandboxing requires a certain amount of observed testing before a general, public license is issued. Sandboxing allows the industry to push forward with innovation while reducing the risk of damage to individual investors or market integrity. Such sandboxes represent a HKSAR policy that encourages activity in the local economy rather than mainly serving international client institutions—although it does signal that Hong Kong is in step with a policy first seen in its main point of reference, London.[53]

---

[46]See e.g., Campbell (2017).

[47]Schmidt and Bain (2019).

[48]SFC (2017a).

[49]Chan (2018a).

[50]'Money' is the concept that triggers application of the Payment Systems and Stored Value Facilities Ordinance, CAP 584, L.N. 145 of 2004, amended 2015. Money is also a prerequisite to 'taking deposits' under the Banking Ordinance, CAP 155, 1986, E.R. 1 of 2013.

[51]SFC (2018).

[52]SFC (2018).

[53]FCA (2015).

Each of the three Hong Kong financial regulators have established regulatory sandboxes. The HKMA set up a supervisory sandbox in 2016 and later created a chatroom. The HKMA sandbox is linked to those of the SFC and the Hong Kong Insurance Authority (IA) to create 'a single point of entry for pilot trials of cross-sector fintech products.' The principles for use of the HKMA sandbox are that the bank's management provide clear definitions about the scope, phases and timing of the project, show measures to protect the interests of customers during the trial, establish sufficient risk management controls, display readiness of operative systems, and conduct adequate monitoring of the trial.[54] As at the end of 2019, the HKMA reported 43 pilot projects had used its supervisory sandbox.

The SFC created its regulatory sandbox in 2017 'to provide a confined regulatory environment for qualified firms to operate regulated activities under the SFO.'[55] The SFC's regulatory sandbox 'is available to both licensed corporations and start-up firms that intend to carry on a regulated activity under the SFO. The qualified firm must be fit and proper, utilise innovative technologies and be able to demonstrate a genuine and serious commitment to carry on regulated activities through the use of Fintech.'[56] The SFC reserves the right to more closely monitor the admitted firm's activity, subject it to special licensing requirements and restrict the range of customers to which services or products may be offered.

The IA launched its Insurtech Sandbox in 2017 'to facilitate a pilot run of innovative Insurtech applications by authorized insurers to be applied in their business operations.'[57] The administrative principles for use of the IA sandbox are essentially identical to those of the HKMA supervisory sandbox. The mutual benefits seen by the IA are to allow insurers testing new Insurtech products to 'gain real market data and information of user experience in a controlled environment before launching them into the market,' while giving the IA 'inputs … for refining its supervisory requirements, taking into account the latest technological applications by the insurance industry.'

3.6 InsurTech

Unlike other regulators, the HK IA has directly benefited local firms through its acceptance of insurers using new technology. Under a guideline that expressly permits virtual delivery of insurance service over the internet,[58] it has authorized two local

---

[54]These are listed on the HKMA website for its Fintech Supervisory Sandbox, www.hkma.gov.hk/eng/key-functions/international-financial-centre/fintech-supervisory-sandbox.shtml.

[55]SFC (2017b).

[56]SFC (2017b).

[57]Information on the IA's sandbox is available at the IA's Insurtech Corner, www.ia.org.hk/en/aboutus/insurtech_corner.html#1

[58]Guideline Eight, On the Use of Internet for Insurance Activities.

firms to provide fully virtual insurance services, Bowtie Life Insurance and Avo Insurance.

4 The Social Costs of Automating Finance

To remain competitive both regionally and globally, financial centers must embrace financial technology, or fintech, which can perform data-intensive, repetitive tasks with well-defined objectives[59] faster and cheaper than can humans. Although the firms developing such automation will undoubtedly create some jobs, particularly in the IT sector, the applications developed will reduce significantly the pool of available mid-level jobs for the financial and related service providers, a core activity of the HKSAR economy. Displaced financial services employees will have a hard time finding alternatives with similar pay scales and skill sets in the geographically small territory of Hong Kong. Events in 2019 demonstrated[60] that Hong Kong's strong economic inequality has already translated into a fragile social structure. Heavy shedding of jobs in the financial sector would exacerbate the situation.

As observed above, a common response to such observations is that the fear of job loss is 'Luddite' and that past waves of automation simply led to a shifting structure of the workforce and enhanced overall welfare. It was indeed true that between the late 19th century and the mid-20th century entire economies shifted from agriculture and labor-intensive manufacturing to a modern industrial infrastructure (which did not yet include computers), but this was accompanied by an exploitation of workers that fed into revolutions and related wars with human costs of unprecedented magnitude.[61] Moreover, the shift toward computer-assisted manufacturing and services since 1970 did not create replacement jobs for displaced labor and was accompanied by a strong uptick of income inequality and a steady decline in labor's share of corporate profits.[62] A 2019 Brooking Institution study found that in the coming wave of automation, '[a]mong the most vulnerable jobs are those in office administration .... Such jobs are deemed 'high risk,' with over 70 percent of their tasks potentially automatable.'[63] A 2019 study undertaken at the MIT-IBM Watson AI Lab agrees with the Brookings

59 'Anima Anandkumar, director of machine learning research at Nvidia, a maker of graphics processing units, said workers should evaluate the future of their own roles by asking three questions: Is my job fairly repetitive? Are there well-defined objectives to evaluate my job? Is there a large amount of data accessible to train an AI system?' Liu (2019).

60 BBC (2019).

61 This observation is made by Yuval Harari, as he observes, 'it took more than a century of terrible wars and revolutions to experiment with these models, separate the wheat from the chaff, and implement the best solutions,' as agricultural gave way to industrial society, and 'given the immense destructive power of our civilization, we just cannot afford more failed models, world wars, and bloody revolutions' in the 21st century. Harari (2018), p. 34.

62 Ford (2015), pp. 37–41.

63 Muro et al. (2019), p. 5.

study, finding automation hollowing out mid-level tasks, as would be expected from the nature of both automation and the economic reasons for applying it:

> Employment has, proportionally, increased among the lowest compensated occupations in the low-wage tercile while employment has, proportionally, increased among the highest compensated occupations in the high-wage tercile. In the mid-wage tercile, there are, proportionately, fewer workers, a reflection of falling mid-wage employment.[64]

Similar automation at a major Hong Kong bank would force employees down, up or out. If the routine aspects of a banking process are automated, the smaller set of tasks supporting the machines would be lower-paying, which would put even more economic pressure on employees in the world's most expensive city. The affected mid-level employees would not all be able to transfer into the smaller number of higher-level jobs, if these are in fact created.

Thus exit would be the likely option. Such exit in, say, the US, Germany or Japan, would lead to higher efficiency and lower costs in financial institutions, while encouraging employees displaced by automation to shift into different industries, such as services and industries that have either already been automated in the past or require too high a quota of human involvement for machine participation to be efficient. But in Hong Kong, the key industries of finance, logistics and tourism, plus related professional services, comprise most of the economy.[65] Financial services employ about 260,000 people in Hong Kong, accounting for about 7% of the workforce, but generating about 19% of GDP in 2017.[66] In the same year, logistics employed nearly triple that amount at about 730,000 and generated 21% of GDP and tourism also employed about 260,000 and generated only about 5% of GDP. Services, including professional services that are greatly geared toward finance, employed nearly 540,000, comprising about 12% of GDP and employment. Other activities are so fragmented that they are not broken out in separate statistics. Manufacturing is noticeably missing from the Hong Kong economy.

Hong Kong's shift from a manufacturing economy in the 1960s to a financial economy in the 1990s significantly increased income inequality, as measured by the Gini coefficient, which rose from 0.43 in 1971 to 0.539 in 2016, resulting in the income distribution in Hong Kong being about as economically balanced as a South American country.[67] Unlike many poor regions, however, only about 15% of Hong Kong residents can hope to own a home.[68] The 2019 protests and accompanying anti-mainland Chinese sentiment have reduced the viability of tourism as a strong

---

[64] Fleming et al. (2019), p. 17.

[65] HKSAR Census and Statistics Department (2019).

[66] The discussion of the Hong Kong economy relies on figures from the HKSAR Census and Statistics Department, available at https://www.censtatd.gov.hk/hkstat/sub/sp80.jsp?tableID=188&ID=0&productType=8

[67] See e.g., Chen (2014) and Oxfam Hong Kong (2018).

[68] See e.g., Harris (2017).

support for the HKSAR economy,[69] and the importance of the Region as an IFC may be reduced, although the 2019 listing of Alibaba may indicate otherwise.[70] Everything we now know indicates that automation in the financial industry will both reduce the number of routine, mid-level jobs and exacerbate income inequality by creating more lower-level positions while making operations more efficient for those who own and manage these institutions.

As digitalization allows more and more processes to be brought within computers and limited artificial intelligence can take on more routine cognitive work, the most recent phase of automation will affect so-called white-collar jobs more severely than in the past. This process will tend to 'hollow out' the mid-level tasks in the value chain,[71] allowing those who own the firm or perform highly specialized tasks within it to earn more because they can take a higher portion of the profits as well as pass on the fruits of increased efficiency to shareholders.

Hong Kong does not have much of a choice on whether or not to automate. This would be true even if HKSAR policy leaders were fully aware that RPA and CRPA will likely increase social instability. If Hong Kong financial institutions and policy leaders resist automation, institutions in naturally competing centers such as Singapore, Shenzhen and Shanghai could simply take the business, which would also reduce employment without benefiting either top management or shareholders. Options to deal with the reduction in jobs would be to either diversify activity in Hong Kong or make the border with mainland China more porous, so that Hong Kong residents could shift into Guangdong to follow jobs, much like someone might do from New York or London into other areas of the US or UK. Given the growing sentiment against mainland China of many Hong Kong residents, a collaborative spirit and relationship and a more porous border between Hong Kong and mainland China appears unlikely until required by Hong Kong's Basic Law.[72]

5 A Socially Sensitive Fintech Policy for Hong Kong

The problems and opportunities of automation are now being addressed globally, and are not restricted to fintech. The hollowing out of the middle-income jobs in many industries will displace workers, and various proposals have been made to deal with the coming disruption. Muro et al. suggest governments implement programs to:

1. 'Invest in reskilling incumbent workers,

---

[69]According to the Hong Kong Tourism Board, visits to Hong Kong dropped in August and September 2019 by 39% and 34%, respectively. See https://partnernet.hktb.com/en/research_statistics/latest_statistics/index.html.

[70]Lockett and Hammond (2019).

[71]This finding of Fleming et al., referred to above, is also affirmed in a study conducted a Brookings Institute, which uses the phrase 'hollowing out' in its findings on automation. See Muro et al. (2019), p. 24.

[72]See e.g., Hui (2018).

2. Expand accelerated learning and certifications,
3. Make skill development more financially accessible,
4. Align and expand traditional education,
5. Foster uniquely human qualities.'[73]

Under existing programs, the HKSAR already funds university-level skill development and continuing professional education, making it much more affordable than in the US,[74] but existing education cannot be said to 'foster uniquely human qualities' such as innovation and creativity. However, even if the programs for training and reskilling were exceptional, the limited size and range of the Hong Kong economy would significantly impede transition to a new workplace. Yet, the cultural transition to the rest of China is for many in Hong Kong out of the question, particularly following the strong localist sentiment whipped up by 2019 protests and riots.[75] Such transition would be legally possible. In 2018, mainland China abolished its work permit requirement for Hong Kong residents, so they would be able to seek positions within the rest of China.[76] This will allow the obviated employees of financial institutions to seek work in the Mainland.

In light of this tangible dilemma, HKSAR policymakers should not trail blindly behind the financial industry as it automates processes and sheds employees to raise competitiveness. Until recently, the HKSAR could brag that it did not plan, but merely followed the flow of money—'market leads, government facilitates.'[77] That blew up badly in 2019, even if the economic policy failures were cloaked as a problem of 'Chinese oppression'.[78] Hong Kong's enthusiastic embrace of fintech follows the market just as many of its earlier policies did. However, in this case, market tracking should be accompanied by sober planning with regard to the probable consequences of fintech. Policymakers should allow the financial institutions themselves to develop fintech's potential while shifting their own focus and funds to Hong Kong society. The HKSAR should seek solutions for the probable impact of financial automation on those Hong Kong residents holding mid-level banking jobs with digitally rich, routine organization.

6 Conclusion

On the example of the HKSAR, this chapter has examined the introduction of fintech, its regulation, and the particular challenges these present for an IFC generally, and an

[73]Muro et al. (2019), pp. 50–56.

[74]Undergraduate tuition in all Hong Kong universities is supported with public funds and was in 2018 uniform at about HK$42,000 (about US$5,400), considerably less than that of an average US university.

[75]See e.g., Ren (2019).

[76]Lam (2018).

[77]Donald (2014), pp. 44–45.

[78]See e.g., Yip (2018).

IFC with limited economic breadth specifically. Fintech offers automation opportunities for financial institutions, and such automation will in many cases both replace human labor and provide services at a speed and quality that human labor could not. Studies show a hollowing out of mid-level jobs resulting from this automation. Financial institutions competing globally will not be able to ignore the advantages of fintech automation, but a large portion of the savings they achieve in this way will have direct, negative consequences on employees.

In its customary laissez-faire spirit, the HKSAR has actively embraced fintech while ignoring social consequences. Moreover, its regulation generally tracks leading international positions on such questions as cryptocurrency, ICOs and electronic payment, but largely overlooks local impact. While Hong Kong regulators have done a good job of positioning the HKSAR as a respectable IFC in its fintech regulation, they have also neglected promotion of activities that would stimulate the local economy, such as SME finance through equity crowdfunding. As such, the regulatory portfolio will stimulate job-reducing fintech in major firms while missing opportunities to alleviate the local woes automation will create.

Automation will unquestionably create some new, highly skilled positions in finance, but it will also translate into a reduction of necessary employees. That is the economic logic of the initiative. This is particularly true for the internationally active banks that employ a large number of people to perform the routine tasks with digital information that are susceptible to RPA and CRPA. In a large and varied economy, persons who lose their positions at banks may seek engagement in other sectors of the economy. In an IFC with limited economic breadth, such mobility is significantly restricted.

Hong Kong is a special administrative region of a country with a very large and growing economy, but presents the highly unusual case of an IFC in which much of the population is culturally alienated from its own country. Thus, displaced workers may refuse to seek new positions in the larger workplace for cultural or political reasons. The protests and riots of 2019 have shown that the HKSAR population does not hesitate to express violently its dissatisfaction with perceived social ills. This should be taken as a warning by the HKSAR government, which has blithely followed a 'market leads, government facilitates' philosophy of laissez-faire for decades.

Together with its active encouragement of fintech, the HKSAR should seek out the best, viable programs to assist persons who will be displaced through fintech automation. While such preparation does smack of the type of social planning that the HKSAR has so assiduously avoided, circumstances dictate that it now begin to act socially, rather than merely as facilitative for the largest and most visible businesses.

References

BBC (2019) Hong Kong protests: Rule of law on 'brink of collapse', police say. Available at https://www.bbc.com/news/world-asia-china-50384360. Accessed 31 March 2020

Browne R (2018) HSBC says it's made the world's first trade finance transaction using blockchain. CNBC, 14 May 2018. Available at www.cnbc.com. Accessed 31 March 2020
Campbell D (2017) Blankfein says it's too soon for a bitcoin strategy. Bloomberg (30 November)
Chan N (2018a) Keynote speech at treasury markets summit 2018: 'cryptoassets and money'. Hong Kong Monetary Authority (21 September)
Chan N (2018b) Launch of the faster payment system. InSight (17 September)
Chen L, Lee J (2017) Bitcoin tumbles as PBOC declares initial coin offerings illegal. Bloomberg (4 September)
Chen L (2014) Beyond the umbrella movement: Hong Kong's struggle with inequality in 8 charts. Forbes (8 October)
Davenport T (2019) A marriage of robotic process automation and machine learning. Forbes (6 June)
Dekhne A et al. (2019) Automation in logistics: big opportunity, bigger uncertainty. McKinsey & Company. https://www.mckinsey.com/industries/travel-transport-and-logistics/our-insights/automation-in-logistics-big-opportunity-bigger-uncertainty. Accessed 31 March 2020
Donald D (2014) A financial centre for two empires: Hong Kong's corporate, securities and tax laws in its transition from Britain to China. Cambridge University Press, Cambridge
Donald D (2015) Bridging finance without fragmentation: a comparative look at market connectivity in the US, Europe and Asia. European Business Organization Law Review 16(2):173–201
Ernst & Young (2016) Capital markets: innovation and the FinTech landscape. Available at: https://www.ey.com/Publication/vwLUAssets/EY-capital-markets-innovation-and-the-finTech-landscape/$FILE/EY-capital-markets-innovation-and-the-fintech-landscape.pdf. Accessed 31 March 2020
Financial Conduct Authority (FCA) (2015) Regulatory sandbox
Financial Services Development Council (FSDC) (2016) Introducing a regulatory framework for equity crowdfunding in Hong Kong
Fleming M et al. (2019) The future of work: how new technologies are transforming tasks. MIT-IBM Watson AI Lab (31 October)
Ford M (2015) Rise of the robots: technology and the threat of a jobless future. Basic Books, New York
Gartner Research (2018) Robotic process automation: 8 guidelines for effective results (27 June)
Harari YN (2018) 21 Lessons for the 21st century. Spiegel & Grau, New York
Harris R (2017) Actually, Deutsche Bank was right, it's time to bail on Hong Kong's housing market. South China Morning Post. Available at: https://www.scmp.com/business/money/markets-investing/article/2098174/actually-deutsche-bank-was-right-its-time-bail-hong. Accessed 31 March 2020
Heritage Foundation (2019) Index of economic freedom 2019. Available at www.heritage.org. Accessed 31 March 2020
Hong Kong Special Administrative Region (HKSAR) (2016) Report of the steering group on financial technologies
Hong Kong Monetary Authority (HKMA) (2018) Authorization of virtual banks a guideline issued by the Monetary Authority under Section 16(10)
Hui M (2018) A part of Hong Kong is effectively becoming mainland Chinese territory. Quartz (4 September)
KPMG (2017) Value of fintech. Available at: https://assets.kpmg/content/dam/kpmg/uk/pdf/2017/10/value-of-fintech.pdf. Accessed 31 March 2020
Lam C (2018) The Chief Executive's 2018 policy address: striving ahead rekindling hope. Available at: https://www.policyaddress.gov.hk/2018/eng/pdf/PA2018.pdf. Accessed 31 March 2020
Lam J (2018) China work permit requirement for Hong Kong, Macau and Taiwan jobseekers on the mainland to be abolished. South China Morning Post (3 August)
Leibniz GW (2001) from the original in 1710) Theodicy: essays on the goodness of God, the freedom of man, and the origin of evil. Wipf and Stock Publishers, Eugene Oregon

Liu J (2019) High-paid, well-educated white collar workers will be heavily affected by AI, says new report. CNBC (27 November)

Lockett H, Hammond G (2019) Alibaba stock jumps 6% in Hong Kong trading debut. Financial Times (27 November)

Malito M (2018) Don't worry, robots aren't going to steal your job — yet. MarketWatch. Available at: www.marketwatch.com. Accessed 31 March 2020

Miguel S et al. (CCAF) (2019) The ASEAN Fintech Ecosystem Benchmarking Study. The Cambridge Centre for Alternative Finance, Cambridge

Monetary Authority of Singapore (MAS) (2015) Facilitating securities-based crowd funding

Muro M et al. (2019) Automation and artificial intelligence: how machines are affecting people and places. Brookings Institution, Washington

Oxfam Hong Kong (2018) Hong Kong inequality report. Available at: https://www.oxfam.org.hk/tc/f/news_and_publication/16372/Oxfam_inequality%20report_Eng_FINAL.pdf. Accessed 31 March 2020

Piketty T (2013) Capital in the twenty-first century. Harvard University Press, Cambridge MA

Rauchs M et al. (2018) Distributed ledger technology systems: a conceptual framework. The Cambridge Centre for Alternative Finance. Available at: www.jbs.cam.ac.uk/faculty-res. Accessed 31 March 2020

Ren S (2019) Losing the Hong Kong that I love. Bloomberg (25 November)

Schmidt R and Bain B (2019) SEC Chief's crypto skepticism sets up Facebook clash over Libra. Bloomberg (27 August)

Securities and Futures Commission (SFC) (2014) Notice on potential regulations applicable to, and risks of, crowd-funding activities

Securities and Futures Commission (SFC) (2017a) Press release, statement on initial coin offerings

Securities and Futures Commission (SFC) (2017b) Circular to announce the SFC regulatory sandbox

Securities and Futures Commission (SFC) (2018) Press release, SFC warns of cryptocurrency risks

Snyder B (2019) Our misplaced fear of job-stealing robots. Insights by Stanford Business (7 March). https://www.gsb.stanford.edu/insights/misplaced-fear-job-stealing-robots. Accessed 31 March 2020

Soriano M et al. (2019) The ASEAN fintech ecosystem benchmarking study. Cambridge Centre for Alternative Finance (CCAF), Asian Development Bank Institute (ADBI) and FinTechSpace (September)

Strogatz Steven (2018) One giant step for a chess-playing machine. The New York Times (26 December)

World Bank Group (2019) Doing business report 2019. Available at: www.doingbusiness.org. Accessed 31 March 2020

World Economic Forum (2019) The global competitiveness report 2019. Available at: http://www3.weforum.org/docs/WEF_TheGlobalCompetitivenessReport2019.pdf. Accessed 31 March 2020

World Economic Forum (2018) The global competitiveness report 2018. Available at: http://www3.weforum.org/docs/GCR2018/05FullReport/TheGlobalCompetitivenessReport2018.pdf. Accessed 31 March 2020

World Economic Forum (2017) The global competitiveness report 2017–2018. Available at: http://www3.weforum.org/docs/GCR2017-2018/05FullReport/TheGlobalCompetitivenessReport2017%E2%80%932018.pdf. Accessed 31 March 2020

World Economic Forum (2016) The global competitiveness report 2016–2017. Available at: http://www3.weforum.org/docs/GCR2016-2017/05FullReport/TheGlobalCompetitivenessReport2016-2017_FINAL.pdf. Accessed 31 March 2020

World Economic Forum (2015) The global competitiveness report 2015–2016. Available at: http://www3.weforum.org/docs/gcr/2015-2016/Global_Competitiveness_Report_2015-2016.pdf. Accessed 31 March 2020

World Economic Forum (2014) The global competitiveness report 2014–2015. Available at: http://www3.weforum.org/docs/WEF_GlobalCompetitivenessReport_2014-15.pdf. Accessed 31 March 2020

Yip H (2018) Beijing is foisting a white elephant on Hong Kong. Foreign Policy (14 September)

Z/Yen Group (2007) ~ (2019) The global financial centres index (Nos 1–24). Available at: https://www.longfinance.net/publications/long-finance-reports/. Accessed 31 March 2020

Fintech Law and Practice: A Korean Perspective

Sunseop Jung

Abstract After reviewing the financial regulatory system and market structure in Korea, this chapter examines the recent development of fintech in the area of banking, capital markets, and payment services. In the banking sector, the main focus is on the development of internet-only banking. Under the strict regulations on the separation of financial capital and industrial capital, technological companies' entry into the banking business causes serious banking law debates. In capital markets, the application of the fintech model in capital markets such as equity and debt-based crowdfunding and robo-advisors is widely discussed. Easy payment & remittance and crypto-assets are a concern for both legal practitioners and the business sector. The legal character and function of crypto-assets is also a significant issue in Korea. In Korea, institutional efforts to introduce new financial products and services in accordance with the combination of technology and finance are being developed in various fields such as banking and securities. Particularly noteworthy is the introduction of new means of payment. The regulatory sandbox newly introduced by Korea will have an impact on the Korean financial regulatory system, which has traditionally been very conservative. This chapter is based on the law of Korea as of 30 June 2019.

Keywords Fintech · Sandbox · Internet-only bank · Equity-based crowdfunding · Robo-advisor · Easy payment and remittance · Crypto-assets · Korean law

1 Introduction

Fintech is developing a variety of new products and services by combining finance and technology. This development is particularly strong in the payment sector, as well as traditional financial services, such as banking, capital markets, and insurance. Regarding the development of fintech, the strict approach in the formulation and interpretation of the Korean financial law is again a problem. The basic approach

S. Jung (✉)
School of Law, Seoul National University, Seoul, Gwanak-Gu, Korea
e-mail: jungss@snu.ac.kr

M. Fenwick et al. (eds.), *Regulating FinTech in Asia*, Perspectives in Law, Business and Innovation, https://doi.org/10.1007/978-981-15-5819-1_4

to financial regulation in Korea is symbolized by the phrase 'no express permission means implicit prohibition.' Unlike most financially advanced countries, there is still a very restrictive legal interpretation in Korea if there is no explicit permission.

In a sense, it is natural that legal risks result from the time lag between law and market development. In particular, in a situation where new technology combines with traditional finance, like fintech, this problem can become more serious. This legal uncertainty creates a chilling effect to discourage entrepreneurs from innovating their way of financial transactions. However, finance is the product of technological development. Technology has important implications for the profitability, cost, risk, competitiveness, and position of financial institutions.[1] Technology affects the way of trading financial products and the structure of financial market infrastructure. As noted by a US regulator, '[w]hat is different today is the speed and tremendous impact of technological innovation *in* and *on* banking, and the potential for technology to disrupt not just an institution or two, but banking as we know it.'[2] In response, financial supervision and regulation should be changed to accommodate new risks and new methods to manage such risks.

This chapter is composed of seven sections. Section 2: Structure of Fintech and Financial Services Regulatory System will overview the financial regulatory system and market structure in Korea. This section will provide the background for further discussions in the following parts in this chapter. Section 3: Banking will examine the development of internet-only banks[3] in Korea. Under the strict regulations on the separation of financial capital and industrial capital, technological companies' entry into the banking business causes severe banking law debates. Section 4: Capital Markets will review various legal issues concerning the application of the fintech model in capital markets. Particularly noteworthy was the discussion on equity and debt-based crowdfunding and robo-advisors. Section 5: Payment and Settlement will examine 'easy' payment and remittance and crypto-assets.[4] The legal nature and function of crypto-assets is also a major issue in Korea. In Sect. 6: Fintech and Regulation, we look at various means to minimize legal risk and increase predictability around the regulatory sandbox. We will also discuss ways of embracing financing

[1] Balling et al. (2002), p. 1.

[2] McWilliams (2018), pp. 1–2.

[3] In this chapter, 'internet-only bank' refers to a bank which operate through electronic media such as the internet without any off-line offices. This type of internet bank is also referred to as 'pure-play, internet-only bank, online-only bank, or virtual bank.'

[4] Several terms are used for virtual currency such as cryptocurrency; digital currency; virtual asset, crypto-asset, and digital token. However, the term 'crypto-asset' has become common recently in international organizations. See Financial Stability Board (2018).

The term 'virtual currency' is used in the law of New York State and Japan (23 NYCRR Sect. 200.2 (p); Japan Payment Services Act, Art2(5)). Some institutions including the Financial Action Task Force(FATF) and Hong Kong Securities and Finance Commission(HKSFC) are using the term 'virtual assets'. FATF, International Standards on Combating Money Laundering and the Financing of Terrorism and Proliferation: The FATF Recommendations, Updated October 2018; HKSFC, Regulatory standards for licensed corporations managing virtual asset portfolios, 1 November 2018.

for vulnerable groups that could be caused by fintech. Section 7: Conclusion will summarize the above discussions and review the main points of this chapter.[5]

2 Structure of Fintech and Financial Services Regulatory System

2.1 Overview

This section will provide an overview of the financial regulatory system and market structure in Korea. This section will provide the background for further discussions in the following parts in this chapter. Korea's financial law is based on the division of banking, capital markets, and insurance business. However, its regulatory system is based on an integrated supervisory model.

Fintech, which means a combination of technology and finance or 'technology-enabled innovation in financial services,'[6] still operates within the traditional financial market framework. Traditional legal concepts and regulatory measures that do not know new technological developments are applied to various fields of fintech without any modification or supplement. A more critical issue is the expertise of the people responsible for these regulations and supervision.

The new business model based on technological development can be subject to entry regulation under the financial regulatory laws and regulations if it corresponds to the definition of traditional financial services. If a company is to start such financial services activities without authorization, it will be subject to strict sanctions, e.g., criminal penalties.

2.2 Financial Regulatory System

2.2.1 Financial Services Laws

Financial regulatory laws in Korea are based on a *multiple sector by sector approach.* Three pillars of the Korean financial services law are the Banking Act 1950,[7] the Financial Investment Services and Capital Markets Act 2009 ('FISCMA'),[8] and the Insurance Business Act 1962.[9]

[5]In the insurance sector, we are discussing legal issues involving P2P insurance model and autonomous vehicles including self-propelled vehicle, drone and autonomous vessel in Korea. This chapter does not cover insurance issues.

[6]European Commission (2018).

[7][Enforcement date May 5, 1950] [Law No. 139, May 5, 1950].

[8][Enforcement date February 4, 2009] [Law No. 8635, August 3, 2007].

[9][Enforcement date January 15, 1962] [Law No. 973, January 15, 1962].

The Banking Act 1950 regulates 'business of lending funds raised by bearing debts owed to many and unspecified persons, by the receipt of deposits or the issuance of securities and other bonds' (Article 2(1)(i)). The Special Act on the Establishment and Operation of internet-only Bank 2018[10] was enacted in order to prescribe special cases that apply to internet-only banks in comparison with general banks. The Banking Act regulates only the business of lending money raised by deposits. Loans based on non-deposit-financed funds are regulated by the Act on Registration of Credit Business, etc. and Protection of Finance Users 2002 ('Credit Business Act 2002')[11] and the Specialized Credit Finance Business Act 1997.[12] In Korea, credit card companies are also subject to the Specialized Credit Finance Business Act 1997. The Banking Act 1950 or the Credit Business Act 2002 may be applied to payment transactions in connection with bank deposit accounts or P2P lending.

The FISCMA 2009 regulates the financial investment industry and the capital market.[13] This Act was enacted to consolidate six major capital market-related laws, including the Securities Transaction Act, Futures Trading Act, Indirect Investment Asset Management Business Act, Trust Business Act, Merchant Banks Act, and Korea Securities and Futures Exchange Act (FISCMA, Addendum Article 2). The FISCMA covers securities issuance, investment dealing and brokerages, collective investment businesses and investment advisory businesses. This Act may be applied to securities-based crowdfunding and robo-advisors.

The Insurance Business Act 1962 regulates the insurance business and sale of insurance products, including life and non-life insurance. This Act may be applied to the way how to insure autonomous vehicle and P2P insurance as an insurance business model.

The Electronic Financial Transactions Act 2007[14] is also very important in relation to the emergence of fintech, in particular new types of payment instruments. This Act regulates 'electronic financial transactions' which means 'any transaction whereby a financial company or an electronic financial services provider provides financial products and services through electronic devices and users use them in a non-facing and automated manner without any direct contact with employees of the financial company or electronic financial services provider (Article 2(i)). The Electronic Financial Transactions Act does not explicitly define 'financial products and services' that are subject of electronic financial transactions. According to the FSS, as the scope of electronic financial services should be viewed as a broad concept when considering the popularization, diversification, and protection of users of electronic financial transactions, credit information, asset custody, or transaction history service

[10][Enforcement date January 17, 2019] [Law No. 15856, October 16, 2018].

[11][Enforcement date October 27, 2002] [Law No. 6706, August 26, 2002].

[12][Enforcement date January 1, 1998] [Law No. 5374, August 28, 1997]

[13]For more on the structure of the FISCMA, see Park (2011), pp. 91–141.

[14][Enforcement date January 1, 2007] [Law No. 7929, April 28, 2006].

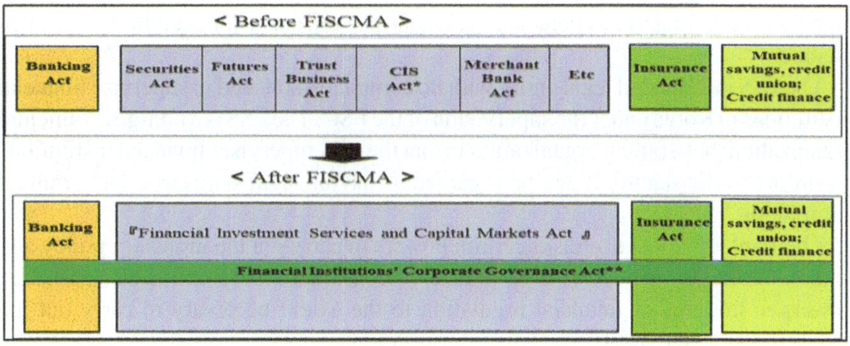

Fig. 1 Financial Regulatory Laws in Korea (Ministry of Finance and Economy)

through the internet corresponds to electronic financial service.[15] However, the Electronic Financial Transactions Act is to regulate only electronic payment transactions using electronic devices for two reasons (Fig. 1).

Firstly, the scope of the electronic financial services regulated by the Electronic Financial Transactions Act is limited to electronic funds transfer services, issuance, and management of electronic debit payment instruments, issuance and management of electronic prepaid payment instruments, and electronic payment settlement agency services (Article 2(iv), Article 28(2)).

Secondly, while the Electronic Financial Transactions Act provides general rules for electronic financial transactions and special rules for electronic payment instruments, there is no regulation regarding electronic banking, securities, insurance, or other traditional financial transactions.

2.3 *Financial Regulatory Bodies*[16]

The financial supervisory system consists of the Financial Services Commission (FSC) and the Financial Supervisory Service(FSS). The FSC is a central administrative body established by the Act on the Establishment, etc. of Financial Services Commission[17] to independently perform the tasks related to financial policy and regulation. It is characterized by the independence of the authority by separately stipulating the method of exercising administrative authority. The FSC consists of nine

[15]FSS (2017), p. 10.

[16]for more on Korea's financial regulatory system, see Jung (2017), pp. 734–736.

[17][Enforcement date April 1, 1998] [Law No. 5490, December 31, 1997]. This act was enacted as Act on the Establishment, etc. of Financial Supervisory Organizations in 1997. However, the name of the was changed to the current Act on the Establishment, etc. of Financial Services Commission in 2008. [Enforcement date February 29, 2008] [Law No. 8863, February 29, 2008].

members, including a chairperson, a vice-chairperson, and a non-standing committee member.

The FSS is a 'special legal entity with no capital' established to supervise financial institutions in Korea under the supervision of the FSC. The FSS is a non-governmental organization, but a public organization in that the FSS supervises financial institutions according to the statute. It can be regarded as having legal status as a 'government corporation.'

The Bank of Korea exercises certain powers to carry out the monetary policy and to monitor the payment system. Korea Deposit Insurance Corporation also has some powers in the area of financial regulation to the extent necessary to carry out the restructuring of the insolvent financial institutions.

3 Banking

3.1 Overview

Until now, fintech in Korea's banking sector has been mainly concerned with internet-only banks and P2P lending except for new types of payment instruments. Issues on the legal and regulatory treatment of new types of payment instruments will be discussed in Sect. 5: Payment and settlement. In a sense, P2P lending is not directly related to the Banking Act as there is no element of deposit-taking. However, as lending is an essential element of the legal definition of banking in Korea, this chapter will review the legal issues regarding P2P lending in this section.

3.2 Internet-Only Banks

3.2.1 Definition

In Korea, internet-only banks have been known as the symbolic presence of fintech.[18] Even though there could be various types of internet bank, internet-only banks in Korea refers to banks without any offline offices. As of the end of November 2018, there are only two internet-only banks that were authorized in 2016 and 2017 by the Banking Act 1950 under the same principle as traditional banks.

The FSC restricts the method of business of internet-only bank to 'method of electronic financial transaction' only as a condition of the authorization.[19] The 'electronic financial transaction' means 'any transaction whereby a financial company

[18] Jung (2017), pp. 52–53.

[19] The FSC may impose necessary conditions for stabilizing financial markets, securing the soundness of banks and protecting depositors in granting banking authorization (Article 8(4)). The Special Act on the Establishment and Operation of Internet-only Bank 2018 defines 'internet-only bank'

or an electronic financial business entity provides financial products and services through electronic apparatus ('electronic financial business') and users use them in a non-facing and automated manner without any direct contact with employees of the financial company or electronic financial business entity' (Electronic Financial Transactions Act, Article 2(1)). This means that the bank trades through electronic devices (CDs, ATMs, computers, telephones, etc.), and the users do not face bank employees in an automated manner. Currently, the internet-only banking in Korea is a completely non-offline-store type.

However, in very exceptional situations, internet-only banks can do face-to-face business or operation.[20] It was an issue of debate whether it is a violation of the condition to meet the customer only where an internet-only bank is trying to conduct a bank transaction by electronic financial transaction method. Still, the customer is unable to complete the transaction by electronic financial transaction method. In this regard, the banking supervisory body judged that it was difficult to meet the condition on the method of electronic financial transaction considering the necessity of financial consumer protection such as depositors in Article 1 of the Banking Act.

The internet-only bank established under the Special Act on the Establishment and Operation of Internet-only bank 2018 shall be deemed to be an established bank under the Banking Act (Article 3(2)).

3.2.2 Shareholding Restriction

One of the main issues involving internet-only banks was whether to ease the strict regulation on the separation of financial and industrial capital in the case of an internet-only bank. The strict regulation on the separation of financial capital and industrial capital were regarded as a hindrance to technology companies' entry into the banking business, in particular, internet-only banking. The separation of industrial and financial capital has long been an issue of hot debate in Korea.[21]

Traditionally, the combination of banks and industries has been problematic in terms of (1) conflict of interest, (2) spread of risk, and (3) concentration of economic power.[22] However, there was a strong argument that industrial capital such as IT companies could strengthen control over the banks to introduce the finance technology to the banking sector, in particular in the case of internet-only banks.[23]

The National Assembly enacted the Special Act on the Establishment and Operation of Internet-only bank 2018 to ease the strict regulation in the context of an internet-only bank. This new Act has two special provisions for internet-only banks. Firstly, minimum capital of an internet-only bank is 25 billion Korean won compared

---

as 'a bank that mainly conducts banking business in the manner of electronic financial transactions (transactions pursuant to Article 2 (1) of the Electronic Financial Transactions Act)' (Article 2).

[20] FSC/FSS (2016).

[21] Lee et al. (2018), p. 75.

[22] Jung (2017), p. 62.

[23] Jung (2017), p. 62.

to 25 billion Korean won in the case of traditional banks (Banking Act Article 8(2)(i)) (Article 4(1)). Secondly, while the Banking Act restricts the shareholding limit of non-financial business operators at 4%(Article 16-2, Article 16(1)(2)), non-financial business operators may hold stocks of an internet-only bank within 34% of the total voting rights of such bank (Article 5(1)).

As a consequence, the strict regulations on the separation of financial capital and industrial capital was eased for an internet-only bank. The term 'non-financial business operators' is the key concept in the regulation of the shareholding limit for the separation of industrial and financial capital. The criteria are as follows:

Firstly, the gross capital of non-financial companies is at least 25% of the gross capital of the person and its affiliates, or Secondly, the total assets of non-financial companies among the person and its affiliates are at least 2 trillion won (Banking Act, Article 2(1)(ix)).[24]

---

[24]The term 'non-financial business operators' means any of the following persons:

(a) The same persons where the total amount of gross capital (referring to the gross amount of assets less the gross amount of debts on the balance sheet; hereinafter the same shall apply) of the persons who are non-financial companies (referring to companies that operate business that is not financial business determined by Presidential Decree; hereinafter the same shall apply) is not less than 25/100 of the total amount of gross capital of the persons who are companies;

(b) The same person where the amount of total assets of the persons who are non-financial companies is not less than the amount prescribed by Presidential Decree, which is not less than two trillion won;

(c) An investment company under the Financial Investment Services and Capital Markets Act (hereinafter referred to as 'investment company') where a person referred to in item (a) or (b) holds more than 4/100 of the total number of its issued stocks (referring to cases where the same person owns stocks in his/her own name or any other person's name or has voting rights on such stocks through a contract, etc.; hereinafter the same shall apply);

(d) A private equity fund under the Financial Investment Services and Capital Markets Act (hereinafter referred to as 'private equity fund'), which falls under any of the following cases:

(i) Where a person referred to in any of items (a) through (c) is a limited partner who holds not less than 10/100 of shares in the total investments in the private equity fund (in such cases, shares of the relevant partner and those of other partners who have a special relationship with such partner shall be included in the calculation of shares);

(ii) Where a person referred to in any of items (a) through (c) is a general partner of the private equity fund (Provided, That, this shall not apply where a person falls under any of items (a) through (c) as a consequence of an investment by a general partner who does not fall under any of items (a) through (c) in stocks or shares of a non-financial company through another private equity fund but limited partners of the relevant private equity fund (including the relevant partner and other limited partners who have a special relationship with such partner) have not made an investment in another private equity fund);

(iii) Where the sum of shares in the private equity fund, acquired by affiliated companies (referring to affiliated companies defined by the Monopoly Regulation and Fair Trade Act; hereinafter the same shall apply) that belong to different enterprise groups subject to limitations on mutual investment (referring to an enterprise group subject to limitations on mutual investment under the Monopoly Regulation and Fair Trade Act; hereinafter the same shall apply), is not less than 30/100 of total investments in the private equity fund; (e) A special purpose company where a private equity fund referred to in item (d) (including a person referred to in any of items (a) through (c) of this

3.3 *Identification Certificate/Real-Name Confirmation*

3.3.1 Duty to Identify 'Real Name' for Financial Transactions

In Korea, the Act on Real Name Financial Transactions and Confidentiality 1997[25] requires a financial company to identify the real name of a party to a financial transaction. The purpose of this Act is 'to realize economic justice and to facilitate the sound development of the national economy by implementing real-name financial transactions and ensuring the confidentiality thereof through normalized financial transactions' (Article 1).[26] The real name law, which distinguishes it from Know Your Customer requirement for the purpose of anti-money laundering (AML) and is a system unique to Korea. AML and CFT is subject to the jurisdiction of the Financial Intelligence Unit under the Act on Reporting and Use of Certain Financial Transaction Information 2001.[27]

Financial companies shall execute financial transactions with customers under their real names (Real Name Act, Article 3(1)). 'Financial transactions' refers to 'transactions in which financial companies receive, sell and purchase, repurchase, mediate, discount, issue, redeem, return, are entrusted with, register, or exchange financial assets, or in which financial companies pay interest, money discounted, or dividends of those financial assets or carry out such payment as an agent, or other transactions involving financial assets as determined by the Ordinance of the Prime Minister[28]'(Article 2(3)). 'Financial assets' include deposits, trusts, stocks, bonds, beneficiary certificates, equity, notes, checks, debts, and other similar securities, which are dealt with by a financial company' (Real Name Act Article2(ii)). However, it does not cover insurance policy and loan products.

'Real name' means 'a name entered in a resident registration card, a name entered in a business registration certificate or any other name as determined by Presidential Decree' (Article 2(4)). A fine for negligence not exceeding 30 million Korean won shall be imposed on an executive or employee of a financial company who violates real name identification requirement (Real Name Act, Article 7).

subparagraph, among persons who have acquired stocks or shares of the special purpose company under Article 249-13 (1) 3 (b) or (c) of the Financial Investment Services and Capital Markets Act) acquires and holds more than 4/100 of stocks or shares of the special purpose company or exercises a de facto influence over the major managerial matters of the special purpose company, such as appointment or dismissal of its executives. For more, see Jung (2017), pp. 83–85.

[25][Enforcement Date December 31, 1997] [No. 5493, December 31, 1997].

[26]Supreme Court of Korea, March 19, 2009. 2008Da45828.

[27][Enforcement Date November 28, 2001] [No. 6516, September, 2001].

[28]There is nothing stipulated in the Enforcement Regulations of the Financial Real Name Act.

3.3.2 Reform

In the context of internet-only banks, the problem was how to identify the real name of the parties to financial transactions. The method and procedures for identifying real name is prescribed by the Presidential Decree (Real Name Act, Article 3(7)). Initially, the FSC permitted only a face-to-face real name identification method. The customer should appear in person before the counter of a bank to identify himself/herself with an identification card. Is it possible to operate a bank specialized on the internet under such a system? On December 1, 2015, the FSC permitted non-face-to-face real name identification with high-tech methodologies.[29] The alternative consists of two steps:

The first step is mandatory. Financial companies should use at least 2 of (1) copy of identification card, (2) video call, (3) verification when transferring means of access, (4) use of an existing account, (5) biometric Authentication/verification.

The second step is an additional requirement. Financial companies should, in addition to the first step, select at least 1 of (6) use of verification results of other companies (mobile phone verification), (7) a variety of personal information, and (8) different methods designed by those companies.

The acceptance of the non-face-to-face real name identification method is recognized as the institutional starting point of internet-only banks and other fintech businesses in Korea.

3.4 P2P Lending

3.4.1 Definition

P2P lending or debt-based crowdfunding refers to a structure in which a group of investors extends small loans to the borrower through the internet platform. P2P Lending Guidelines[30] defines P2P lending as 'a loan facility to a person who wishes to receive a loan through an online platform based on the funds of a person who provides collateral for the borrower and receives a fee, or purchases the right to receive principal and interest payments from the borrower's loan (hereinafter referred to as 'investor')' (Guideline, Definition). P2P lending may be divided into two types: direct loans and indirect loans. In Korea, most P2P lending transactions are taking the type of indirect loan. For this, an internet platform or P2P vendor which brokers borrowers and investors from the internet establishes a lender for loan execution.

After the full implementation of the guideline, the growth has somewhat eased, but the monthly growth rate is steadily growing to 8–10%.[31]

---

[29] FSC (2015a); see also, Korea Federation of Banks (2016), pp. 38–39.

[30] These guidelines were originally published on February 2017 (enforcement date: February 27, 2017). See FSC/FSS (2018b); see also, FSC/FSS (2018a).

[31] FSC/FSS (2018a).

3.4.2 Guidelines

Currently, there is no direct and express regulation on P2P lending in Korea. There are only guidelines published by the FSC and the FSS. However, these guidelines do not have legally binding power.[32]

The P2P Lending Guidelines set a lending limit for individual ordinary investors between 5 and 40 million Korean won depending on the income of the investors (Guideline 2.7). However, these limits do not apply to corporate investors and individual professional investors.[33] P2P loan brokers should segregate client assets from assets of P2P platform or moneylenders by trusting investors' assets to a reputable institution such as a bank (Guideline 2.6).

According to a survey result by the FSS for 178 P2P lenders in Korea, it was found that many companies raised concerns about the potential cases of fraud and embezzlement.[34] The FSS warned that damage to investors has been spreading due to fraud or embezzlement of some P2P companies. The FSS also asked the prosecutors to investigate 20 companies for which illegal activities were detected. Other companies have also been advised to improve their internal controls and adhere to the P2P loan guidelines.

Legislative discussions are underway to regulate P2P lending. 2 bills to regulate P2P lending have been submitted to the National Assembly.[35]

3.4.3 Structure

Figure 2 shows the general structure of P2P lending in Korea. There are two reasons for this structure. Firstly, money-lenders can transfer their credit right to financial companies and other regulated entities only. As a result of the amendment of the Credit Business Act on May 2015, moneylenders and credit financial institutions cannot transfer their credit rights under loan contracts to those who are not appointed by the Presidential Decree, such as registered moneylenders, credit financial institutions, etc. (Article 4, Paragraph 3 of Article 9). The qualifying transferee includes the Korea Deposit Insurance Corporation, the Korea Asset Management Corporation, the Korea Housing Finance Corporation, and the Agricultural Cooperative Asset Management Company. It is natural that a financial institution tries to collect

[32]'[Guidelines] are intended to advise financial institutions on matters that should be considered when dealing with derivatives transactions. ..., even if the transaction is against a guideline that prohibits ..., it cannot be regarded as an invalidation of the transaction itself.' Supreme Court, September 26, 2013, 2011Da53683,53690.

[33]The terms 'ordinary investors' and 'professional investors' are defined in the FISCMA. Classification criteria are risk-taking ability of the investors including expertise in financial investment products and the amount of assets owned (FISCMA, Article 9(5)). For more, see Kim and Jung (2013), pp. 151–155.

[34]FSS (2018).

[35]Bill on Online Loan Brokerage Business (July 20, 2017); Bill on Online Loan Business and User Protection (February 23, 2018). For more, see Ko (2018).

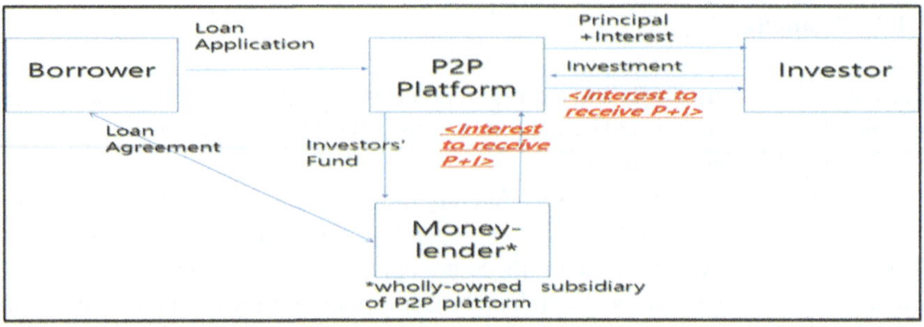

Fig. 2 Debt-Based P2P Lending

loans through the sale of non-performing loans. However, the Act restricts the illegal moneylenders and investors from purchasing NPLs indiscreetly and collecting them illegally.[36] A person who has transferred a credit right under a loan contract in violation of this regulation shall be subject to imprisonment for up to three years, or a fine of up to 30 million Korean won (Article 19 (2)(v)). Taking this into consideration, authorized moneylenders were included between the borrower and the investors in the loan structure, as shown in Fig. 2.

Secondly, if <*Interest to receive P* + *I*>, which was sold to investors by the money-lender, is characterized as *security*, this structure shall be subject to *public offering regulation* under the FISCMA. The structure of transferring < *Interest to receive P* + *I* > to investors by the money-lender takes the structure of loan participation. The lead bank (in this case, the moneylender) retains a partial interest in the loan, holds all loan documentation in its own name, services the loan, and deals directly with the customer for the benefit of all participants.[37] The main issue is whether < *Interest to receive P* + *I* >, partial interest on the loan is whether or not it corresponds to the concept of security.[38] Under this structure, the money-lender has a direct contractual relationship with the borrower, while the investors have a contractual relationship with the money-lender as Lead Bank, not with the borrower. P2P platform-linked money-lender is subject to FSC and FSS regulation (Presidential Decree for the Act on Registration of Credit Business, etc. and Protection of Finance Users < Presidential Decree No 28257, Aug. 29, 2017 > , Article 2).

---

[36] Jung (2017), pp. 193–194.

[37] Vogel, Herger and Reynolds (2013), p. 3.

[38] Ko (2015), p. 28.

4 Capital Markets

4.1 Overview

In the capital market field, fintech is mainly focused on securities-based crowdfunding, robo-advisors, and the use of new instruments such as crypto-assets for fund-raising or investment purposes. The FISCMA has already enacted special rules on crowdfunding and robo-advisors. Legal issues on crypto-assets for fund-raising or investment purposes are examined in Sect. 6: Payment and Settlement below.

4.2 Securities-Based Crowdfunding

4.2.1 Structure

Crowdfunding can be classified into three types, including securities-based, loan-based, and donation-based.[39] Securities-based crowdfunding consists of equity-based and debt-based, according to the type of securities issued under the facility. Korea adopted the regulation to allow a securities-based crowdfunding program in 2015, which enables start-ups and small and medium-sized companies to raise capital from investors.[40]

As of January 2018, a total of 274 companies (298 projects) raised 45.2 billion Korean won (1.6 billion Korean won average per issuer) through crowdfunding for two years.[41] While the business experience of 59.7% of the total issuers was less than three years, the amount of 77.2% of the transactions was less than 200 million Korean won. The FSC estimates that securities-based crowdfunding has been established as a channel for procuring small-scale funding for companies in the early stages of their start-up, in various industries, such as IT, manufacturing, and cultural contents.[42]

The main concern in the regulation of crowdfunding is whether to regulate online platforms as brokers and whether to include securities-based crowdfunding within the realm of a public offering. In Korea, the deregulation claim for crowdfunding was accepted. However, there has been controversy about the level of adequate investor protection. The entry regulation for crowdfunding brokers involved in crowdfunding and disclosure requirements for public offering securities has been relaxed. However, it is claimed that there is still a need to further mitigate restrictions on investment limits of individual investors and the scope of qualifying issuers.

[39]Loan-based crowdfunding or P2P lending is discussed in Sect. 3. Banking above of this chapter. The legal structure of crowdfunding varies from country to country. See, e.g., Ulrich and Bholat (2016); United States Government Accountability Office (2011).

[40][Enforcement date January 25, 2015] [Law No. 13448, July 24, 2015].

[41]FSC/FSS et al. (2018).

[42]FSC/FSS et al. (2018).

4.2.2 Regulation

(a) **Definition**

The FISCMA defines crowdfunding as 'public offering or sale of debt securities, equity securities and investment contract securities issued by the qualifying issuers, on another person's account in whatever name by the method prescribed by Presidential Decree' (FISCMA Article 9(27).

(b) **Types of Securities: Online small-value securities**

The types of securities which can be issued under such a crowdfunding program include debt securities, equity securities, and investment contract securities, which are referred to as 'online small-value securities' in the FISCMA. The FISCMA classifies securities into six types, such as debt securities, equity securities, beneficiary certificates, investment contract securities, derivatives-linked securities, and depositary receipts depending on the type of rights recognized in securities.[43] The other types of securities, including beneficiary certificates, derivatives-linked securities, and depositary receipts cannot be used for securities-based crowdfunding program. Beneficiary certificates are securities which represent a beneficial interest in a trust. Derivatives-linked securities denote securitized derivatives. Depositary receipts bear a right related to the deposited underlying securities in a depository. As there is no case of investment contract securities in Korea, online small value securities may be either debt securities or equity securities.

(b) **Qualifying Issuers**

'Qualifying issuers' include non-listed small and medium-sized business starters with less than seven years of business experience. However, venture companies, technological innovation-type SMEs, etc., which take the initial time to develop technology, may use the crowdfunding program regardless of the business experience. While equity-listed companies and gaming industry etc. cannot use this program, the scope of issuers can be expanded by the FSC.

(c) **Method of Issuing Online Small Value Securities**

A 'Method prescribed by Presidential Decree' means the method of issuing online small-value securities after making arrangements for the exchange of opinions between the issuer and investors, and mutually among investors on the website of a crowdfunding broker including a site opened by the crowdfunding broker at a cyberspace through an application used by mobile communications terminals or any other similar application program (FISCMA Presidential Decree, Article 14-4(1)).

---

[43]For more detailed discussion on the definition of securities in Korea, see Kim and Jung (2013), pp. 65–95.

4.2.3 Crowdfunding Brokers

(a) **Entry Regulation**

The FISCMA defines crowdfunding brokerage as 'online brokerage of public offering or sale of debt securities, equity securities and investment contract securities issued by the qualifying issuers, on another person's account in whatever names by the method prescribed by Presidential Decree' (FISCMA Article 9(27). Crowdfunding broker is an investment broker engaging in the crowdfunding brokerage (FISCMA Article 9(27). Entry regulation for crowdfunding broker is *registration*, instead of *permission* for general investment brokerage business (FISCMA Articles 117-3,117-4). No one shall engage in the brokerage of crowdfunding unless he/she has been registered as a crowdfunding broker (FISCMA Article 117-3). Capital requirement is at least 50 million Korean won.

(b) **Conduct of Business Regulation**

The FISCMA also exempts most conduct of business regulation for crowdfunding broker such as suitability, appropriateness, duty to explain, the appointment of a compliance officer, prudential regulation, etc. and general principles for proper business activities of crowdfunding broker (FISCMA Article117-7(1)). Instead, the FISCMA provides for alternative investor protection regime for crowdfunding as follows:

First, the annual limit of the issuing amount is 700 million Korean won per issuer.

Second, the FISCMA also provides for an annual limit of investment (annual and per issuer), which classify 4 groups of 5million/10million/20million/no limit based on sophistication of the investors.

Third, a lock-up period to prevent losses caused by the circulation of high-risk securities, and to encourage a long-term investment culture, all crowdfunding securities shall be deposited or separately kept in custody with KSD, and cannot to be resold or transferred for six months unless the buyer is a professional investor. The lock-up period for issuers and major shareholders is one year.

Fourth, if the amount of subscription falls short of the target amount, the issuer shall cancel the issuance thereof.

Fifth, crowdfunding brokers should segregate investors' money and securities.

Sixth, investment advice, and acquiring crowdfunding securities by crowdfunding broker is also prohibited.

Seventh, the FISCMA provides for responsibilities of Providers of Electronic Message Board Services such as Naver and Daum) to limit the method of advertisement to Electronic Message Board Services, to give guidance and recommendations to comply with the obligations prescribed in Article 117-9, to take measures to prevent damage to investors, such as restricting access by the violator, and deleting information posted in violation of the Act, and to report to the FSC on the fact that the violator has violated the FISCMA.

(c) **Primary Market Disclosure Regulation**

The FISCMA exempts registration statements and prospectus requirements for a public offering of online small-value securities of less than 700 million Korean won issued under the crowdfunding program. Instead, issuers should post terms of the issue, financial condition, business plan, etc. on the website of the crowdfunding broker. Crowdfunding brokers have to confirm the issuer's financial condition, personal background of the executives of the issuer, use of the fund, etc. before brokering crowdfunding. Issuers, issuers' representatives and directors, CPA, credit companies etc. who confirmed the correctness of business plan and other documents will assume liability for damages caused by false descriptions in the relevant documents. And damages may be calculated based on the presumption of damages under Article 126 of the FISCMA (FISCMA Article 117-10).

4.3 Robo-Advisors

In Korea, a robo-advisor is called an 'electronic investment advice devices' in Korean law (FISCMA Presidential Decree Article 99(1((i-ii); Financial investment Services Regulation Article 4-73-2). FISCMA, in principle, requires the use of manpower for the investment advisory business or the discretionary investment business except for electronic investment advice devices that meet certain requirements (Article 98(1(iii)). Electronic investment advice devices denote automated computerized information processing equipment with all of the following requirements (FISCMA Presidential Decree Article 99(1((i–ii); Financial investment Services Regulation Article 4-73-2):

- To analyze the investment propensity of the investors through the electronic investment advice device considering the investor's purpose of investment, asset situation, and investment experience.
- To prepare a system for prevention or recovery of accidents and disasters;
- not to concentrate investment assets included in the investment advice or discretionary investment assets in one issue or asset.
- To rebalance the contents of investment advice or portfolio following assessment of operation based on safety and profitability of Investment advice and portfolio at least once a quarter.
- To have one or more professional personnel in charge of maintenance of the electronic investment advice devices.
- To conduct the requirements review process by the deliberation committee composed of external experts.

With regard to robo-advisors, one of the significant issues was whether it is possible to make non-face-to-face investment discretionary management contract with ordinary investors. Initially, it was prohibited because the FISCMA required face-to-face execution of the duty to explain (Financial Investment Business Regulation Article 4-77(18)). This regulation was revised to allow non-face-to-face performance of the duty to explain either using video calls or through online interaction, etc.

5 Payment and Settlement

5.1 Overview

As in other countries, fintech is the most developed in the payment sector in Korea. Preference for cash as a payment instrument has been the highest in Korea, together with Japan. Recently, the proportion of cash use is rapidly declining both in wholesale and retail transactions, as discussed below. Credit cards are now one of the most widely used means of payment. The use of various easy payment & transfer services is increasing rapidly. Korea is one of the countries with the most active transactions of crypto-assets. As of November 23, 2018, there is no law or regulation expressly regulating crypto-assets except guidelines and self-regulatory practices.[44]

5.2 Easy Payment and Transfer

5.2.1 General

The use of easy payment and transfer services has increased significantly. This may be due to the government's deregulation and the expansion of the provision of smartphones to improve service provision conditions. Mainly, the expansion of the use of easy payment service reflects the preference for credit cards as means of payment. According to the results of the survey by the Bank of Korea in 2017, while cash (36.1%) and credit cards (31.4%) accounted for the majority based on the proportion of usage by type of payment, credit card (34.5%) followed by cash (20.3%) took the majority in terms of the amount paid.[45] It is illegal for merchants to refuse payment by credit cards or to differentiate credit card users compared to cash payers (Specialized Credit Finance Business Act 1997, Article 19(1)). A violation of this prohibition is subject to a criminal penalty, a sentence of less than one year or a fine of less than 10 million Korean won (Specialized Credit Finance Business Act 1997, Article 70(4)(iv)).

---

[44]Financial Intelligence Unit (2018); Korea Blockchain Association (2017).

[45]Bank of Korea (2018), p. 51.

In terms of regulation, easing measures such as allowing electronic payment agent's credit card information retention (October 2014) and abolishing the obligation to use an accredited certificate[46] for the electronic financial transaction (March 2015) became important occasions. Retention of credit card information by an electronic payment agent is made possible by amendment of credit card merchant's standard terms of credit association (August 28, 2014). A 'technology neutrality principle,' which does not mandate the use of specific technologies or services was introduced on October 15, 2014 by amending the Electronic Financial Transactions Act. The obligation to use accredited certificates for electronic financial transactions was abolished (Electronic Financial Transactions Supervision Regulation Article 37).[47]

5.2.2 Easy Payment Service

An easy payment service refers to 'a service in which a purchaser of an online commerce inputs payment information such as credit card information or account information at the first time or the minimum number of times, and payment is completed only by authentication of a password at the time of payment.'[48] A payment user can store his or her payment information in advance in a server of a payment service provider or a financial institution or charge a certain amount of money in a virtual account of a service institution. This service is regulated as payment gateway services under the Electronic Financial Transactions Act. The payment gateway service or 'electronic payment settlement agency service' means 'any service to transmit or receive payment settlement information in purchasing goods or using services by electronic means or to execute as an agent or mediate the settlement of prices thereof' (Electronic Financial Transactions Act, Article2(xix)). Any person who intends to provide this service shall register himself/herself with the FSC except banks and other financial institutions (Article28(2)(iv)).

5.2.3 Easy Transfer Service

Easy transfer service means 'a service to transfer prepaid money, which is charged by way of transfer of money through a mobile device, to a recipient by using a telephone number, SNS, etc.'[49] This service is using electronic prepayment instruments under the Electronic Financial Transactions Act. Any person who intends to provide this service shall register himself/herself with the FSC except banks and other financial institutions (Article28(2)(iii)).

---

[46]Accredited certificate or public key certificate was a type of electronic signature which was required in electronic financial transactions in Korea.

[47]FSC (2015a).

[48]Bank of Korea (2018), p. 79.

[49]Bank of Korea (2018), p. 79.

5.3 Crypto-Assets

5.3.1 Overview

Crypto-assets have been described as the emergence of new means of payment based on technology advances in the industry. There is also an evaluation that the new monetary system has been established by removing the influence of the state by converting the state-led legal system into a monetary system based on private autonomy. However, as the possibility of being abused by financial crimes has been confirmed through the Silk Road case[50], it is necessary to emphasize the necessity of regulating the crypto-assets from the perspective of strengthening transparency and prevention of money laundering. It is pointed out that crypto-assets may be exploited for money laundering due to their speed, ease, and anonymity. The G-7 Summit also emphasizes the need for measures to ensure transparency in financial flows through appropriate regulation of virtual currencies and new means of payment.

The term 'currency' or 'money' is used in the sense of a new means of payment, but it is somewhat stronger in terms of being recognized and used as a new means of investment or funding. The function as a new funding instrument, such as the Initial Coin Offering (ICO), is to enable the unrestricted borrowing of a business. It means a significant change. In Korea, concerns about the large-scale loss of users due to the surge in crypto-assets transaction volume began to appear, while emphasizing the necessity of upbringing from an industrial policy perspective.[51]

5.3.2 Self-regulation by Crypto-Asset Companies

The FSC recommended self-regulation by crypto-asset companies on September 4, 2017. An industry association, Korea Blockchain Association, prepared the self-regulation scheme on December 2017.[52] This scheme includes conduct of business, protection of users, rules to protect users including duty to explain, prohibiting insider trading, market manipulation, regulation for virtual currency companies and their executives and employees only, not users, custody of cash and virtual currency in case of hacking or bankruptcy of virtual currency companies,[53] regular external audit on custody situation, identifying real name of users, prohibiting trading of minors and non-residents and system stability and information protection.

---

[50] Hout and Bingham (2013), pp. 385–391; Lacson and Jones (2016), pp. 40–61.

[51] For more on the situation in Korea, see Jung (2018), pp. 6–19.

[52] See Kim and Han (2018), pp. 50–68.

[53] While cash should be deposited 100% to separate bank account, at least 70% of virtual currency is going to be deposited in cold wallet.

Name of Bill	Subject	Definition
Bill on Cryptocurrency Trading (Bill No. 2011786, February 6, 2018);	Crypto-currency	Any type of digital unit used as a medium of exchange or digital value storage that can be created or obtained by computer technology or production efforts, based on decentralized, non-centralized, based on distributed, non-centralized repository and administrator-based computer cryptography, excluding a digital unit that is used only within an online gaming platform and has no market or no use other than its gaming platform, digital units that cannot be exchanged for money, electronic money, goods, services, etc., and electronic money according to the Electronic Financial Transactions Act
Bill on Virtual currency business (Bill No. 2011752, February 2, 2018)	Virtual currency	A property value that can be used for the provision of goods or services and pay for many and unspecified persons or sold or bought by many and unspecified persons (electronic equipment or otherwise recorded by electronic means, except for foreign currencies and electronic payment instruments pursuant to Article 2 of the Electronic Financial Transactions Act except virtual currency), which can be transferred by electronic methods
Bill to amend the Electronic Financial Transactions Act (Bill No. 2008288, July 31, 2017)	Virtual currency	A token issued in electronically stored form or data thereon, which can be used as a medium of exchange or electronically stored value, excluding digital token or data thereon which cannot be exchanged for legal tender, electronic money, goods, or services, or electronic money
Bill to amend the Public Service Ethics Act (Bill No. 11763, February 5, 2018) (Article 4(2)(iii)(ta))	Virtual currency	A token issued in electronically stored form or data thereon, which can be used as a medium of exchange or electronically stored value, excluding digital token or data thereon which cannot be exchanged for legal tender, electronic money, goods, or services, or electronic money
Bill to amend the Act on Reporting and Using Specified Financial Transaction Information (Bill No. 2012592, March 21, 2018) Article 2(i)(ha)	Virtual currency	A token which can be transferred electronically or data thereon that is recognized as a medium of exchange or store of value by the counterparty

Fig. 3 Definition of Crypto-assets in Korea

5.3.3 Legal Issues

(a) Legal Tender

Crypto-assets are not legal tender under the Bank of Korea Act 1950. The Bank of Korea shall have the exclusive right to issue legal tender within the territory of the Republic of Korea (Bank of Korea Act, Article 47). The Bank of Korea notes and coins issued by the Bank of Korea shall pass as legal tender current freely for all transactions (Bank of Korea Act, Articles 48&53). However, crypto-assets can be used as a medium of exchange where the parties concerned agreed on the way of payment by crypto-assets.

5.3.4 Capital Markets

(a) Securities and Derivatives

If tokens 'represent assets such as participations in real physical underlying, companies, or earnings streams, or an entitlement to dividends or interest payments', '[i]n terms of their economic function, the tokens are analogous to equities, bonds or derivatives.'[54] The term 'securities' in the FISCMA means financial investment instruments issued by a Korean national or a foreigner (FISCMA, Article 4(1)). If there are no issuers and direct legal relationship between issuers and asset holders, those crypto-assets cannot be securities. Can a virtual currency be a derivative? The Australian regulator, for instance, concluded that '[i]f a token is priced based on factors such as another financial product or underlying market index or asset price moving in a certain direction before a time or event which resulted in a payment being required as part of the rights or obligations attached to the token, this may be a derivative.'[55] In this regard, it is noteworthy that the Hong Kong Securities and Futures Commission (HKSFC) announced a policy statement to make fund managers and sales companies for the crypto-assets subject to financial regulation on November 1, 2018.[56]

(b) **Underlying Assets of Derivatives**

The term 'underlying assets' in the FISCMA means financial investment products such as securities and derivatives, currency including foreign currency, commodities, credit risk, and other risks that is natural, environmental, or economic phenomena, which can be computed or assessed by price, interest, indicator, or unit in a reasonable and appropriate manner (FISCMA, Article 4(10)). It is not generally understood than crypto-assets are securities or derivatives. Currency, including foreign currency in the FISCMA, means legal tender. Commodities in the FISCMA denotes tangible and deliverable assets. There could be no question that the term credit risk does not cover

[54]Swiss Financial Industry Supervisory Authority (2018).

[55]Australian Securities and Investments Commission (2018).

[56]HKSFC (2018).

crypto-assets. The issue is whether crypto-assets can be corresponding to 'other risks that are natural, environmental, or economic phenomena, which can be computed or assessed by price, interest, indicator, or unit in a reasonable and appropriate manner.' The problem is valuation. As noted by the SEC staff, 'Would funds have the information necessary to adequately value cryptocurrencies or cryptocurrency-related products, given their volatility, the fragmentation and general lack of regulation of underlying cryptocurrency markets, and the nascent state and current trading volume in the cryptocurrency futures markets?'[57] FSC has the opinion that 'virtual currency does not conform to the elements of the underlying assets under the FISCMA.'[58]

In the US, the situation is different. The term denoting underlying asset in the US is commodity under the Commodity Exchange Act 1936, which is defined as 'the agricultural commodities enumerated in Sect. 1a(4) of the Commodity Exchange Act, 7 USC 1a(4), and all other goods and articles, except onions as provided in Public Law 85-839 (7 USC 13-1), a 1958 law that banned futures trading in onions, and all services, rights, and interests in which contracts for future delivery are presently or in the future dealt in.'[59] CFTC interprets bitcoin as a commodity.[60] The court also interprets bitcoin and other crypto-assets as a commodity.[61]

(c) **Collective Investment Scheme: Investable Assets with Property Value**

The FISCMA stipulates managers may invest fund assets on 'investable assets with property value' (Article 6(5)). It should be noted that firstly, the collective investment assets should be valued by the market value of the assets under management (Article 238 (1)), and secondly, if there is a demand for redemption, fund managers should repurchase the collective investment securities with money acquired by disposing of collective investment assets (Article 235(5)). In the US, questions are raised as to whether these requirements can be met for crypto-assets, including bitcoins.[62] In this regard, it was noted that such problems are not necessarily limited to bitcoins, and bitcoins should be judged on a case by case basis.[63] In Korea, there is no express interpretation by the the FSC and FSS.

The HKSFC announced a policy statement to make fund managers and sales company for crypto-assets subject to financial regulation on November 1, 2018.[64] HKSFC is going to impose an authorization requirement for a company that operates a portfolio in crypto-asset (Type 9 regulated activity: asset management), whether or not a virtual asset falls under the definition of a security or futures contract. HKSFC

[57] Securities and Exchange Commission (2018).

[58] Lee (2017), Financial Supervisory Commission.

[59] US Commodity Future Trading Commission (2018).

[60] In the Matter of Coinflip, Inc., d/b/a Derivabit, and Francisco Riordan, CFTC Docket No. 15-29, September 17, 2015(bitcoin options contracts); In the Matter of: BFXNA INC. d/b/a BITFINEX, CFTC Docket No. 16-19, June 2, 2016(leveraged or margined bitcoin trading).

[61] CFTC v. My Big Coin Pay, Inc., Case No. 1:18-cv-10077 (D. Mass. Filed Jan. 16, 2018); CFTC v. McDonnell et al., No. 18-CV-361, 2018 WL 1175156, at *12 (E.D.N.Y. Mar. 6, 2018).

[62] Securities and Exchange Commission (2018).

[63] CBOE Global Markets (2018).

[64] HKSFC (2018).

also announced that companies which sell crypto-assets will be subject to registration requirement and conduct of business regulation such as suitability principle (Type 9 or Type 1 regulated activity: dealing in securities).

ICO[65]

Initial coin offerings ('ICO'), also known as token launch or token generation, is 'a term describing a limited period in which a company sells a predefined number of digital tokens (crypto coins) to the public, typically in exchange for major cryptocurrencies (as of today, mostly Bitcoins and Ether).'[66] While they are known as ICOs since they bear similarities to traditional initial public offerings (IPOs), ICOs are specific transactions that differ from IPOs particularly in terms of the nature of the rights acquired by the investor since tokens do not, in principle, have the same characteristics as equity securities.[67] Tokens(coins) issued in the course of ICOs can have different legal natures, including securities, digital currency, and utility token in accordance with economic functions and substances. In many countries, such as the US and Switzerland, the financial regulators do not restrict the issuance of tokens issued by the ICO and are not corresponding to securities.[68] France proposed a Bill to require issuers of ICOs to acquire approval.[69] The FSC prohibited all types of ICO in Korea on September 29, 2017.[70] The FSC also emphasized the importance of consistent application of securities regulation such as disclosure of digital tokens and regulation of trading platforms, etc., and mentioned the necessity of joint international action in the annual meeting of the BOD and AGM of the International Organization of Securities Commissions(IOSCO).[71] In the AGM of the FATF, the FSC emphasized as Korea currently prohibits ICOs, there is no need to introduce the anti-money laundering system for ICO related businesses.[72]

An ICO can be understood as something between an IPO and securities-based crowdfunding in structure and functions. Therefore, it is not possible to deny the possibility that it is used for avoiding or bypassing regulation of securities public offering and crowdfunding regulation. However, there may be arguments that, in the case of ICO, the perception of traditional means of investment or funding should

---

[65] Jung (2018), pp. 14-16.

[66] Price Waterhouse Coopers (2017), p. 1.

[67] Autorité des Marchés Financiers (2017), p. 2.

[68] See, e.g., SEC, Release No. 81207/July 25, 2017 Report of Investigation Pursuant to section 21(a) of the Securities Exchange Act of 1934: The DAO; SEC, Release No. 10445/December 11, 2017 In the Matter of MUNCHEE INC., Respondent. ORDER INSTITUTING CEASE-ANDDESIST PROCEEDINGS PURSUANT TO section 8A OF THE SECURITIES ACT OF 1933, MAKING FINDINGS, AND IMPOSING A CEASE-AND-DESIST ORDER; Swiss FINMA, Guidelines for enquiries regarding the regulatory framework for initial coin offerings (ICOs), 16 February 2018; MAS clarifies regulatory position on the offer of digital tokens in Singapore, 1 August 2017.

[69] PROJET DE LOI relatif à la croissance et la transformation des entreprises(ASSEMBLÉE NATIONALE CONSTITUTION DU 4 OCTOBRE 1958 QUINZIÈME LÉGISLATURE Enregistré à la Présidence de l'Assemblée nationale le 19 juin 2018), Art 26 L552-4.

[70] FSC/FSS et al. (2017).

[71] FSC (2018).

[72] Korea Financial Intelligence Unit (2018).

be fundamentally changed, as it allows no obligation to repay. In general, it can be summarized that the nature of the transaction depends on the transaction structure and form of ICO, especially the rights of token holders. In this respect, it is argued that ICO should be allowed in Korea.

From a long-term point of view, two fundamental questions must be answered. Firstly, it is how to protect users or investors. Can we completely abandon the protection of investors, including agency problems or fraudulent transactions, that are concerned with traditional regulations on investment instruments such as securities and derivatives? It is necessary to answer the question of whether the investor's principle of self-responsibility can be fully applied again and rule for investor protection wholly excluded from the object of regulation because of the form of token or coin. Secondly, it is whether the FISCMA and Company Regulations should be applied. The FISCMA and the Companies Regulations are establishing various safeguards related to the protection of shareholders and creditors as well as the defense of existing corporate control rights. Is it possible to completely exclude the application of such a protective device just because the instrument takes the form of a coin? It may be a welcome development as a new means of financing that does not affect shareholder rights or creditors' property. However, there is no denying the possibility that it will be abused as a financial instrument for which the capital market law or company regulations cannot be applied.

5.3.5 Forfeiture

In Korea, it is also questioned whether the prosecutors may forfeit crypto-assets. In April 2017, the Prosecutors' Office seized the accused's cash worth 1.46 billion won and 216 Bitcoins by transferring the crypto-asset to a government wallet. The defendant was indicted for distributing pornographic materials. Seized Bitcoin was worth KRW500 million when he was arrested.

At first, the court decided that 'it is not appropriate to forfeit because Bitcoins are in the form of electronic files without physical entities, unlike cash.'[73] The Court of Appeal ordered to seize KRW2.4 billion worth Bitcoins and decided that 'we cannot conclude that Bitcoin does not have any economic value just because it does not have a physical entity,' and it can be converted to legal tender at exchanges and some businesses are using the digital currency as means of payment'[74] The Supreme Court accepted the decision of the Court of Appeal in that 'bitcoin is intangible assets with property value.'[75]

---

[73] Suwon District Court, Sep 7, 2017. 2017GoDan2884.

[74] Suwon District Court, Jan 30, 2018. 2017No7120. Court orders forfeiture of Bitcoins for first time, reported in The Investor, January 31, 2018.

[75] Supreme Court, May 30, 2018. 2018Do3619.

5.3.6 AML

Korean anti-money laundering ('AML') agency, the Financial Intelligence Unit ('FIU') announced Guideline on anti-money laundering for virtual currency, January 30, 2018 (effective until Jan. 30, 2018) on January 2018.[76] This Guideline is (1) to apply Enhanced Due Diligence(EDD) for crypto-assets companies, and also check whether such companies explain that crypto-asset is not legal tender, the contents of crypto-asset, the risks of crypto-asset trading and other relevant matters as to allow the user to understand them, and obtain relevant confirmation from the users; (2) to activate Suspicious Transaction Report (STR) with regard to crypto-asset trading; and (3) to strengthen internal control system on AML.

This guideline is regarded as the most critical policy tool to stabilize crypto-asset transactions in Korea. In the National Assembly, a Bill to amend the Act on Reporting and Using Specified Financial Transaction Information (Bill No. 2012592, March 21, 2018) was proposed to include crypto-asset companies and crypto-assets transactions within the structure of AML regulation.

5.3.7 Bills

There are 3 Bills to regulate crypto-assets business including Bill on Cryptocurrency Trading (Bill No. 2011786, February 6, 2018); Bill on Virtual currency business (Bill No. 2011752, February 2, 2018); Bill to amend the Electronic Financial Transactions Act (Bill No. 2008288, July 31, 2017). These Bills are to regulate cryptocurrency business, including dealing, brokering, issuing, and managing; to prohibit unfair trading in relation to cryptocurrency trading, including market manipulation and money laundering; to introduce investment recommendation regulation for cryptocurrency such as duty to explain; and to establisha self-regulatory organization. The Bill to amend the Public Service Ethics Act (Bill No. 11763, February 5, 2018) is to add crypto-assets to the types of property to be registered under the Act.

6 Fintech and Regulation

6.1 Overview

The basic features of the financial regulatory system in Korea can be summarized in two ways. Firstly, it is based on a rule-based rather than a principles-based approach. Secondly, there exists very narrow administrative discretion to waive the application

[76]This Guideline was amended on June 27, 2018, 6.27, and will be implemented for one year from July 10, 2018. This Guideline is using the term 'virtual currency' as it was made in early 2018. For more, see Lee et al. (2018), pp. 42–48.

of financial regulation, even in very exceptional cases. The basic approach to financial regulation in Korea is symbolized by the phrase 'no express permission means implicit prohibition.'

6.2 *Regulatory Sandbox*

The term regulatory sandbox refers to 'a 'safe space' in which businesses can test innovative products, services, business models and delivery mechanisms without immediately incurring all the usual regulatory consequences of engaging in the activity in question.'[77] The regulatory sandbox is to reduce the legal risks arising from the time lag between the speed of financial market development and the legislation. This is because the test business itself is inevitably prohibited in cases where it is uncertain whether new products or transactions are in violation of existing regulations.

In this regard, the Korean government proposed short term and long-term plans.[78] In the short term, the FSC introduced (1) outsourcing test to authorized financial companies, (2) appointed representative, (3) no-action letter, which needs no further legislative change. In the long term, the FSC will introduce, (4) restricted or tailored authorization (based on the UK or Australian model), (5) waiver of financial regulation, in particular, entry regulation through legislation.

The current approach is an administrative solution to legal risks with limited or no legal certainty. The Korean government is considering a legislative solution in this context. Korea enacted the Act to Support Financial Innovation in December 2018.[79] This Act defines 'innovative financial services' as 'services provided during the course of carrying out business related to financial services or related services, which are distinguished from the contents, method, and form of existing services' (Article 2 (4)). A person who can apply for the designation of innovative financial services is a financial company or a company under the Commercial Code with domestic offices (Article 5). In reviewing the application for the designation of innovative financial services, the FSC shall take into consideration criteria such as innovation of service, consumer convenience, and adequacy of financial consumer protection measures (Articles 4(2),19). The FSC may designate innovative financial services according to the results of the examination by the Innovation Finance Review Committee. If designated, the scope of the service users and regulations excluded for the services should be included (Article 4(2)). The provider of innovative financial services (the innovative financial service provider) may carry out the service within the scope specified regardless of other laws and regulations (Article 16). In this regard, the following three points are noted.

---

[77] UK Financial Conduct Authority (2015), Regulatory Sandbox, 1 (November 2015). For more on the legal treatment of regulatory sandbox in Korea, see Jung (2017), pp. 6–15.

[78] FSC (2016).

[79] [Enforcement Date April 1, 2019] [Law No 16183, December 31, 2018]

Firstly, the new Act introduced indemnity clauses. Those involved in a regulated sandbox shall not be disadvantaged if positively and actively engaged in business without intent or gross negligence (Article 30). Secondly, if designated, the innovative financial service providers have the right to exclusively operate innovative financial services for two years (Article 23). Thirdly, the innovative financial service provider shall prepare and observe measures for financial consumer protection and risk management (Article 19(1)).

7 Conclusion

In Korea, institutional efforts to introduce new financial products and services in accordance with the combination of technology and finance are being carried out in various financial fields such as banking and securities. Particularly noteworthy is the introduction of new means of payment. The regulatory sandbox newly introduced by Korea will have an impact on the Korean financial regulatory system, which has traditionally been very conservative.

References

Australian Securities and Investments Commission (2018) Initial coin offerings and crypto-currency. Information Sheet 225

Autorité des Marchés Financiers (2017) Discussion paper on initial coin offerings

Balling M, Lierman F, Mullineux A (eds) (2002) Technology and finance: challenges for financial markets, business strategies and policy makers. Routledge, London

Bank of Korea (2018) Payment and settlement report 2017(in Korean)

CBOE Global Markets (2018) Letter: Engaging on Fund Innovation and Cryptocurrency-related Holdings (the "Staff Letter"), March 23, 2018

European Commission (2018) Press release: FinTech: Commission takes action for a more competitive and innovative financial market. https://ec.europa.eu/digital-single-market/en/news/fintech-commission-takes-action-more-competitive-and-innovative-financial-market. Accessed 31 March 2020

Financial Intelligence Unit (2018) Guideline on anti money laundering for virtual currency

Financial Stability Board (2018) Crypto-asset markets potential channels for future financial stability implications

Lee (2017), Financial Supervisory Commission, Bitcoin, not an underlying asset under domestic law derivative trading prohibited. Newsis. http://www.newsis.com/view/?id=NISX20171206_0000169057. Accessed 31 March 2020 (in Korean)

FSC (2015) Press release: Electronic financial transactions supervision regulation amended (in Korean)

FSC (2015) Press release: Rationalization of real name identification method when opening account (in Korean)

FSC (2016) Basic approach to financial regulation testbed (Regulatory Sandbox) (in Korean)

FSC (2018) Press release: Vice Chairman of the FSC attended the meeting of BOD and AGM of the International Organization of the Securities Commissions (in Korean)

FSC/FSS (2016) Interpretation: It is possible for an Internet-only bank to be able to handle limited face-to-face sales and business operations under certain conditions (in Korean)
FSC/FSS (2018a) Press release: Extended P2P loan guidelines (in Korean)
FSC/FSS (2018b) P2P lending guidelines (in Korean)
FSC/FSS et al. (2017) Press release: Hosted 'virtual currency related agency joint TF' to check the status of implementation by institution
FSC/FSS et al. (2018) Press release: Major trends and future plans of crowd funding for small and medium businesses (in Korean)
FSS (2017) Commentary on electronic financial supervisory regulation (in Korean)
FSS (2018) Press release: P2P loan check result and future plan (in Korean)
HKSFC (2018) Regulatory standards for licensed corporations managing virtual asset portfolios
Hout M, Bingham T (2013) 'Silk Road', the Virtual Drug Marketplace: A Single Case Study of User Experiences, Int J of Drug Policy 28(5):385–391. http://dx.doi.org/10.1016/j.drugpo.2013.01.005. Accessed 31 March 2020
Jung (2017) Technological development and financial regulation: possibility in Korean law of the so-called 'Regulatory Sandbox'. BFL No. 85 (in Korean)
Jung (2017b) Banking law. Jiwon Publishing, Seoul (in Korean)
Jung (2018) Legal issues of virtual currency. BFL No. 89 (in Korean)
Kim and Han (2018) Legal issues on cryptocurrency transaction and self-regulation. BFL No. 89 (in Korean)
Kim and Jung (2013) Capital markets law, 3rd edn. Dusung Publishing, Seoul, Jabonsijangbob
Ko (2015) Legal review on peer-to-peer lending in Korea. Korean Journal of Banking and Financial Law 8(2) (in Korean)
Ko (2018) Main contents and issues of a bill on online loan business and user protection (on file with the author) (in Korean)
Korea Blockchain Association (2017) Self-regulation scheme (in Korean)
Korea Federation of Banks (2016) Commentary on financial real name transaction service (in Korean)
Korea Financial Intelligence Unit (2018) Press release: The results of attending the FATF plenary. The 1st Plenary Meeting of the 30th Session OECD, October 14-18, Paris(in Korean)
Lacson W, Jones B (2016) The 21st century dark net market: lessons from the fall of silk road. International Journal of Cyber Criminology 10:40-61 http://cybercrimejournal.com/Lacson&Jonesvol10issue1IJCC2016.pdf. Accessed 31 March 2020
Lee, Kim, Ko (2018), Korea. In: McLean A and Miller P (eds) Getting the deal through: Fintech 2019. https://gettingthedealthrough.com/area/92/jurisdiction/35/fintech-south-korea/. Accessed 31 March 2020
Lee, Lee, Cho (2018) Virtual currency and anti-money laundering. BFL No. 89 (in Korean)
McWilliams J (2018) Fintech and the new financial landscape https://www.fdic.gov/news/news/speeches/spnov1318.pdf. Accessed 31 March 2020
Park J (2011) Consolidation and reform of financial market regulation in Korea: financial investment services and Capital Markets Act. National Taiwan University Law Review 6:91–141
PriceWaterhouseCoopers (2017) Initial coin offerings: a strategic perspective
Securities and Exchange Commission (2018) Staff Letter: Engaging on Fund Innovation and Cryptocurrency-related Holdings
Swiss Financial Industry Supervisory Authority (2018) Guidelines for Enquiries Regarding the Regulatory Framework for Initial Coin Offerings
US Commodity Future Trading Commission (2018) CFTC Backgrounder on Oversight of and Approach to Virtual Currency Futures Markets http://www.cftc.gov/idc/groups/public/@newsroom/documents/file/backgrounder_virtualcurrency01.pdf. Accessed 31 March 2020
Ulrich A and Bholat D (2016) Peer-to-Peer Lending and Financial Innovation in the United Kingdom, Staff Working Paper No. 598, Bank of England
United States Government Accountability Office (2011) Person-to-Person Lending: New Regulatory Challenges Could Emerge as the Industry Grows, GAO-11–613

UK Financial Conduct Authority (2015) Regulatory Sandbox, 1 (November 2015)
Vogel J, Herger G, Reynolds L (2013) FDIC New York Region Regulatory Teleconference: Loan Participations New York Regional Call. https://www.fdic.gov/news/conferences/ny/2013-04-04.pdf. Accessed 31 March 2020

Does China Need the Regulatory Sandbox? A Preliminary Analysis of Its Desirability as an Appropriate Mechanism for Regulating Fintech in China

Fan Liao

Abstract A regulatory sandbox is a safe space in which businesses can test innovative products, services, business models and delivery mechanisms without immediately incurring all the normal regulatory consequences of engaging in the activity in question. The fundamental purpose of the regulatory sandbox is to facilitate the development of fintech, especially the 'disruptive innovation' activities of the start-up enterprises. In this sense, the regulatory sandbox is a sub-category of the regulation of fintech. Fintech is technology-enabled financial innovation, synonymous with the term 'internet finance' in the Chinese context. A different but related term, the regulatory technology (regtech), in a broad sense refers to a combination of the 'compliance technology' by the market players with the 'regulatory technology' by the regulators. In nature, the regulatory sandbox is conditional, limited, and controlled deregulation. It was primarily a reaction to the somehow overly burdensome regulatory requirements after the Global Financial Crisis (GFC), thus leaving a 'lifeline' for financial innovation and, in particular, fintech. The situation is very different in China, where the major problem for internet finance it not over-regulation but under-regulation. With a vast territory, diversified areas, and numerous institutions, China does not feature a much developed and high concentrated financial market like that of the UK, Singapore, or the HK SAR. Nor does it have an integrated financial regulatory system. And, most importantly, the existing mechanisms in China are capable of performing equivalent or even more functions than the sandbox, which, if copied in China, would be redundant. In short, the regulatory sandbox is admittedly a remarkable innovation in terms of regulatory ideas and approaches conducive to financial innovation, especially fintech. However, with its specific background, exterior conditions, and intrinsic limitations, it is by no means an inevitable choice or universal model for the regulation of fintech. Based on the actual circumstances, it's not desirable for China to introduce the sandbox, at least for the time being.

Keywords Regulatory sandbox · Financial technology (fintech) · Regulatory technology (regtech) · Disruptive innovation · Adaptive regulation

F. Liao (✉)
Institute of International Law, CASS, Beijing, China
e-mail: liaofan@cass.org.cn

M. Fenwick et al. (eds.), *Regulating FinTech in Asia*, Perspectives in Law, Business and Innovation, https://doi.org/10.1007/978-981-15-5819-1_5

1 Introduction

The term 'regulatory sandbox' first appeared in a report of the UK Government Office for Science issued in March 2015.[1] In a feasibility study report in November 2015 titled *Regulatory Sandbox*, the UK Financial Conduct Authority (FCA) elaborated on this concept. According to that report, a regulatory sandbox is 'a 'safe space' in which businesses can test innovative products, services, business models and delivery mechanisms without immediately incurring all the normal regulatory consequences of engaging in the activity in question.'[2] The regulatory sandbox program was officially launched in the UK in June 2016. So far, 375 enterprises have applied to the FCA, with 139 accepted to test innovative products, services, business models, and delivery mechanisms.[3] Inspired by this, countries and regions such as Australia, Singapore, and the HK SAR have come up with their own versions of sandboxes. Calls for initiating the regulatory sandbox in Chinese mainland are often heard recently. Given the situation, this chapter endeavors to review the theoretical foundation and practical development of the regulatory sandbox, so as to draw some preliminary conclusions.

As stated in the FCA report, the fundamental purpose of introducing the sandbox is to promote the development of financial technology (fintech), in particular, to support the 'disruptive innovation' by start-ups.[4] In this sense, the regulatory sandbox constitutes a sub-topic of the regulation of fintech. Based on this understanding, I would first like to make a brief clarification of three basic concepts and their relations, i.e., fintech, internet finance, and regtech.

According to the *Financial Stability Implications from FinTech: Supervisory and Regulatory Issues that Merit Authorities' Attention* ('FSB Report') issued by the Financial Stability Board (FSB) in June 2017, fintech refers to 'technology-enabled innovation in financial services that could result in new business models, applications, processes or products with an associated material effect on the provision of financial services'.[5] This definition was accepted and adopted by the Basel Committee in its report *Sound Practices: Implications of Fintech Development for Banks and Bank Supervisors* in February 2018.[6]

The term 'financial technology' is not yet seen in any law, regulation, or official regulatory document in China. A similar expression in the Chinese context is 'internet finance.' According to the *Guiding Opinions for Promoting the Healthy Development of Internet Finance* ('Guiding Opinions') promulgated by the People's Bank of China (the Chinese Central Bank) in conjunction with nine other ministries and commissions, internet finance is 'a new business model where traditional financial

---

[1]Government Office for Science (2015), p. 52.

[2]FCA (2019a), p. 2.

[3]Calculated by the author based on the information from the FCA website. See FCA (2019b).

[4]FCA (2019a), p. 5.

[5]FSB (2017), p. 7.

[6]Basel Committee on Banking Supervision (2017), p. 8.

institutions and internet companies make use of internet technologies and information and telecommunication technologies to enable finance, payment, investment and infomediary services.'[7]

As to the relationship between fintech and internet finance, there are basically two types of opinions in China. One is that the two terms refer to roughly the same thing, and internet finance can be seen as a localized expression of fintech.[8] While the other view holds that fintech is different from internet finance in terms of technical elements as well as business scope, and internet finance is but a phase or branch of fintech.[9]

According to the author, the meanings of internet finance and fintech do differ in appearance. When put into practical use, however, neither can be understood according to their apparent meaning. That might be the reason why the FSB report chose to avoid the full expression 'financial technology' and go straight to the term 'fintech' from the very beginning. Both fintech and internet finance involves a combination of finance and technology, and the final foothold is finance.

On the one hand, internet finance covers both the 'finance + internet' model by the traditional financial institutions and the 'internet + finance' model by internet companies. On the other hand, the definition of fintech by the FSB focuses on the services provided rather than the providing entity or the technology itself and stresses that fintech will not fundamentally change the essence of intermediation in the financial system or the required economic functions.[10]

In addition, 'internet finance' is a broad and evolving concept. To some extent, Big Data, blockchain, artificial intelligence, biometric identification, etc. can all be seen as derivative technologies based on and covered by internet technology in a broad sense.[11] Furthermore, China has already established a basic regulatory framework for internet finance covering both the financial institutions and the internet companies, with no substantial difference from the basic contents and points of focus regarding the regulation of fintech in the FSB report.[12] In particular, Box A of Annex C to the report ('Case study on FinTech credit') is titled 'China's regulatory framework for internet finance,'[13] obviously treating fintech and internet finance as the same. Given this 'international recognition,' there is not much need to differentiate between the two concepts. Thus this chapter supports the first type of opinion mentioned above, taking fintech and internet finance as interchangeable terms in the context of China.

Another important concept related to fintech and, in particular, to its regulation is regulatory technology or regtech. The exact meaning of regtech is yet to be agreed upon, but there are, broadly speaking, two kinds of understandings. The narrow

[7] People's Bank of China et al. (2015).

[8] See, e.g., Zhu and Chen (2016), p. 22; Zhu (2018), pp. 56–57.

[9] See, e.g., Yang and Zhang (2017), p. 5.

[10] See FSB (2017), pp. 6–7.

[11] As can be seen from the relevant contents on the official website of the World Internet Conference (2019).

[12] See FSB (2017), pp. 23–27.

[13] See FSB (2017), p. 42.

understanding regards regtech as part of fintech. As stated by the FCA, 'RegTech is a sub-set of finTech that focuses on technologies that may facilitate the delivery of regulatory requirements more efficiently and effectively than existing capabilities.'[14] This definition understands regtech mainly from the perspective of market players, i.e., how do the participants in the financial market use new technologies to save compliance costs and meet regulatory requirements.

A broader understanding, as articulated by Douglas Arner, considers regtech to be more than a branch of fintech. According to this understanding, regtech can be seen as encompassing three distinct but complementary market sectors and groups of participants. Firstly, financial institutions and the financial industry are increasingly applying technology to meet the demands of regulators, especially demands upon large financial institutions in developed markets arising from new post-crisis regulations. Secondly, regulators are faced with the need to use technology to address the challenges of monitoring and enforcing increasingly demanding regulatory requirements on fast-changing, rapidly growing, and cross-border markets. Thirdly, policymakers and regulators will face the challenge of rapidly transforming financial systems in the coming years, and of building the necessary infrastructure to support their regulation, which will necessitate the increasing use of and reliance on regtech.[15] In short, regtech, on the one hand, refers to the increasing use of technology to meet regulatory requirements, while, on the other hand, it means that the regulatory authorities employ technologies to monitor and implement the increasingly burdensome regulatory tasks. Thus regtech has two dimensions, i.e., market v. regulation, or market players v. regulatory authorities.

According to the author, regtech in the narrow sense is better termed as 'compliance technology' rather than 'regulatory technology.' Not sufficient to convey the two-fold meaning of the participation of both the market players and the regulatory authorities, it is in particular unable to embody the needs and trend for the regulatory authorities to innovate regulatory conceptions and approaches. Thus, this chapter understands regtech in the broad sense.[16]

---

[14]FCA (2016), p. 3. Following this logic, the FCA divides Regtech into four categories, i.e., technology that allows more efficient methods of sharing information, including alternative reporting methods, sharing utilities, the cloud/cloud computing, and online platforms; technology that drives efficiencies by closing the gap between intention and interpretation, including semantic tech and data point models, shared data technology, application program interface (APT), and Robo-Handbook; technology that simplifies data, allows better decision making and the creations of adaptive automation, including Big Data analytics, risk and compliance monitoring, modelling/visualization technology, and machine learning and cognitive technology; and technology that allows regulation and compliance process to be looked at differently, including blockchain/distributed ledger, inbuilt compliance, biometrics, and system monitoring and visualization. See FSB (2017), pp. 7–9.

[15]See Arner et al. (2017), pp. 383-384.

[16]This stance is also in consistent with the majority of Chinese financial law scholars. See, e.g., Yang and Zhang (2017), p. 9; Wei and Xu (2017), p. 65; Lin et al. (2017), pp. 59–60; Xu (2018), pp. 8–9; Yang (2018), pp. 77–78.

2 Historical Background and Theoretical Foundation of the Regulatory Sandbox

2.1 Historical Background

It is worth mentioning from the outset that the regulatory sandbox, to a great extent, was a 'counteraction' or 'correction' to the much strengthened or even burdensome regulatory requirements after the GFC of 2008. Given that the relevant laws and rules cannot be revised in a timely manner to alleviate the market players of the regulatory burdens, this is actually a circuitous way to leave some leeway for financial innovation, so as to keep the vitality and international competitiveness of the financial market.[17] As emphasized by a commentator, 'implementing a regulatory sandbox does not substitute for otherwise warranted regulatory reforms. In particular, the abolition of some Crisis-driven rules should be discussed openly as regulators and politicians may have overreacted to the crisis, and adopted, at least some, unwise rules.'[18]

Since the Great Depression in the 1930s, the evolution of the financial regulatory system and rules has roughly been a reaction to the various financial crises. Such a crisis-driven model has two interconnected features or defects. First, facing the post-crisis public outcry and pressure, financial regulation tends to go too far, imposing overly rigid and burdensome requirements upon market players. Second, due to the lagging nature of the law, it is often difficult to adjust the regulatory rules in time when the market recovers, thus fettering financial operations.

The GFC is no exception. The post-crisis financial regulatory reforms increased banks' compliance obligations and altered their commercial incentives and business structures. In particular, the universal banking model has been directly challenged with ring-fencing obligations and increased regulatory capital changing the incentive or capacity of banks to originate low-value loans. For example, Basel III substantially raised the capital adequacy requirements for banks. While this enhanced market stability and risk-absorbing capacity, it also diverted capital from Small and Medium Enterprises and private individuals. Many private individuals then turned to P2P lending platforms or other innovations to fulfill their need for credit.[19]

In this sense, post-crisis regulation has catalyzed fintech in at least two ways. On the one hand, in the face of the more onerous and rigid regulatory rules, financial institutions need new technologies to reduce compliance costs as well as meet the regulatory requirements and compliance obligations. This is more about the 'technology' aspect of fintech or the employment of fintech by the established financial institutions. On the other hand, in the increasingly rigid regulatory environment, traditional financial institutions have cut off certain operations, leaving gaps to be

[17] Government Office for Science (2015), p. 5.

[18] Zetzsche et al. (2017), p. 94.

[19] See Arner et al. (2016), pp. 1288-1289.

filled by new players. This is more about the 'financial' aspect of fintech or the competition from the fintech enterprises against the traditional financial institutions.

2.2 Theoretical Foundation

As a regulatory experiment and innovation, the regulatory sandbox is based on two correlated theories, i.e., disruptive innovation and adaptive regulation. As described by the US scholar Clayton Christensen, disruptive innovation includes not only technological innovation but also business model innovation; any innovation that starts in less important or subordinate market but eventually succeeds in overturning the mainstream market and rewriting the competition rules can be said to be a disruptive innovation.[20] A brief comparison would tell that fintech, in essence, fits well into the concept of disruptive innovation.[21] In fact, in explaining the reason for introducing the sandbox, the FCA made it quite clear:

> Disruptive innovation is a key part of effective competition, which is why we launched Project Innovate. Project Innovate aims to support innovation that offers new products and services to customers and challenges existing business models. To do this, we engage constructively with innovative businesses, and seek to remove unnecessary regulatory barriers to innovation…… Half of the promising 'disruptive' fintech start-ups in Europe are in the UK. To remain Europe's leading fintech hub, we have to ensure that we continue to be an attractive market with an appropriate regulatory framework.[22]

The traditional financial market is comparatively fixed and closed, with a rather high threshold of entry and rather clear borderlines between the different financial sectors. While this feature is helpful for providing the necessary stability and safety to the financial market and financial system, it nonetheless tends to result in a lack of competition in the relevant market, making the financial service providers less motivated to improve the service quality and meet the customers' needs. Fintech, with its inherent 'disruption' or 'subversion' of the existing financial business models, not only blurred the lines between different financial sectors but even blurred the lines between finance and non-finance. Thus it poses substantial competitive pressure upon traditional financial institutions and sectors. That is exactly why the FCA stresses that 'disruptive innovation is a key part of effective competition as mentioned above.

Given that fintech has the nature of disruptive innovation, its regulation has to take account of both the two aspects, i.e., disruption and innovation. On the one hand, standard regulatory requirements may prove unbearable for start-ups and impede innovation. On the other hand, a totally laissez-faire approach easily contributes to the 'barbarian growth' of fintech, augments and expands its disruption, and even results in systemic risk. The chaotic development of internet finance in China before 2015 was a telling example of the latter. Before the promulgation of the *Guiding Opinions*

[20]See Guo (2016), p. 8.

[21]See Xu (2018), pp. 8–9.

[22]FCA (2019a), pp. 2, 5.

in 2015, Chinese authorities took a near laissez-faire approach to internet finance, advocating it as a symbol of 'Mass Entrepreneurship and Innovation.' Although this approach did succeed in fostering such megafirms as Alipay and WeChat Pay, lots of problems followed, with the massive P2P failures stood most striking.

In this sense, fintech entails some form of adaptive regulation and regulatory experimentalism.[23] Take the capital market as an example. Technological development in the 21stcentury has deeply changed its microstructure, and such changes are, in turn, transforming the regulatory ecosystem as a whole. Just as the modes and means of disseminating information have multiplied, so have opportunities with which fraud can be conducted and markets manipulated. Furthermore, changes in the market ecosystem and competitive dynamics are changing the incentives for market participants and gatekeepers in ways that may not always bolster financial stability or investor protection. Issuers are able to raise as much capital via nonpublic devices and private placement infrastructure as through IPOs; exchanges are no longer sources of capital but increasingly seekers of liquidity; and broker-dealers are able to connect investors in ways that they increasingly resemble exchanges.[24] All these have posed new challenges to regulatory agencies, regulatory ideas, and regulatory approaches.

The concept of adaptive regulation originated in administrative law.[25] When applied to the financial market, it roughly means allowing for more regulatory discretion as well as more regulatory resources, including technological tools that can match the complicated financial activities of the market players. However, the 'fashionable' need of reacting to the development of fintech put aside, the argument for more regulatory discretion in financial regulation has long existed. The so-called principle-based regulation, for example, recognizes the significance of continuous regulatory discretion. In this respect, the striking feature of adaptive regulation lies in that it views financial regulation itself as a process with ceaseless adaption, emphasizes on the continuous interaction between the regulators and regulated, and allows for more trial and error.

The basic idea of adaptive regulation is that the regulatory authorities can innovate not only with regard to the substance of market rules but also in terms of their tactics. They can, within the scope of their discretion, adjust their rulemaking in ways that enable more knowledgeable, speedy, but incremental rulemaking that is often well-suited to a world of constant microstructural change. Different from one omnibus package of reforms, adaptive regulation is more of iterative decision-making following a structured, multistep protocol: (1) definition of the problem, (2) determination of goals and objectives for management, (3) determination of the baseline,

[23]It needs to be made clear, though, that adaptive is not a concept specifically designed for Fintech. It is actually a regulatory concept and approach in a broader sense.

[24]See Brummer (2015), pp. 1051–1052.

[25]See, e.g., Baxter (2011), p. 253 (arguing that conceptual frameworks for regulating complex markets are moving away from directive models in favor of adaptive approaches); McCray et al. (2010), p. 951 (surveying US federal regulatory programs concerning the environment, health, and safety to ascertain which ones have included adaptive features).

(4) development of conceptual models, (5) selection of future actions, (6) implementation and management actions, (7) monitoring, and (8) evaluation and return to step (1).[26]

In fact, no matter if it is individual pilot programs, or more systemized innovation hubs (enterprise zones for financial market compliance and regulatory adaptation), they are all the practical application of regulatory experimentalism. The launch of the Project Innovate and the establishment of the Innovation Hub by the FCA in 2014 was indeed an application of regulatory experimentalism. The regulatory sandbox is but a continuation and enhancement.[27]

3 Practical Development and Preliminary Judgment of the Regulatory Sandbox

3.1 Practical Development

Just as fintech is nothing mysterious, so is the regulatory sandbox. As an import from computer technology, the word 'sandbox' appears somewhat exotic, but its primary functions are not substantially different from such concepts as pilot programs for financial innovation or incubators for high-tech enterprises which we are more familiar with. In fact, for a better understanding of the sandbox in the context of the financial markets, a better parallel may be with clinical drug trials, as the sector is similarly regulated to prevent consumer harm while testing new innovation.[28]

Take the AI investment advice service (robo-advice), for example. A sandbox could allow a firm to make its advice platform available to a limited number of consumers. As a safeguard, once the advice is issued, but before transactions are executed, financial advisers would review the advice. This would allow firms to learn how consumers interact with their advice platform and how their algorithm performs compared to human assessment.[29]According to the FCA, the purpose of creating the regulatory sandbox is to: (1) reduce the time and, potentially, the cost of getting innovative ideas to market; (2) enable greater access to finance for innovators; (3) enable more products to be tested and, thus, potentially introduced to the market, and (4) allow the FCA to work with innovators to ensure that appropriate consumer protection safeguards are built into their new products and services.[30]

The regulatory sandbox is open both to the authorized firms, i.e., those licensed financial institutions, and to the unauthorized firms, i.e., start-ups that have not yet

---

[26]McCrayetal. (2010), pp. 1043–1044.

[27]As part of the expanded Project Innovate, regulatory sandbox is managed by the newly established 'sandbox unit'. See FCA (2019a), p. 3.

[28]See Arner et al. (2017), p. 409.

[29]FCA (2019a), p. 2.

[30]FCA (2019a), pp. 2–3.

obtained a financial license, with the same criteria for entry. Similar to those of the FCA Innovation Hub, the criteria for entry into the sandbox cover five aspects, namely scope of business (is the planned new solution designed for or supports the financial services industry?), genuine innovation (is the new solution novel or significantly different to existing offerings?), consumer benefit (does the innovation offer a good prospect of identifiable benefit to consumers), need for sandbox (does the business have a genuine need for testing within the sandbox framework?), and background research (has the business invested appropriate resources in developing the new solution, understanding the applicable regulations, and mitigating the risks?).[31]

But authorized firms and unauthorized firms have different 'pain points.' The problem facing unauthorized firms is that due to the license requirement for the financial business, they will have to incur potentially significant one-off costs and apply for authorization before they can meaningfully explore consumers' appetite for a product/service or if there are any significant risks posed to consumers. On the other hand, authorized firms and technology firms that provide outsourced services to such firms are mainly concerned about the FCA's reaction to new solutions; they are interested in early dialogue, clarity about how to apply rules and the risk of the FCA taking enforcement action at a later date.[32] The FCA thus provides distinct options for the two groups.

For unauthorized firms, the key point of the sandbox is to forge a tailored entry/authorization process, so as to allow testing by firms who need to become authorized to try their new products or services. Sandbox firms will first be authorized with restrictions, allowing them to test their ideas but no more (restricted authorization). Once the firm is able to meet 'full' requirements, restrictions can be lifted. Such a restricted authorization option allows firms to become authorized in their own right while only having to meet authorization requirements that are proportionate to the testing activities. This process should also be quicker than applying for 'full' authorization. When launching full commercial activity, firms will have to apply to have restrictions lifted in order to carry on relevant regulated activities, but they will not have to apply for a new authorization.[33]

For authorized firms, options provided by the FCA include no enforcement action letters (NALs), individual guidance, and waivers. These options may also be used by technology companies when they find authorized firms that are interested in testing their products or services. Under the first option, the FCA issues a letter stating that no FCA enforcement action will be taken against testing activities where it is reasonably satisfied that the activities do not breach its requirements or harm its objectives. However, the FCA reserves the right to close the trial, and its commitment not to take enforcement action applies to the period from the issue of the NAL until the testing is completed or closed by the FCA.[34]

---

[31] FCA (2019a), p. 7.

[32] FCA (2019a), p. 8.

[33] FCA (2019a), p. 8.

[34] The US Consumer Financial Protection Bureau (CFPB) implemented a similar policy towards financial innovation in February 2016. See CFPB (2016).

In addition to NALs, the FCA can issue individual guidance to a firm on the interpretation of applicable rules in respect of testing activities the firm may be carrying out. If the firm acts in accordance with this guidance, it will give them certainty that the FCA would not take action against them. The third option is for the FCA to waive or modify certain regulatory rules for the sandbox firms. Where it is clear that testing activities do not meet FCA rules, but the firm can meet the waiver test and the rules are within the FCA's power to waive, the FCA can waive or modify particular rules for sandbox firms. However, the FCA is limited in what it can waive by EU legislative requirements.[35]

3.2 Preliminary Judgment

Based on the foregoing analysis, it is safe to say that the FCA sandbox is a mechanism with a clear idea but mixed contents. In it, there is not only such regulatory innovation as restricted authorization but also a regulatory practice that has long been there (waiver of specific rules) or has been borrowed from the US (NALs). Subsequent sandboxes launched in Australia, Singapore, and the HK SAR also differ a lot in their emphases and details, hardly indicating any 'unified model.' Nevertheless, taking the FCA sandbox as the focus, with necessary observations on those other markets, we can still make some preliminary judgments on the features, requirements, and limitations of the regulatory sandbox.

First, at least so far, the regulatory sandbox is not an inevitable choice or universal model for the regulation of fintech. The United States, with the most developed financial industry and fintech, has not generally adopted the sandbox model but followed the more moderate approach of innovation hub instead.[36] Among the countries and regions already having their sandboxes, the UK, Singapore, and the HK SAR all feature a much developed and highly concentrated financial industry suitable for somehow unified testing and management. Besides, Australia, Singapore, and the HK SAR all have strong historical links with the UK and are deeply influenced by the English law. The 'path dependence' factor might have had some role to play.

Second, countries and regions testing sandboxes usually have a comparatively integrated financial regulatory system, with a comparatively integrated regulatory authority being responsible for the administration of the sandbox. More specifically, both the UK and Australia follow the 'Twin Peaks' approach, with the FCA and the Australian Securities and Investments Commission (ASIC) being responsible for

[35] FCA (2019a), p. 9.

[36] In the US, so far there have been only sporadic practices of regulatory sandbox at the state level. For example, Arizona took the lead in launching a sandbox in March 2018. In July 2018, the Treasury Department, in a report submitted to the President, suggested that measures including sandbox be taken to support fintech and financial innovation. See Beyoud (2018). This suggestion has incurred strong opposition from the New York State Department of Financial Services, whose head issued a harshly worded statement on its website, claiming that 'Toddlers play in sandboxes. Adults play by the rules'. See Department of Financial Services (2018).

the conduct regulation and consumer protection regarding all financial institutions. Singapore goes even farther. The Monetary Authority of Singapore (MAC) unifies the central banking and financial regulatory functions, comparable to a combination of the so-called 'One Bank, Two Commissions' of China.[37]

The situation in the HK SAR is slightly different. The Hong Kong Monetary Authority (HKMA) has a comparatively narrow scope of authority, responsible only for the foreign exchange arrangement and banking regulation. Accordingly, however, the HK sandbox is only open to local banks, not to start-ups and technology companies.[38]

Third, the regulatory sandbox relies heavily on the two-way interaction on the basis of individual cases. The sandbox is an experiment for the regulatory authority as well as for the firms testing in the sandbox.[39] It is as a test of fintech and financial innovation as that of regtech and regulatory philosophy. Thus mutual confidence and smooth communication between the regulatory authority and the testing firms are of paramount importance. In fact, no matter it's the tailored authorization conditions for the fintech firms, or the NALs and individual guidance issued to the traditional institutions, or the various safeguard measures for the protection of consumers,[40] they all need to be negotiated and agreed upon by the 'cat' and 'mouse' on a case-by-case basis, with much specificity and elasticity.

For example, the FCA will assign a dedicated case officer to sandbox firms who support the design and implementation of the test. Such close contact enables case officers to help firms understand how their innovative business models fit within the regulatory framework while ensuring that appropriate safeguards are built into innovative products and services during and after testing.[41] According to the author, such an operation model entails corresponding regulatory ideas or even culture, which happen to be boosted by the UK with a tradition of light-touch regulation and principle-based regulation.

Last but not least, the regulatory sandbox has its visible boundary and limitations, mainly in terms of waivers and entry conditions. As to the former, the FCA's waiving power is subject to the criteria listed in the FSMA, and it may not waive any regulatory requirement coming from EU law. And, as to the latter, sandbox firms will have to meet the relevant authorization requirements to be able to carry out the relevant financial activities. Although as mentioned above, requirements for the restricted authorization would be proportionate to the testing activities, a threshold nonetheless exists. This makes it difficult for firms with certain business models to meet the

---

[37]That is, the People's Bank of China as the central bank, China Banking and Insurance Regulatory Commission (CBIRC) as the regulatory authority for the banking and insurance business (as a result of the merger of the former CBRC and CIRC in April 2018), and China Securities Regulatory Commission (CSRC) as the securities regulator.

[38]See, e.g., Zhang (2017), pp. 24–25.

[39]FCA (2017), p. 3.

[40]FCA (2019a), pp. 9–10.

[41]FCA (2017), p. 4.

initial regulatory requirements to become authorized, causing small-scale testing to be particularly difficult.

For example, some sandbox firms proposed to underwrite insurance products during their tests, which would have required them to be authorized as insurers. In many instances, these firms are unable to meet the initial regulatory requirements to become an insurer while in the sandbox. Similar difficulties were encountered by firms looking to operate multilateral trading facilities (MTFs) as these firms must hold a substantial level of initial regulatory capital and have in place systems and controls that have been stress tested to a high standard. Such challenges mean it has been difficult for firms to become authorized as either an insurer or an MTF to test their propositions within the sandbox framework, particularly in the case of smaller start-ups.[42] Such start-ups, however, are often in the most urgent need of money. In this regard, the role that the sandbox can play is quite limited.

4 Does China Need the Regulatory Sandbox? a Preliminary Conclusion

In nature, the regulatory sandbox is conditional, limited, and controlled deregulation. It seeks to make a better balance between innovation and regulation, innovation and standardization, and innovation and risks. It is a kind of adaptive regulation based more on principles than on rules. Compared to traditional regulatory approaches, the sandbox attaches more importance to the activeness of the regulators, with an eye on the establishment of effective communication, cooperation, and interaction between the regulators and the regulated. As put by one commentator, it embodies a transfer from passive regulation to cooperative regulation.[43]

Due to its intrinsic limitations, however, the regulatory sandbox cannot deal well with massive and/or breakthrough innovations. First, being highly 'individualized,' the sandbox relies heavily on the case-by-case tailoring and continued interaction between the testing firms and the regulatory authorities/personnel, resulting in little if any general experience. Second, the power of the regulatory authorities to streamline the authorization requirements or waive/revise the rules in question is limited. In other words, the room for lowering the regulatory threshold is quite narrow. Therefore, options provided by the regulatory authorities to the testing firms, especially the smaller start-ups, are limited. This is exactly why the FCA suggested in the *Sandbox Report* of 2015 that relevant UK legislation be amended to introduce a new regulated activity of 'sandboxing' for testing, which could enable the FCA to create a new sandbox regime (with new authorization requirements and rules) that is more flexible than the current regime in areas where EU legislation does not apply or where the UK can have additional rules to those that exist under EU legislation.[44]

[42]FCA (2017), p. 18.

[43]See Zhang (2018), p. 82.

[44]FCA (2019a), p. 14.

In addition, as mentioned above, the creation of the regulatory sandbox was somehow a 'counteraction' or 'correction' to the much strengthened or even overly burdensome regulatory requirements after the GFC, thus leaving a 'lifeline' for financial innovation and in particular fintech. The situation is remarkably different in China. Before 2015, due to the nearly laissez-faire attitude of the regulatory authorities, internet finance in China had grown rapidly. Indeed, apart from the payment area, there was little genuine innovation, but widespread circumventive or even illegal activities taking advantage of regulatory gaps and loopholes. A nationwide overhaul started in 2016 and had been expected to end in March 2017. Due to the workload and complexity of the action, however, the deadline has been postponed more than once. Now the deadline for overhauling the P2P business is set as June 2019.[45] The author agrees with one commentator that the major problem for China's internet finance/fintech is not over-regulation, but rather under-regulation.[46] In this regard, it does not seem urgent for China to introduce a sandbox.

Furthermore, at least seen from the practical development of the regulatory sandbox so far, it does not seem to suit China well. With a vast territory, diversified areas, and numerous institutions, China does not feature a much developed and high concentrated financial market like that of the UK, Singapore or the HK SAR. Besides, although there have been various cross-sector financial operations in China, its regulatory model remains largely a multi-regulator one on the basis of entity regulation (as opposed to functional regulation). In this context, a unified implementation of the sandbox would raise the question of who takes the lead and how to coordinate. However, if the 'One Bank, Two Commission' launch their respective sandboxes instead, this would seem to be running counter to the very nature and original intention of financial innovation.

Last but most importantly, the existing mechanisms in China are capable of performing equivalent or even more functions than the sandbox, which, if copied in China, would be totally redundant. First, since 2013, China has been building the Pilot Free Trade Zones (PFTZs) in Shanghai and some other areas. With the testing experiences accumulated and the testing mechanism formulated, those PFTZs are more than enough to serve as the 'experimental field' for fintech and regtech. In fact, financial innovation has been so indispensable to and characteristic of the PFTZs that a well-known scholar compared the Shanghai PFTZ to the UK innovation hub as a model of adaptive regulation. [47] In addition, the State Council has been authorized by the Standing Committee of the National People's Congress (NPC) to suspend when necessary the implementation of certain statutory provisions within the various PFTZs. This indeed provides potential room for experimentation far broader than the FCA sandbox. Furthermore, this kind of authorization is not limited to matters related to the PFTZs. According to Article 13 of the Law of the People's Republic of China on Legislation, the National People's Congress and its Standing Committee may authorize to temporarily adjust or suspend the application of certain statutory

[45]See Li (2018).

[46]See Sun (2017).

[47]See Brummer (2015), p. 1048.

provisions in certain areas within a fixed period of time. This means that even if the relevant regulatory experiments concerning fintech need to go beyond the territorial scope of the PFTZs, there is still a legal basis for that.

To be sure, the regulation of fintech should be inclusive and prudential. Inclusive regulation has its footing on the innovative aspect of fintech, including enhancing financial inclusion, increasing transaction efficiency, and promoting market competition, while prudential regulation eyes the risk aspect of fintech, as manifested in technological and operational risk, data security risk, and information asymmetry risk. Fundamentally speaking, inclusive and prudential regulation is to look at the essence of fintech, taking into account all the three keywords of finance, technology, and innovation. It endeavors to strike a balance between innovation and normalization, efficiency and security, and institutional rigidity and operational flexibility. First, based on the nature of the 'disruptive innovation' of fintech, the idea of adaptive regulation should be established to improve on the flexibility and effectiveness of regulation. Second, in order to cover the relevant risks more comprehensively, the regulatory system and mechanisms should be improved. Third, regulatory technology should play its peculiar role, so as to encounter technology-enabled financial innovation with technology-enabled regulatory innovation.

That being said, the regulatory sandbox is not necessarily the appropriate mechanism to deliver such inclusive and prudential regulation of fintech in China. Admittedly the regulatory sandbox is a remarkable innovation in terms of regulatory ideas and approaches conducive to financial innovation, especially fintech. However, with its specific background, exterior conditions, and intrinsic limitations, it is by no means an inevitable choice or universal model for the regulation of fintech. Based on the actual circumstances, it's not desirable for China to introduce the sandbox, at least for the time being.

References

Arner D et al. (2016) The evolution of fintech: anew post-crisis paradigm. Georgetown Journal of International Law 47:1345–1393

Arner D et al. (2017) Fintech, regtech, and the reconceptualization of financial regulation. Northwestern Journal of International Law and Business 37:383–384

Basel Committee on Banking Supervision (2017) Sound practices: implications of fintech development for banks and bank supervisors. https://www.bis.org/bcbs/publ/d415.pdf. Accessed 31 March 2020

Baxter L (2011) Adaptive regulation in the amoral bazaar. South African Law Journal 128:253–272

Beyoud L (2018) Treasury report endorses fintech bank charters, sandboxes. https://news.bloomberglaw.com/banking-law/treasury-report-endorses-fintech-bank-charters-sandboxes-1. Accessed 31 March 2020

Brummer C (2015) Disruptive technology and securities regulation. Fordham Law Review 84:977–1052

CFPB (2016) Policy on no-action letters. https://files.consumerfinance.gov/f/201602_cfpb_no-action-letter-policy.pdf. Accessed 31 March 2020

FCA (2016) Feedback statement, call for input on supporting the development and adopters of regtech. https://www.fca.org.uk/publication/feedback/fs-16-04.pdf. Accessed 31 March 2020
FCA (2017) Regulatory sandbox lessons learned report. https://www.fca.org.uk/publication/research-and-data/regulatory-sandbox-lessons-learned-report.pdf. Accessed 31 March 2020
FCA (2019a) Regulatory sandbox. https://www.fca.org.uk/publications/documents/regulatory-sandbox. Accessed 31 March 2020
FCA (2019b) Regulatory sandbox-cohort 1, regulatory sandbox-cohort 2, regulatory sandbox-cohort 3, regulatory sandbox-cohort 4, regulatory sandbox-cohort 5. https://www.fca.org.uk/firms/regulatory-sandbox. Accessed 31 March 2020
FSB (2017) Financial stability implications from fintech: supervisory and regulatory issues that merit authorities' attention. http://www.fsb.org/wp-content/uploads/R270617.pdf. Accessed 31 March 2020
Government Office for Science (2015) Fintech futures: the UK as a world leader in financial technologies. https://assets.publishing.service.gov.uk/government/uploads/system/uploads/attachment_data/file/413095/gs-15-3-fintech-futures.pdf. Accessed 31 March 2020
Guo (2016) Research on disruptive innovation of Internet industry. Unpublished Doctoral Dissertation, University of Science and Technology of China (in Chinese)
Li (2018) In depth promotion of special rectification of Internet financial risks [Hulianwang jinrong fengxian zhuanxiang zhengzhi shenru tuijin]. Financial Times
Lin et al. (2017) Data logic, technology application and development path of regtech [Jianguan keji de shuju luoji, jishu yingyong ji fazhan lujing]. South China Finance 10:44–50
McCray L et al. (2010) Planned adaptation in risk regulation: an initial survey of US environmental, health, and safety regulation. Technol Forecast Soc Chang 77:951–959
People's Bank of China et al. (2015) Guidance on promoting the healthy development of Internet finance [Guanyu cujin hulianwang jinrong jiankang fazhan de zhidao yijian]. http://www.cbrc.gov.cn/showFfjzDoc/E02EFF7A63564F8B9DF4ED2B3A736310.html. Accessed 31 March 2020
Department of Financial Services (2018) Statement by DFS superintendent Maria T. Vulloon treasury's endorsement of regulatory sandboxes for fintech companies and the OCC's decision to accept fintech charter applications. https://www.dfs.ny.gov/about/statements/st1807311.htm. Accessed 31 March 2020
Sun (2017) ICO is not the same as blockchain the regulation of sandbox is not suitable for China [ICO budengtong yu qukuailian jianguan shahe bingbu shihe zhongguo]. www.yicai.com/news/5344227.html. Accessed 31 March 2020
The World Internet Conference (2019) http://www.wuzhenwic.org/. Accessed 31 March 2020
Wei and Xu (2017) The theoretical framework and development of regtech [Jianguan keji regtech de lilun kuangjia ji fazhan yingdui]. Shanghai Finance 10:63–69
Xu (2018) The nature of 'disruptive innovation' of fintech and new ideas of regtech [Jinrong keji de 'pohuaixing chuangxin' benzhi yu jianguan keji xin silu]. Oriental Law 2:4–13
Yang (2018) Regtech: regulatory challenges and dimensional construction of fintech [Jianguan keji: jinrong keji de jianguan tiaozhan yu weidu jiangou]. Social Sciences in China 5:69–95
Yang and Zhang (2017) The path transformation of the regtech and China's choice [Jinrong keji jianguan de lujing zhuanhuan yu zhongguo xuanze]. Law Science 8:3–14
Zetzsche D et al. (2017) Regulating a revolution: from regulatory sandboxes to smart regulation. Fordham Journal of Corporate and Financial Law 23:31–103
Zhang (2017) The international model of 'regulatory sandbox' and the development path of Mainland China [Jianguan shahe de guoji moshi he zhongguo neidi de fazhan lujing]. Financial Regulation Research 5:22–35
Zhang (2018) Regulatory sandbox and its compatibility with China's administrative law system [Jianguan shahe ji yu woguo xingzheng fa tixi de jianrong]. Zhejiang Academic Journal 1:77–86
Zhu (2018) Comprehensive analysis framework of fintech's development and evolution in China [Woguo fintech fazhan yanjin de zonghe fenxi kuangjia]. Financial Regulation Research 1:55–67
Zhu and Chen (2016) Research on the potential risk and regulatory response of fintech [Fintech de qianzai fengxian yu jianguan yingdui yanjiu]. Financial Regulation Research 7:18–32

Thai Regulatory Approaches to Technology-Driven Innovation in Financial Services

Pawee Jenweeranon

Abstract In recent years, Thai policymakers have adopted laws aimed at keeping pace with contemporary technological developments. This can be seen from the issuance of a number of legislative measures regulating innovative products and services that cannot be effectively dealt with under existing laws and regulations, including those related to financial services. More specifically, Thailand 4.0 has been presented by the government as a policy to transform Thailand into a more innovation-driven or technology-driven economy. In accordance with the policy, there is an agenda to develop a technology cluster and future industries which are related to digital, Internet of Things (loT), Artificial Intelligence, and embedded technologies. The aim is that by using digital tools and IoT as platforms, it will be possible to enhance productivity, quality, and innovation in various economic activities. This can be considered as an important step for Thailand in responding to the rapid development of innovation and technology in various sectors. This chapter reviews these efforts, with a particular emphasis on fintech, as well as considering supplemental initiatives that might be useful to develop further the fintech ecosystem in Thailand. Finally, the chapter considers recent government efforts to intervene and strengthen industry associations as an example of 'soft law' mechanisms in.

Keywords Financial technology · Fintech · Regulatory approaches · Thailand

1 Introduction

In recent years, Thai policymakers have tried to introduce laws to keep pace with technology. This can be seen from the issuance of legislation that responds to innovative products and services and that are regulated within the framework of existing laws and regulations.

Thailand 4.0 is the policy adopted by the government to transform Thailand into a more innovation- and technology-driven economy. One of the five agendas is to

P. Jenweeranon (✉)
Faculty of Law, Thammasat University, Bangkok, Thailand
e-mail: paweejen@tu.ac.th

M. Fenwick et al. (eds.), *Regulating FinTech in Asia*, Perspectives in Law, Business and Innovation, https://doi.org/10.1007/978-981-15-5819-1_6

develop a technology cluster and future industries which are related to digital, the Internet of Things (IoT), Artificial Intelligence, and embedded technologies. The aim is to increase the use of digital tools and loT as platforms to enhance productivity, quality, and innovation in various economic activities. This policy is reflected in the positive trend to promote and support the development of fintech in Thailand recently.

To this extent, there are regulatory attempts from key regulators to support emerging technologies, the notification of the Capital Market Supervisory Board regarding regulations on offer for sale of securities through an electronic system or network issued by the Thai Securities and Exchange Commission (SEC) in May 2015; the consultation paper regarding a regulatory framework to regulate peer-to-peer lending via electronic method issued by the Bank of Thailand in September 2016; the Payment System Act B.E.2560 (2017) which complies with the National E-payment Master Plan and the recent Royal Decree on Digital Asset Business B.E.2561 (2018) issued by the Bank of Thailand and became effective in early 2018; and, the Royal Decree on Digital Asset Businesses B.E.2561 (2018) which is a law issued by the king, upon the advice of the cabinet under the Constitution of Thailand B.E.2560 (2017) Section 172. A Royal Decree is intended to be an emergency measure for national security, public safety, or national economic stability. Also, the amendment of the banking agent regulation by the Bank of Thailand, which is the latest attempt to address the financial exclusion problem, can reflect the active role of Thai authorities to solve the problem.

These laws, as well as subordinate regulations issued by responsible authorities, can reflect the active role of policymakers to make related laws/regulations and can be used to support technology properly, to protect all stakeholders, and to mitigate potential risks.

2 Equity-Based Crowdfunding Regulations

Thailand has exhibited a positive trend towards equity-based crowdfunding as many stakeholders in the country have recognized that it is a tool for economic development by extending access to finance for SMEs and start-ups. Therefore, equity-based crowdfunding is eligible to be operated legally in Thailand. According to the involvement of stakeholders, there are not only private but also public agencies involved in the mechanism of crowdfunding in Thailand.

Regarding the private sector, there are the main three main stakeholders involved in the equity-based crowdfunding ranging from (1) SMEs and start-ups who need funding; (2) funding portals who are intermediaries and act as crowdfunding platforms; and (3) investors who are both retail and non-retail investors and would like to invest in SME and start-up businesses.[1]

[1] Securities and Exchange Commission. Available at: https://www.sec.or.th/th/pages/lawandregulations/crowdfunding.aspx. Accessed 31 March 2020 (in Thai).

Regarding the public sector, there have been signals of support and promotion from the SEC as the main government agency, which is directly responsible for issues relating to equities and securities. In addition, from the perspective of company registration, various public sector agencies, such as the Department of Business Development (DBD)[2] and the Ministry of Finance, have also supported and cooperated with the SEC to register companies, which would like to use equity-based crowdfunding.

Since the mechanism of equity-based crowdfunding returns equity to investors, so it is recognized as a type of fundraising through equity. Therefore, the main law which regulates equity-based crowdfunding is the Securities and Exchange Act B.E. 2535 (1992). With reference to this act, the SEC is the main regulator, which is able to initiate policy and issue other related regulations.

The series of notifications issued by the SEC allows business operators wishing to act as crowdfunding platforms and protects all stakeholders such as funders as well as fundraisers who might be involved in crowdfunding-related activities. The Thai SEC is the authority that grants licenses and considers a platforms' application, as well as checking compliance with regulations.

Regarding the first response towards equity-based crowdfunding, a first notification came into effect on May 16, 2015, allowing a qualified company to raise funds from the public by offering shares via the internet platform structured by a funding portal approved by the SEC,[3] under the following requirements and restrictions.[4] To this extent, there are three main notifications issued by the Capital Market Supervisory Board. The first is the notification no. TorChor. 7/2558 regarding regulations on offer for sale of securities through an electronic system or network. The second is the notification no. KorChor. 3/2558 regarding exemption from filing of a registration statement for securities offered through the provider of electronic system or network. The third is the notification no. TorChor. 8/2558 regarding rules, conditions, and procedures for offering for sale of shares by shareholders of limited companies.

Specifically, the requirements for being a crowdfunding platform under Thai law provided in Chapter 3 clause 12 and 13 of the notification no. TorChor. 7/2558 are as follows:

1. Filing an application with the SEC Office in accordance with Form 35-FP together with the documents specified in the application.
2. Being incorporated under Thai law.
3. Having paid up registered capital not less than five million Baht (around 0.15 million USD).
4. Not having a reasonable ground to believe that the applicant has financial condition problems or has any deficiency and/or not appropriate for being crowdfunding platform.

---

[2]Department of Business Development, providing information on the cooperation between the Securities and Exchange Commission and the Department of Business Development supporting equity-based crowdfunding. Available at: https://www.dbd.go.th/ewt_news.php?nid=11649. Accessed 31 March 2020 (in Thai).

[3]Baker and Mckenzie (2016a).

[4]Jenweeranon (2015).

5. The person who are the directors, managers should not be prohibited by the rule regarding personnel in the capital market business.
6. Having the place for operating crowdfunding platform business.
7. In cases that the applicant is a company having operated other businesses, other businesses shall not have conflict of interest with the crowdfunding portal platform.

Regarding disclosure duties requirements of the issuing company for the offer for sale of newly issued securities, the duties to disclose information concerning issuance or offering for sale of securities are provided in notification of the Capital Market Supervisory Board No. TorChor. 28/2551 regarding application for and approval of an offer for sale of newly issued shares in accordance with Section 35 of the Securities and Exchange Act B.E.2535, which gave the power to the Capital Market Supervisor Board to specify in the notification.

Basically, the notification no. TorChor.28/2551 provides that a public limited company that desires to make an offer for sale of newly issued shares to the public has the duty to disclose information by filling related documents and complying with the procedure specified in this notification; however, there is new regulation which is a notification of the Capital Market Supervisory Board No. KorChor 3/2558 which provided the exemption for filing the registration statement for a public limited company in case that the value of securities that offered to retail investors is not more than twenty million baht (600,000 USD) during twelve months from the first offer and not more than forty million baht (1,200,000 USD) as from the first offer; however, the value of securities that offered to each retail investor shall not exceed fifty thousand baht (1,500 USD) for each company.

For the offer for sale of newly issued shares by a limited company under the Civil and Commercial Code, Section 34 in accordance with Section 56 of the Securities and Exchange Act B.E.2535 (1992) and the notification of the capital market supervisory board no. TorChor. 44/2556 a limited company shall prepare the financial statement and related document specified in Section 56 of the act. In brief, the duties of a limited company are less than the duties provided for a public limited company. However, there is no regulation to exempt the disclosure duties for an issuing company in case the issuing company is a limited company.

With regards to the limit for securities offerings, basically, for a limited company, the limitation of the value of an offer for sale of securities to retail investors is limited to twenty million Baht per 12 months from the first offer and a total value shall not exceed forty million Baht as from the first offer. The offer for sale to each investor shall not exceed 50,000 Baht according to the notification of the Capital Market Supervisory Board No. TorChor. 7/2558 clause 7.

Additionally, in the case of the sale of shares through a crowdfunding portal offered by a shareholder of a limited company under Section 34 of the Securities and Exchange Act B.E.2535, the notification of the Capital Market Supervisory Board No.TorChor. 8/2558 provides the type of investors as follows:

1. Individual Investors,
2. Institutional Investors and/or

3. The shareholders of that limited company; however, it does not allow the public announcement of the offer for sale of shares by a shareholder of a limited company.

In case of a sale of securities through a crowdfunding portal offered by a public limited company, this is not governed by the notification no. TorChor. 7/2558. This means that for a public limited company that offers a sale of newly issued shares specifically to limited investors or to the public, we do not need to consider the limitation for securities offering in notification no. TorChor.7/2558 but have to consider the general regulation, which is the notification no. TorChor. 28/2551 for approval of offer for sale of newly issued shares. However, clause 9 of notification no. TorChor. 7/2558 provides the presumption that an offer for the sale of newly issued securities by a public limited company via a crowdfunding portal in the manner of clause 7 (similar to the limit for securities offerings in case of a limited company) shall be deemed to have been approved by the SEC Office.

In May 2017, the Thai SEC issued a consultation paper on the amendment of securities offering through a crowdfunding portal. The initial idea was to allow a funding portal to use blockchain and smart contracts in the financial allocation. This also facilitated start-ups and SMEs in accessing finance. Also, the Thai SEC considers facilitating stakeholders by providing secondary market crowdfunding securities to enhance liquidity.[5]

After the Thai SEC issued the aforementioned regulations to allow applicants in submitting an application for becoming a crowdfunding portal, there was still no equity-based crowdfunding platform that started operations in Thailand. One of the reasons for this is related to market conditions, such as the quantity and quality of innovation in the Thai market. There are not many business operators that are familiar and genuinely understand the concept of equity crowdfunding.

Moreover, as one of the applicants (dreamakerequity.com) expressed, the reason for the delay in the approval process by the Thai SEC is because the platform has been facing difficulties in preparing the IT infrastructure to meet the requirements set by the SEC.

In addition, some scholars further contend that the paid-up capital requirement for being an equity-based crowdfunding platform in Thailand is significantly lower than in other countries. As well as, the limit for securities offerings, especially that limits as the offer for sale to each investor shall not exceed 50,000 Baht, may not suit SMEs/fundraisers.

---

[5]Thai SEC News (2017). Available at: https://www.sec.or.th/TH/Pages/News_Detail.aspx?SECID=6739. Accessed 31 March 2020.

3 P2P Lending Regulations

Peer to Peer (P2P) Lending has been increasing in significance around the world. Likewise, it has been the focus of attention in Thailand, as a result of the following three factors, which reflect the concerns of borrowers, lenders, and the government.

3.1 The Channel of Access to Finance for SMEs as Borrowers' Necessity

P2P Lending is necessary to SMEs as it expands access to finance. In addition, according to PricewaterhouseCoopers's data,[6] up to 21% of Thai people do not have enough access to financial services. To reduce the gap and promote access to finance to more than 25% of Thais, P2P Lending is supposed to be a much more significant tool in Thailand. In addition, P2P Lending could be one of the factors to reduce the time consuming of lending transactions given its relatively simple procedures, at least when compared with traditional financial institutions.

3.2 The Channel of Investment for Investors as Lenders' Necessity

Concerning PeerPower, one of the ten fintech platforms selected in the competition organized by the Office of the SEC, investors are able to gain better loan interest rates from P2P lending than a saving interest from financial institutions. According to the Nation newspaper,[7] chief executive of PeerPower, Phornvanich Vorapol, reflected that 'at present, investors and savers in Thailand earn a relatively low return on their funds, averaging 0.5% for savings accounts, 2–2.5% for fixed deposits and 4–4.5% for corporate bonds. Therefore, P2P lending is not only crucial to borrowers who need money but also investors who have money and want to invest to gain a better return.

3.3 The Channel of Investment Promotion Policies as the Government's Necessity

The country's main financial and security regulators, the Bank of Thailand and the SEC, recognize that P2P lending presents both opportunities and risks. However,

---

[6]Denwitthayanan (2016).

[7]Limsamarnphun (2017).

the Board of Investment (BOI), the government sector that has responsibility for promoting foreign and domestic investment, added fintech as one of the digital services for investment promotion in Thailand.[8] According to the BOI's announcement in 2014,[9] the fintech business operators, are eligible to receive a corporate income tax exemption and other investment benefits. Consequently, P2P lending, as one of the finTech platforms, is essential for the government's investment promotion policies.

At the moment, there is no law regarding P2P Lending in Thailand. However, there have been efforts to regulate this issue by governmental authorities in the country. According to the latest Supervision Report of the Bank of Thailand in 2015,[10] there are the following three organizations that have been exchanging information regarding fintech and cyber threats, especially in P2P Lending: the Bank of Thailand; the SEC; and the Office of Insurance Commission.

Moreover, in 2016, the Bank of Thailand also launched the latest consultation paper on a framework to regulate P2P Lending on September 30 to receive comments from P2P Lending operators and related stakeholders. Even though this paper is not a legal instrument, it is significant to the P2P Lending in the light of the matchmaker model. It indicates (1) requirements to disclose P2P Lending platforms, (2) a regulation related to agreements between a lender and borrower, and (3) qualifications of P2P Lending operators for non-financial institutions as well as qualifications of investors and borrowers interested in joining P2P Lending.[11]

In sum, before 2019, the main law related to the operation of the P2P platform in Thailand was the Financial Institutions Business Act B.E. 2551 (2008). In relation to this Act, there was a problematic issue regarding Paragraph 1 of Section 9 of the Act enforcing lenders to be a public limited company and granted a license by the Minister of Finance on the advice of the BOT.[12] In light of the exception of this provision, there are regulations to facilitate 'nano-finance' businesses in Thailand, which the Bank of Thailand declared are exempt from Section 9 of the Act. However, P2P lending platforms are not freely entitled to operate because three regulations to facilitate the Nano finance businesses could not support the unique characteristics of fintech.[13]

[8]Baker and McKenzie (2016c).

[9]Board of Investment (2016).

[10]Bank of Thailand (2015).

[11]Jenneeranon (2016).

[12]Financial Institution Business Act B.E. 2551 (2008), Section 9. Available at: https://www.bot.or.th/English/AboutBOT/LawsAndRegulations/SiteAssets/Law_E24_InstitutIns_Sep2011.pdf . Accessed 31 March 2020. The commercial banking business, finance business or credit foncier business may be undertaken only by a juristic person in the type of public limited company and upon having obtained a license from the Minister by the advice of the Bank of Thailand. In granting such license, the Minister may prescribe rules as deemed appropriate.

[13]There are the following three regulations regarding the Nano finance business: (1) Notification of Ministry of Finance regarding type of business in accordance with Section 5 of the Declaration of the Revolutionary Council (No. 58); (2) Notification of Ministry of Finance regarding the financial institution and applicable interest rate (No. 13) 2015; and (3) Notification of the Bank of Thailand

However, the Bank of Thailand recently issued Notification no. 4/2562,[14] which set out requirements for being a P2P lending platform operator, as well as restrictions on certain issues with the primary objective of protecting related stakeholders, such as investors and borrowers. The Notification imposes requirements for being a P2P lending platform operator; for example, an operator must be incorporated under Thai laws, have paid-up capital of not less than 5 million baht, and have not less than 75% Thai ownership. The Notification also includes restrictions on investment and types of investors. Additionally, participating in the regulatory sandbox is compulsory for businesses that are interested in applying for P2P lending operational licenses from the BOT.

Concerning other relevant regulations, the Committee for the Protection of Credit Information also announced a public hearing for the Draft of Credit Information Business Operation Act B.E... (...) which included P2P lending business as a member under the definition provided in Section 3 of the act. This is because the current terminology of 'member' under this act included only 'a financial institution that a credit information company.' From the official document presented by the committee, the objective of this amendment is to support SMEs and start-ups in accessing finance.[15]

4 New Payment Services Regulations

The Bank of Thailand is the main authority for supervising all related activities with regard to all types of payment services. Before the Payment System Act B.E.2560 (2017) became effective there were complicated procedures as well as overlapping of supervising duties of related authorities, such as the Ministry of Finance and the Bank of Thailand.

The New Payment System Act B.E.2560 (2017) of Thailand is a part of the National e-Payment Master Plan, which aimed to promote the use of e-Payment in all industries. In particular, the Bank of Thailand is a pivotal authority to support two projects, which is part of this master plan, namely the PromptPay project and Card Usage Expansion project.

This concept corresponds with a growth rate (volume) of e-Payment presented by the Bank of Thailand from 2011-2016. In particular, mobile banking is an e-Payment channel with the highest growth rate of 97% during these years. In the meantime, the Bank of Thailand together with the National Broadcasting and Telecommunication Commission (NBTC) took part in pushing the Telecommunication Association of Thailand under the Royal Patronage (TCT) and the Thai Banker's Association (TBA)

SorNorChor 1/2015 regarding rule procedures and conditions for operating 'Nano-finance' business for non-bank institution.

[14]Available at: https://www.bot.or.th/Thai/FIPCS/Documents/FPG/2562/ThaiPDF/25620096.pdf. Accessed 31 March 2020.

[15]Committee for the Protection of Credit Information (2016).

to sign a memorandum of understanding to enhance security standards for financial transactions via mobile phones.[16]

Regarding e-Payment services, before the effective date of the Payment System Act B.E.2560 (2017), a business operator wishing to provide e-money or e-payment services need to get licenses in accordance with related laws (the Royal Decree Regulating Electronic Payment Service Business, B.E. 2551 (2008) issued under the Electronic Transactions Act B.E. 2544 (2001) and the Notification of the Finance Ministry issued under Section 5 of the Revolution Council Decree No. 58 (The Notification of the Electronic Transactions Commission re: Rules, Procedures and Conditions for Undertaking Electronic Payment Service Business B.E. 2559 (2016)).

Accordingly, the Payment System Act B.E.2560 (2017) (the PSA)[17] of Thailand is an example of the attempt by the Bank of Thailand to facilitate fintech players or e-money/e-payment service provider with a single license scheme while preventing risks for all stakeholders. The Payment System Act B.E. 2560 (2017) was published in the Government Gazette on 18 October 2017. The PSA aims to unify existing payment laws and regulations and synchronize certain requirements with international standards as well as allow some flexibility to support or regulate the emergence of new payment system/services in the future. The PSA regulates Systemically Important Payment Systems, Regulated Payment Systems, and Regulated E-Payment Services.

In detail, the act provides a single license scheme—existing licensed e-payment service providers also needed to apply for a new license or registration within 120 days after publication of the Ministry of Finance's notification as a requirement under the Act in order to continue their operation. Also, the PSA imposes a new categorization of regulated payment activities ((1) important payment systems; (2) supervised payment systems; and (3) supervised payment services[18]).

However, under Section 13 of the New Payment System Act B.E.2560 (2017), a regulated payment system business may be operated only by a juristic person that is a limited company or a public limited company or any other juristic person as prescribed in the Notification of the BOT. This is another restriction that is similar to what has been prescribed in other fintech-related regulations/guidelines. To this extent, under the Notification of the BOT, a foreign juristic person is only allowed to operate a card network business. Also, a foreign juristic person needs to establish

---

[16]Bank of Thailand (2016b).

[17]Payment System Act B.E. 2560 (2017). Available at: http://www.krisdika.go.th/wps/wcm/connect/489e9f804507e66882f39aefd8452bbc/PAYMEPA+SYSTEMS+ACT%2C+B.E.+2560+%282017%29.pdf?MOD=AJPERES&CACHEID=448e9f804507e66882f39aefd8452bbc. Accessed 31 March 2020 (tentative translation)

[18]Payment System Act, Section 3 provides that 'vital payment system' means a payment system which is vital to security or stability of payment systems, financial institution systems or financial systems of the country; 'regulated payment system' means a payment system which requires permission from the Minister or registration by the BOT, as the case may be; 'payment service' means the provision of a service offering a medium for payment or a channel of payment of any money, whether tangible or intangible, for paying prices of goods or services or transferring money or making any other financial transaction; 'regulated payment service' means a payment service which requires permission from the Minister or registration by the BOT, as the case may be.

a branch or representative office in Thailand, as well as appoint a representative to operate on behalf of that juristic person.

5 Digital Asset Businesses Regulations

Digital assets have been used as a fundraising instrument, and medium of exchange in Thailand and activities conducted outside the framework of any regulatory framework have been of great concern for the Thai government and regulatory authorities, as these activities pose significant risks for national financial stability and for retail investors. From the SEC Thailand's Viewpoint on ICO published in 2017, the SEC recognized in September 2017 that ICOs do not yet fit neatly with the current regulatory framework while emphasizing its potential in enhancing financial inclusion for start-ups.[19]

At the beginning of 2018, successful ICO projects in the country have spurred the government to regulate such activities to prevent fraudulent activities and other scams.[20] The SEC's first regulatory attempt was to amend the Securities Law to bring ICO projects within the scope of the legislation.[21] Faced with the lengthy duration of the amending process, however, a Royal Decree on Digital Asset Businesses B.E.2561 was instead issued by the King in May 2018.[22]

In September 2016, the SEC issued an announcement regarding ICOs. Even though there are concerns with regards to the misuse of ICOs and public risks related to cyber security-related issues, from the announcement, it was clear that the SEC saw that ICOs have the potential to provide an alternative means of fundraising, especially for tech start-ups. For this reason, the SEC was considering an improved regulatory approach for ICO activities.

The Royal Decree on Digital Asset Businesses was enacted to regulate the offering of digital assets and the undertaking of digital asset businesses, which must obtain an operating license from the SEC to legally conduct such activities. The SEC estimated that there are around 50,000 active users in Thailand involved in crypto-asset-related activities such as investing in Bitcoin or other cryptocurrencies.[23]

Even though the Royal Decree and subordinate rules are at an early stage of implementation, there are many concerns, such as the issuance of scam coins, as well as risks related to cybersecurity. To this extent, the SEC expressed concerns regarding how to educate people to understand the risks in digital asset investment

[19] Securities and Exchange Commission (2017).

[20] Example of successful project: JFinCoin ICO launched by J Ventures at the beginning of 2018.

[21] The Securities and Exchange Act B.E.2535.

[22] A Royal Decree is a law issued by the King, upon the advice of the cabinet under the Constitution of Thailand, often used as an emergency measure to safeguard national security, public safety or national economic stability. B.E.2560 (2017), Section 172.

[23] Interview with Butree Vangsirirungruang, The Securities and Exchange Commission, in Bangkok, Thailand (August 28, 2018).

and prevent additional public confusion. For example, once the SEC listed seven cryptocurrencies that were allowed to be traded in the permitted exchange platform—this led to a misunderstanding of the legal status of the currencies as legal tender under Thai law. This is also because the number of people interested in investing in digital assets, including Bitcoin and other cryptocurrencies, was expected to increase after the Royal Decree on the Digital Asset Businesses became effective in May 2018.

The Royal Decree on Digital Asset Businesses is the main regulation for crypto-asset supervision in Thailand. The decree came into force on 14 May 2018.[24] It was enacted to regulate the activities related to ICO, as well as a cryptocurrency exchange. Such businesses must obtain an operating license from the SEC. Subsequently, the SEC issued a series of subordinate regulations[25] to add specific details, such as the exemptions in the case of utility tokens and stable coins under the existing law.[26]

In general, the Royal Decree set the requirement for digital asset businesses, ICO portal, and businesses which want to engage in an ICO. Under the Royal Decree, digital asset businesses are classified into three main categories: Digital Asset Exchange, Digital Asset Broker, and Digital Asset Dealer. All these businesses shall obtain a license and comply with the rules, conditions, and procedures specified in the notification of the SEC.[27] To this extent, the rules prescribe related details, such as paid-up capital requirement, the requirement that crypto-asset businesses need to be a Thai company, as well as the exemption for some types of crypto-asset (such as a utility token). Any digital business must also fulfill requirements set out in the notification from the Ministry of Finance (e.g., a capital requirement).[28] For instance, digital token portal service providers (ICO portal operator) must be registered with a capital of 5 million Thai Baht (around 150,000 USD) which is significantly lower than paid-up capital requirements which were set for digital asset exchange, digital asset broker (50 million Thai Baht, around 1,500,000 USD), and digital asset dealer (25 million Thai Baht, around 750,000 USD).

With reference to the terminology, the Royal Decree provides a definition of a 'digital asset' along with a definition of 'cryptocurrency' and 'digital token.' As provided in Section 3, digital asset means cryptocurrency and digital tokens, and digital assets businesses are classified into three types as earlier mentioned.

[24]Royal Decree on Digital Asset Business B.E.2561 (2018) (Royal Decree). Available at: https://www.sec.or.th/EN/SECInfo/LawsRegulation/Documents/actandroyal/digitalasset_decree_2561_EN.pdf. Accessed 31 March 2020

[25]Available at: https://www.sec.or.th/TH/pages/lawandregulations/initialcoinofferingregulations.aspx. Accessed 31 March 2020.

[26]The exemption is specified in the notification KorTor 10/2561, KorJor12/2561 and KorTor11/2561 issued by the Securities and Exchange Commission. It became effective on June 16, 2018.

[27]Available at: https://www.sec.or.th/th/pages/lawandregulations/digitalassetbusinessregulations.aspx. Accessed 31 March 2020.

[28]Available at: https://capital.sec.or.th/webapp/nrs/data/7736s.pdf. Accessed 31 March 2020; https://capital.sec.or.th/webapp/nrs/data/8182s.pdf. Accessed 31 March 2020.

With regards to the main authority to supervise related activities for both ICO and cryptocurrency exchange, the SEC is identified as the main authority to supervise and consider all matters related to digital asset activities. The Bank of Thailand supervises, examines, and analyses the financial status and performance, and risk management system of the financial institutions in order to promote financial institutions stability.

Also, from Section 4 of the Royal Decree ‘The Minister of Finance shall be in charge of the enforcement of this Emergency Decree and shall have the power to issue notifications and appoint a competent officer to perform duties in accordance with this Emergency Decree’, accordingly, in practice, the SEC and Ministry of Finance are supervising crypto-asset-related activities.

Regarding anti-money laundering measures, the Anti-Money Laundering Office (AMLO) acts as an authority that is responsible for money-laundering prevention. From the Royal Decree, a crypto-asset business under the Royal Decree is considered as a financial institution under the Money Laundering Act of Thailand (Section 7 of the Royal Decree). This means that crypto-asset businesses have a duty to comply with the Money Laundering Act B.E.2542 (1999) Section 15, which imposes a duty to report any transaction which falls within the scope of Section 15 of the Anti-Money Laundering Act.[29]

In conclusion, digital asset business operators and digital token service providers shall be regarded as financial institutions and thus abide by anti-money laundering regulations.[30] Digital asset businesses must, therefore, undertake know-your-client measures, a client due diligence process, and measures against financial assistance to terrorists or money laundering.[31]

However, it is inevitable that there are regulatory concerns from relevant stakeholders in a number of issues, including the limitation of the types of digital asset businesses under the Royal Decree.

6 The Regulatory Sandbox

Basically, a sandbox initiative has been implemented separately by different authorities in Thailand, namely the Bank of Thailand, the SEC, and the Office of Insurance Commission of Thailand.

The Bank of Thailand became the first authority to adopt a regulatory sandbox scheme in December 2016 to experiment with new products, services, or business models in financial services involving new technologies. Subsequently, the SEC

[29] Available at: http://www.amlo.go.th/amlo-intranet/media/k2/attachments/AMLAZNoZ1-5Z2016_2.pdf. Accessed 31 March 2020.

[30] Royal Decree, Section 7.

[31] Royal Decree, Section 30, along with a duty to report prescribed in the Anti-money laundering Act B.E.2542 (1999) of Thailand, Chapter 2. See Interview with Butree Vangsirirungruang, The Securities and Exchange Commission, in Bangkok, Thailand (August 28, 2018).

launched its regulatory sandbox, and applications were invited in March 2017 for an investment advisor/private fund sandbox and a clearing settlement sandbox in May 2017.

To this extent, in Thailand, this can imply that the SEC and Bank of Thailand, which are the main regulators in this fintech area, have different supervisory powers. Even the SEC and Bank of Thailand have to collaborate with each other to monitor financial products and services. However, the SEC focuses on capital market supervision, and the Bank of Thailand focuses on the supervision of matters concerning financial institutions and other financial services such as e-payments. Laws and subordinate regulations of the authorities are also separated from each other.

Accordingly, In general, in Thailand, there are now three sandboxes launched by government authorities, namely the Bank of Thailand, the SEC, and the Office of Insurance Commission (OIC).

Compared to other sandboxes launched by SEC and OIC, the number of applicants applied for the Bank of Thailand sandbox is significantly higher. Particularly, for the Bank of Thailand sandbox, there have been many applications from traditional banks, and they subsequently got permission from the Bank to exit from the sandbox using new innovation in their business. For example, such permission was granted from the Bank of Thailand for banks to use QR code payment services.

However, the SEC and OCI sandboxes are different from the Bank of Thailand sandbox in that not many applicants participated.

To be more specific, consider as an example, in 2016, the launch of the Bank of Thailand sandbox. This followed the publication of a consultation paper on FinTech Regulatory Sandbox Guidelines ('Draft Guidelines') on September 14th—October 15th.[32] The Bank of Thailand allowed business operators to test their financial products or services in a live but limited environment, without being fully subject to all requirements that are normally applicable. Through the Regulatory Sandbox, the Bank of Thailand aimed to facilitate new financial innovations while still ensuring consumer protection and financial system stability.

With regard to the key issues under the Draft Guidelines, there are six key points related to the implementation of the regulatory sandbox in Thailand.[33]

First, participants in the Bank of Thailand's Regulatory Sandbox can only offer their fintech products or services to consumers within the limited scope as approved by the Bank of Thailand (e.g., the specific period of time, area, and types and number of consumers). These operations involve somewhat more lenient rules, as specified by the Bank of Thailand on a case-by-case basis.

Second, regarding the type of applicants, the following are eligible to apply: (1) financial institutions; (2) companies within the business group of financial institutions; (3) non-financial institutions under the supervision of the Bank of Thailand (e.g., business operators providing personal loans under supervision, nano-finance, etc.); (4) fintech firms; and (5) technology firms. Regarding their qualifications, qualified applicants have to incorporate in Thailand, have directors, executives,

[32]Bank of Thailand (2016a).

[33]Baker and McKenzie (2016b).

and employees with managerial powers with good corporate governance, and have received all relevant licenses as required under the applicable laws.

Third, regarding the types of products or services, the following activities are specified: (1) loans (not including debt instrument issuance); (2) payments and fund transfers; and (3) other financial transactions which have similar characteristics, or innovations. Regarding the qualification of the services, the product or service must be innovative with new technology not already available in Thailand, the product or service can solve financial services problems or must be beneficial to the consumers in, or the financial system of; Thailand.

Fourth, regarding the application process, applicants have to submit a complete set of supporting documents as prescribed by the Draft Guidelines to the Bank of Thailand along with the application. In addition, the consideration process has to take no longer than 60 days from the date on which the Bank of Thailand receives the application and a complete set of supporting documents.

Fifth, requirements during the participation, there are the following four issues to maintain during the participation process: (1) consumer protection measures (e.g., measures regarding consumers' money and assets and consumer data, complaints, and compensations); (2) sufficient risk management systems, including IT and cyber risk management; (3) information disclosure to the customer e.g., restrictions and conditions in using the services, the fact that the service is being tested in the regulatory sandbox; and (4) sufficient and appropriate procedures regarding anti-money laundering and counter-terrorism financing.

Finally, regarding the post-sandbox period, there are three important points: (1) once the test period ends, the lenient rules will no longer apply, unless an extension period is explicitly granted by the Bank of Thailand; (2) if the test results meet the goals, and the participant can comply with normal regulatory requirements, the applicant must apply for approval under the normal regulatory scheme to provide the services with a broader scope; and (3) an applicant must stop its service if the test results do not meet the goal, or the applicant does not comply with the conditions agreed to during participation in the sandbox.

Due to the fact that the regulatory sandbox is issued under an executive power, the sandbox acts as an exemption of the existing laws and/or regulations passed by the Congress under legislative power. Some Thai scholars, therefore, argued that this idea is contrary to the doctrine of separation of powers in Thai constitutional law.

To address this problem, it is necessary to consider the issue of the extent and character of the authority of the Bank of Thailand. First, according to the authority of the Bank of Thailand, it is the main organization that is the financial regulator and launches the guideline for the regulatory sandbox in Thailand. With reference to the Bank of Thailand Act B.E. 2551 (2008),[34] Section 7 and Section 8 together with Section 28/9 and 28/10 prescribe that the committee of the financial institution of the Bank of Thailand is able to issue policies and relevant notifications to maintain the stability of financial institution and payment system in Thailand.

---

[34]Bank of Thailand Act B.E. 2551 (2008). Available at: https://www.bot.or.th/Thai/MonetaryPolicy/Monet PolicyComittee/MPR/DocLib1/BOT_decrde.pdf. Accessed 31 March 2020.

The other point is related to the scope of the regulatory sandbox. The direct domestic basis for the announcement of the Regulatory Sandbox was the Financial Institution Business Act B.E. 2551 (2008).[35] With reference to the Section 7 of this Act, a notification of the Bank of Thailand issued under the act shall come into force upon its publication in the Government Gazette. Consequently, the Draft Guideline, which was issued by the Bank of Thailand, complied with this Act.

In addition to these domestic acts granting the authority to the Bank of Thailand and the scope of the regulatory sandbox, the Draft Guideline can also fulfill the consumer protection criteria. Finally, even though the regulatory sandbox is an exemption of the existing laws or regulations under legislative power. This idea is not contrary to the doctrine of separation of powers because it is under the authority of the Bank of Thailand and has a lawful scope of its notification, as well as the consumer protection criteria.

However, the three main authorities currently operating and supervising the sandboxes do not have any coordination mechanism which allows all authorities to work together in considering the sandbox application and coordinating a project. This also reflects a difficulty for the sandbox applicant as the platform (P2P lending platform) expressed that their business model falls within the scope of supervision for both the Bank of Thailand and the SEC sandboxes. Moreover, once they applied for the Bank of Thailand sandbox, it is also difficult for the Bank of Thailand to give advice on matters of law that do not fall within the scope of their supervision. This creates a potential difficulty in achieving the regulatory sandbox's objective of supporting fintech or start-up companies.

In Thailand, there is still a lack of sufficient support for small fintech firms. This can refer to an example of applicants of the Bank of Thailand regulatory sandbox. For the moment, most applicants are big commercial banks or financial institutions, not small fintech or start-up firms.

With regards to the SEC sandbox, the SEC launched two schemes, a regulatory sandbox and temporary regulations that were designed to help enable innovative players. At the present time, all of the players so far have been using the temporary regulations scheme, and there is no one using the regulatory sandbox scheme. This is something that the SEC did not foresee when they decided to implement a sandbox.

To be more specific, the temporary regulations initiative exempted certain types of businesses from certain rules under Thai SEC's supervision for the period of time as specified. Along with the reason that the SEC recently amended their subordinate rules to be more flexible to facilitate and support relevant players in the market. As the aforementioned statement, this means that a regulatory sandbox is not the first preference for those players.

This is different from the sandbox guidelines provided by the Bank of Thailand. Specifically, their sandbox guidelines imposed an obligation for some types of businesses to compulsorily need to experiment with their innovation in the Bank of Thailand sandbox scheme before launching their product. This was the case for the QR code payment service mentioned above, for example.

[35] Financial Institution Business Act B.E. 2551 (2008).

Another example is the practice of e-Know Your Customer (KYC) under the supervision of both the SEC and Bank of Thailand. The requirement, under the notification issued by the SEC, does not require KYC to arrange a face to face customer identification. This is the reason why fintech players who wish to employ an e-KYC in business under the supervision of the Bank of Thailand need to apply to participate in the sandbox.

In addition, there is a proposal for a National Regulatory Sandbox, which was made by the National Science Technology and Innovation Policy Committee. However, since the initiative was first proposed at the beginning of 2018, there has been no substantial progress.

7 Conclusion

Overall, legislation has been issued to support financial technology development in Thailand. The Thai government has taken the approach to encourage Thai fintech players and set the requirements for all players to set up the company under Thai laws. This may benefit Thai fintech platforms. However, this may limit the development of the digital environment in Thailand at the same time, as some foreign companies expressed their concerns about operating their businesses in Thailand. Moreover, because of the considerable gap between Thai and foreign fintech players, this also can make it difficult to adopt financial technology to address specific problems, such as financial inclusion. To be more specific, Thai commercial banks do not want to take risks in offering loans for 'risky' groups, while Thai fintech players may not have the resources to fill the gap, resulting in an unmet need.

In sum, relaxing this requirement might be useful for allowing foreign fintech players to enter the Thai market. This can benefit Thai citizens in many ways, such as boosting e-commerce, reducing transaction fees, and supporting the economic development of the country.

Overall, Thai regulators play an active role in supporting fintech development. In essence, the SEC fintech division and the Bank of Thailand are supportive of providing an environment that is conducive to fintech innovations and deployment. For instance, the SEC took an active approach to regulate innovation by the issuance of Royal Decree on Digital Asset Business, which is the result of concerns that occurred from an ICO-related activity conducted in Thailand at the beginning of 2018. However, related to digital asset businesses related regulation—withholding tax on income from digital assets may possibly obstruct or make foreign firms hesitate to launch their business in Thailand as well as the requirement that digital asset businesses need to register as a Thai company may have a similar chilling effect.

Also, with regards to the infrastructure, Thailand has the potential to achieve success in digital infrastructure development due to many factors such as the number of mobile phone users in Thailand and expanding of free wi-fi coverage in provinces outside Bangkok. More importantly, the Thai government's issuance of a Thailand 4.0 policy as well as other initiatives such as the e-Payment master plan all reflects a sustainable way to improve the digital environment. Even some scholars may propose that digital literacy and digital skills shortage can be crucial factors that obstruct the development fintech industry in Thailand. Still, the problems are being considered by relevant authorities and could be solved in the medium- to long-term.

References

Board of Investment (2016) BOI Announcement no. sor. 1/2559 re: additional amendments of eligible activities for investment promotion in accordance with the BOI announcement No. 2/2557. http://www.boi.go.th/upload/content/Announcement_Sor1-2559_90752.pdf. Accessed 31 March 2020

Baker & McKenzie (2016a) Fintech and the legal landscape. http://www.bakermckenzie.com/-/media/files/insight/publications/2016/02/fintech-and-the-legal-landscape/al_global_fintechlegal landscape_feb16.pdf?la=en. Accessed 31 March 2020

Baker & McKenzie (2016b) Fintech update: Thailand's fintech regulatory sandbox. http://www.bakermckenzie.com/-/media/files/insight/publications/2016/10/fintech-update/al_bangkok_fint echsandbox_oct16.pdf?la=en. Accessed 31 March 2020

Baker & McKenzie (2016c) Thailand: fintech 2016 highlights and beyond. http://www.bakermcke nzie.com/en/insight/publications/2016/12/fintech-2016-highlights-and-beyond/. Accessed 31 March 2020

Bank of Thailand (2015) Supervision report 2558. https://www.bot.or.th/Thai/FinancialInstitutions/Publications/Pages/Supervision-Report.aspx. Accessed 31 March 2020 (in Thai)

Bank of Thailand (2016a) Consultation paper on fintech regulatory sandbox guidelines. https://www.bot.or.th/Thai/FinancialInstitutions/Documents/ConsultativePaper_Regulator ySandbox.pdf. Accessed 31 March 2020 (in Thai)

Bank of Thailand (2016b) Payment system report 2016. https://www.bot.or.th/English/PaymentSystems/Publication/PS_Annually_Report/Documents/Payment_2016_E.pdf. Accessed 31 March 2020

Committee for the Protection of Credit Information (2016) Information public hearing the Draft of Credit Information Business Operation Act B.E…(…). https://www.creditinfocommittee.or.th/Thai/Documents/25591117-Hearing-1.pdf. Accessed 31 March 2020 (in Thai)

Denwitthayanan K (2016) Loan 'Peer-to-Peer Lending' Opportunity or Risk. https://www.pwc.com/th/en/pwc-thailand-blogs/blog-20160922.html. Accessed 31 March 2020

Department of Business Development (2015) Crowdfunding Fundraising Policy https://www.dbd.go.th/ewt_news.php?nid=11649. Accessed 31 March 2020

Jenneeranon P (2016) The regulatory framework for peer-to-peer lending industry in Thailand: a consultation paper issued by the Bank of Thailand. https://www.crowdfundinsider.com/2016/10/91069-regulatory-framework-peer-peer-lending-industry-thailand-consultation-paper-issued-bank-thailand/. Accessed 31 March 2020

Jenweeranon P (2015) The establishment of equity crowdfunding in Thailand & the strengthening of Thai SMEs for the ASEAN Single Market. https://www.crowdfundinsider.com/2015/05/68267-the-establishment-of-equity-crowdfunding-in-thailand-the-strengthening-of-thai-smes-for-the-asean-single-market/. Accessed 31 March 2020

Limsamarnphun N (2017) Peer-to-peer lending platform awaits Bank of Thailand nod. The Nation, Thailand. http://www.nationmultimedia.com/news/business/corporate/30305129. Accessed 31 March 2020

Securities and Exchange Commission (2017) SEC Thailand's viewpoint on ICO. https://www.iosco.org/library/ico-statements/Thailand%20-%20SEC%20-%20Viewpoint%20on%20ICOs.pdf. Accessed 31 March 2020

Securities and Exchange Commission (DATE) Crowdfunding, structure and objectives, http://www.sec.or.th/TH/RaisingFunds/CFD/Pages/principle.aspx. Accessed 31 March 2020
Thai SEC News (2017) the SEC is amending Crowdfunding regulations to support using of technologies in financial allocation management and secondary market for Crowdfunding securities. https://www.sec.or.th/TH/Pages/News_Detail.aspx?SECID=6739. Accessed 31 March 2020

Fintech in Vietnam and Its Regulatory Approach

Hai Yen Nguyen

Abstract In the '4th Industrial Revolution,' the upsurged trend of financial services of non-banking institutions and the intersection of financial services and technology have shaped fintech companies. Such businesses have advantages in technology, deliver financial solutions with modern technologies, and provide customers with a highly accessible and streamlined path to fulfill their financial needs. Vietnam has been considered as a potentially lucrative market for fintech as it has a young and 'tech-savvy' population, high mobile phone and internet penetration rates, and relatively low levels of financial inclusion. Although its fintech market is still fledgling, more than 150 companies have joined with increasing transaction volumes and high growth rates. They have provided customers with financial and banking services such as digital payment, crowdfunding, peer-to-peer lending, remittance, blockchain, personal finance management, and information comparison with modern technologies, lower costs, and more straightforward procedures. Also, the country has been making an effort to spur the development of fintech companies by setting up a fintech steering committee, preparing the national financial inclusion strategy, and cautiously seeking the best approach to regulate fintech. This chapter examines the use of fintech to facilitate socio-economic development in Vietnam and considers the appropriate regulatory framework to achieve such a goal.

Keywords Fintech · Financial service · Regulatory approach · Financial regulation · Vietnam

H. Y. Nguyen (✉)
Hanoi Law University, Hanoi, Vietnam
e-mail: nguyenhaiyen@hlu.edu.vn

M. Fenwick et al. (eds.), *Regulating FinTech in Asia*, Perspectives in Law, Business and Innovation, https://doi.org/10.1007/978-981-15-5819-1_7

1 Introduction

Financial technology, or fintech, combines financial products and services with technology and usually refers to the use of technology to deliver financial solutions.[1] The fintech industry is very dynamic and dramatically changing. More and more fintech start-ups are entering the market every year with innovative business models.

Vietnam has been considered as a potentially lucrative market for fintech. This is because of its young and 'tech-savvy' population, high mobile phone and internet penetration rates, and relatively low levels of financial inclusion.[2] Fintech is the key driver for financial inclusion[3]; it plays an important role in increasing collaboration across sectoral boundaries and promoting the allocation of resources.[4] Therefore, it could be useful for facilitating the socio-economic development of the country. In order to examine the importance of fintech for the financial sector and the possibility of using fintech to facilitate the socio-economic development, it is necessary to consider comprehensive data regarding operating segments, market size, and growth potential of fintech. This chapter presents the current situation of fintech in Vietnam, then submits that fintech plays an important role in spurring financial inclusion, which underlines the sustainable balance of socio-economic development.

Although Vietnam's fintech market is still fledgling, more than 150 companies have joined, and there are increasing transaction volume and high growth rates. These fintech companies have provided customers with financial and banking services such as digital payment, crowdfunding, peer-to-peer lending (P2P lending), remittance, personal finance management, and information comparison with modern technologies, lower costs and simpler procedures.[5] Despite the success and growth of the fintech industry, the expansion of the fintech industry is associated with certain challenges (prevailing challenges covered are investment management, customer management, regulation, technology integration, privacy and security, and on-going difficulties that new and existing fintech business must address).[6]

In the meanwhile, the current operation of fintech companies in the absence of a sufficient regulatory framework has led to risks for all stakeholders in the fintech space and the obstacle for innovation in the country. In fact, fintech in Vietnam has been considered as a new business sector. Therefore, the policy and regulations on fintech are generally insufficient and unclear. Although the country has been making an effort to facilitate the development of fintech companies through setting up the Fintech Steering Committee (in March 2017), issuing many policies, programs, and projects with the focus on creating a favorable environment for the development of diversified fintech products and services, and preparing the National Financial Inclusion Strategy, there has not been a sufficient regulatory framework for fintech

[1] Aner et al. (2016), p. 3.

[2] See Tung (2019), p. 26; see also Vietnam Investment Review (2018).

[3] Tam and Hanh (2018), p. 11.

[4] See UNEP (2016), p. 22.

[5] See Retail New Asia (2019); see also Thong (2019).

[6] See Moshirian et al. (2019), p. 19.

so far. Besides, in the context of many different views on the management of fintech and the diversity of regulatory approaches, Vietnam aims to use regulatory sandbox to pilot fintech products and has been drafting a regulatory sandbox for fintech.

To have a better understanding of the need for regulating fintech in Vietnam, the chapter studies the current regulations on fintech as well as assesses the problems posed by fintech. Based on the consideration of possible regulatory approaches such as 'doing nothing,' cautious permissiveness, structured experimentalism, and the development of a specific new regulatory framework,[7] the chapter proposes a reasonable regulatory approach for fintech to encourage the development of innovation while to ensure public interests in order to facilitate the socio-economic development of the country.

Following this introduction, Sect. 2 introduces the current situation of fintech in Vietnam, to illustrate the growth and potential of the fintech industry, and identifies challenges for fintech development. Section 3 considers the possibility of using fintech to facilitate the socio-economic development through spurring financial inclusion, increasing collaboration across sectoral boundaries, and promoting the allocation of resources. Section 4 examines Vietnam's current regulations on fintech to illustrate that the absence of an appropriate regulatory framework for fintech could hinder the development of disruptive innovation. Section 5 discusses possible regulatory approaches and then proposes an appropriate solution for regulating fintech in Vietnam to facilitate socio-economic development. Section 6 concludes.

2 Current Situation of Fintech in Vietnam

Fintech is considered as a technological innovation that could deliver financial services in Vietnam over the last decade. Although the fintech sector in the country is relatively new (the oldest fintech firm named VTPay operating in the mobile payment sector was established in 2005[8]), the number of fintech start-ups has been rising sharply and reached more than 150 as of October 2019.[9] These fintech companies are providing various financial services such as digital payment, crowdfunding, P2P lending, blockchain, personal finance management, data management, and information comparison for around 47.96 million users with the significant total transaction value at the number of USD 7,372 million by September 2018.[10]

Regarding digital payment, internet and mobile communications payments currently are a central fintech focus and have been a driving force, particularly in developing countries.[11] Vietnam is not an exception. The digital payment sector in the country has been witnessed as one of the fastest-growing sectors, and one of

[7]Zetzsche et al. (2017), p. 1.

[8]Tam and Hanh (2018), p. 14.

[9]Retail New Asia (2019); Thong (2019).

[10]Ernst and Young Vietnam (2018), p. 5.

[11]Aner et al. (2016), p. 19.

the hottest investment trends for start-ups with the total transaction value accounts for 99.9% of the total transaction value of the fintech market in 2017.[12] Cashless payments are booming in Vietnam, more than doubling in value over the first three quarters of 2018. In particular, transactions over mobile apps and digital wallets rose by an impressive 126% and 161% respectively.[13] As of November 2019, thirty-two non-bank institutions have been licensed by the State Bank of Vietnam to provide payment intermediary services (including e-wallet services, online payment gateway, and mobile payment services) to serve the demand for payment of e-commerce transactions and small money transfers.[14] Twenty of them offer e-wallets, including well-known names like MoMo, Bankplus, Vi Viet, VTC Pay, WePay, Vimo, Ngan Luong, and Payoo,[15] with the value of transactions in 2017 reached more than VND 53.1 trillion.[16] The largest mobile wallet provider of the country is MoMo, an e-wallet and mobile payment application developed by M-Service, which offers simple and convenient mobile payment solutions and better user experience in comparison with incumbent players.[17] With MoMo, users can make transactions such as top up and pay their utility bills. MoMo currently supports payments to nearly 100 service providers and online businesses.[18] Besides, there are many online payment gateways operating in Vietnam, such as Ngan Luong, Baokim.vn, and VTCPay, which quickly and conveniently provide a payment solution for e-commerce websites between buyers and sellers. Ngan Luong is the largest payment gateway in Vietnam, which linked to many reputable e-commerce sites such as ebay.vn and chodientu.vn.[19] Moreover, mobile payment is becoming a new trend in Vietnam with the rise of technologies such as QR codes, contactless payments, and the tokenization of card information[20] with 41 licensed providers so far.[21] The Vietnam mobile payment market size was valued at USD 16,054 million in 2016.[22] Currently, around 90% of payment transactions in the country are made in cash, and this has led fintech companies to focus primarily on the development of payment services, with one-third of the companies working on payment services, the highest rate in the ASEAN region.[23]

In recent years, along with a fast-growing start-up movement, the Vietnamese market has developed capital mobilization from the community that is often referred to as crowdfunding. Many crowdfunding platforms have emerged and gained a great

---

[12]See Tam and Hanh (2018), p. 15.

[13]British Business Group Vietnam (2019), p. 2.

[14]The State Bank of Vietnam (2019a).

[15]Vietnam Investment Review (2019).

[16]See Thao (2018).

[17]See The Asian Banker (2018).

[18]See Fintechnews Vietnam (2019).

[19]See VeriMe (2018).

[20]See Nguyen (2019).

[21]See Vietnamnet (2019).

[22]Rake (2018).

[23]Das (2018).

Platform	Year of establishment	Area of focus	Number of projects	Total successful funding	
				In million VND	In USD [a]
Betado	2015	Various	18	1562	68800
Comicola	2015	Publishing	11	1564	68915
Firststep	2014	Various	7	45	1980
Fundstart	2015	Various	6	117	5138

([a] Equivalent amount in USD, calculated at exchange rate USD/VND = 22,700)

Fig. 1 Successful crowdfunding in Vietnam

deal of trust from the community.[24] Charity Map was claimed as the first crowdfunding platform in the country in 2012. Its mission was to solve the mismatch between donors and knowledge about orphanages and other social organizations across Vietnam. Charity Map is the only known donation-based crowdfunding platform that has operated in the country. It had raised more than VND 200 million (equivalent to USD 8.7 thousand) for over 50 social organizations across the country before it closed in 2016.[25] Besides, there are four reward-based crowdfunding platforms that were founded from January 1, 2014, to December 31, 2016, including Comicola, FirstStep, Betado, and Fundstart. During that time, there were a total of forty-two completed crowdfunding projects with total successful funding amounts to nearly VND 3.3 billion (equivalent to USD 143 thousand) as follows (Fig. 1) :[26]

Among them, Comicola is known as a crowdfunding platform for the Vietnamese comic industry with the aim of helping the young comic artist community to share their products with successful funding amounts to nearly VND 2 billion (equivalent to USD 87 thousand) for many projects up to now.[27] Comicola also develops online selling of products related to comic books. This crowdfunding web platform operates quite actively and allows terms of payment like phone cards and online bank transfers, thereby helping users to exploit all its strengths.[28] In addition, equity-based and lending-based crowdfunding platforms have also emerged in Vietnamese markets recently. Funding is an equity-based crowdfunding platform established in 2013 which connects entrepreneurs with the general public, individual, and business investors.[29] By the end of 2016, Fundingvn had completed 80 crowdfunding projects with successful funding amounts to VND 33.3 billion.[30] Huydong and Tima are counted as a lending-based crowdfunding (or P2P lending) platform group (Fig. 2).[31]

[24] See Phan Law Vietnam (2018).

[25] See Bui (2017), p. 27.

[26] See Thuy (2017), p. 42.

[27] See Comicoca (2019).

[28] See Phan Law Vietnam (2018).

[29] See Thuy (2017), p. 26.

[30] See Thuy (2017), p. 42.

[31] See Bui (2017), p. 29.

Fig. 2 Fintech Vietnam Start-up Map 2019 Fintechnews Vietnam (2019)

P2P lending is currently the second-largest fintech segment in Vietnam, with around 40 start-ups.[32] The development of P2P lending platforms as an alternative financing model in the country makes it easier to mobilize capital from investors for small and medium enterprises and individuals who are unable to get access to bank loans.[33] P2P lending experienced a period of fast growth and development, starting with some big names such as Tima, Huydong, Lendbiz, Vaymuon, and Mofin from 2015.[34] With the initial investment of VND 150 billion (equivalent to USD 6.5 million), Tima joined the financial market as the first P2P lending platform in the country. From June 2016, Tima has provided customers across the country with lending services and financial advisories.[35] P2P lending is forecasted to reach a growth rate of 48.2% annually in the 2016–2024 period in research conducted by Transparency Market Research. [36]

Furthermore, there are a vast number of fintech start-ups that have boosted substantial funds. One of them is Money Lover, a finance management application that has

---

[32]British Business Group Vietnam (2019), p. 3; Tan (2019); Duyen and Mai (2019).

[33]Duyen and Mai (2019).

[34]Tan (2019).

[35]See Tima (2017).

[36]See Viet Nam News (2019).

30 languages and 100 currencies and has more than 2.3 million downloads globally.[37] Many other products are emerging, including Blockchain, Bitcoin, or digital banking, which have been provided by fintech companies, such as Cash2vn, Bitcoin Vietnam, VBTC Bitcoin, or Timo and FE Credit.[38]

Vietnam has been considered as an attractive and stable market for fintech as it is highly populated with a population of more than 97 million people by November 2019[39] and 69.3% population within the golden age (from 15 to 64 years old).[40] At 7.1% GDP growth in 2018, the country is one of the fastest-growing economies in Asia and in the world.[41] Vietnam achieved the World Bank's middle-income status in 2010, and is now the sixth-largest economy in the 10-member ASEAN trading bloc.[42] The country is ranked at 48th in 2018 from 82nd in 2016 in terms of ease of doing business, and it ranks ahead of Indonesia (72nd) and Philippines (113th). This is due to a variety of factors, including light regulatory and banking environments.[43]

Also, Vietnam has been considered as a potential market for fintech because of its high internet and mobile phone penetration rates, and relatively low financial inclusion rates. Vietnam's internet penetration rate reached 52% of the population in 2016, while smartphone ownership accounted for 72% in urban areas and 53% in rural areas.[44] More and more people in the country are participating in online activities and remittance activities, especially overseas remittance.[45] Besides, only 59% of the population have a formal bank account, while the rest have no access to banking services, especially the poor and people who live in rural areas.[46] In addition, it is said that consumer lending is an important instrument to boost consumption and contribute to macroeconomic development. However, the majority of Vietnamese people have never used a consumer loan.[47] Approximately 53 million people find it difficult to access consumption loans.[48] Thus, this is the opportunity for P2P platforms to play a bigger role in providing financial services to customers who have not served by the traditional banking system.

Regarding investment into the fintech sector, Vietnamese fintech start-ups have been continuing to be one of the hottest investment sectors in the country, capturing the interest of domestic and foreign investors. The total value of fintech start-up deals

---

[37] Fintechnews Singapore (2015).
[38] Fintechnews Singapore (2019).
[39] See Danso.org (2019).
[40] See Worldometers (2019).
[41] See Countryeconomy.com (2018).
[42] CSIRO's Data61 (2018).
[43] Ernst and Young Vietnam (2018), p. 6.
[44] Fintechnews Singapore (2018).
[45] See Tam and Hanh (2018), p. 16.
[46] Viet Nam News (2018).
[47] Viet Nam News (2018).
[48] VTV News (2018).

in Vietnam in 2016 is USD 129 million, representing 63% of total start-ups investment.[49] Some of the major deals in Vietnamese fintech market are as follows: (1) UTC Investment from South Korea spent USD 10 million to buy 65% stake in VNPT Epay from VMG Media and some individual shareholders.[50] With this price, the valuation of VNPT Epay is USD 36.7 million[51]; (2) Sea, the Singapore based digital entertainment firm formerly known as Garena, one of the most valuable start-ups in South East Asia, said that it has 45.18% capital of VNPAY, a Vietnamese payment solution provider[52]; (3) M-Service received an investment of USD 28 million from Goldman Sachs and Standard Chartered Private Equity in 2016 for e-wallet MoMo, which can be used to pay for transportation, entertainment, food, drink, online shopping, and other products. M-Service has seen double-digit growth in the last two years and has over 5 million users in both urban and rural areas[53]; (4) Credit China Fintech Holdings Ltd, a Hong Kong-based firm, spent USD 12.73 million to acquire 51% capital of Amigo Technologies, one of the five largest developers of IT services and solutions for personal financial services in Vietnam[54]; (5) F88, a pawn shop chain based in Hanoi which offers loans for various assets such as automobiles, motorbikes, mobile phones, laptops, and jewelry, mobilized USD 10 million from Mekong Capital[55]; and other big deals such as MOL Access Portal's acquisition of 50% of Ngan Luong's shares, NTT Data's acquisition of 64% of Payoo's shares, True Money bought 40% stake of 1Pay, and Golden Gate Ventures and GMO Global Payment Fund purchased 25% stake of Bao Kim. These deals are worth up to tens of millions of dollars.[56] Moreover, the Vietnamese fintech market is also really attractive to foreign fintech giants, such as Samsung Pay, Alibaba, Apple Pay, Facebook Payments, Google Wallet, and Amazon Payments.[57] For example, Samsung launched its mobile payment app Samsung Pay allows customers to use the contactless payment technology in September 2017 in partnership with the National Payment Corporation of Vietnam (NAPAS),[58] the first and unique intermediary payment service provider being granted license by the State Bank of Vietnam (SBV) of providing switching and electronic clearing and settlement services in Vietnam.[59] Alibaba also entered into the Vietnamese market by a memorandum of understanding with NAPAS to enable Chinese tourists to use Alipay when traveling across Vietnam.

Thus, with all the above favorable factors, from the rapid rise of the economy, the growing digital penetration, and the investment attractiveness, fintech firms could

---

[49] Ha (2018).

[50] BDA Partners (2017).

[51] Chi (2017).

[52] Chi (2017).

[53] Nikkei Asian Review (2017).

[54] IntellAsia Finance Vietnam (2017), p. 6.

[55] IntellAsia Finance Vietnam (2017), p. 6.

[56] Vietnam Investment Review (2018).

[57] Viet Nam News (2016).

[58] Fintechnews Singapore (2018).

[59] See Banking.org (2018).

play a key role in significantly improving Vietnamese people's access to financial services.[60] However, in comparison with the number of fintech start-ups in some other countries in the ASEAN region like Singapore and Indonesia (nearly 500 fintech start-up companies and about 260 fintech firms as of May 2018 respectively)[61], the number of Vietnamese fintech companies is relatively small, and fintech sector is still in its infancy.

While the fintech industry is still evolving, there are identified challenges for fintech as below. First, it is a challenge for investors to accurately select and evaluate innovative fintech ideas.[62] Without properly managing the portfolios of fintech projects, investors will easily be flooded with countless fintech technologies. Second, customer management plays a very important role when fintech companies have to compete to acquire and retain customers. That is another challenge for fintech companies to address customer needs well by enhancing accessibility, convenience, and custom products.[63] Third, as financial innovations accompany with fintech are becoming more prevalent, regulators have been cautious of the risks that they bring to the financial sector and its participants, then they could tighten fintech management.[64] For example, concerns have arisen from virtual currency. The State Bank of Vietnam has declared that the issuance, supply, and use of bitcoin and other similar virtual currencies is illegal as a means of payment and subject to punishment ranging from VND 150 million to VND 200 million.[65] Many other concerns might include cybersecurity, privacy violations, and securities/trading violations, credit/lending operations, consumer information/consent violations, and intellectual property. Fourth, it is a challenge for fintech firms to integrate innovative technologies into the business model of financial institutions to provide customers with seamless services.[66] Last, it is a constant challenge for fintech services to cover their exposure to privacy and security risks.[67] The focus on privacy and security is justified by the fact that fintech led financial services operate as the most intensive users of data.[68]

---

[60] Vietnam Investment Review (2018).

[61] Fintechnews Singapore (2018a).

[62] See Moshirian et al. (2019), p. 13.

[63] Tung (2018), p. 16.

[64] See Moshirian et al. (2019), p. 14.

[65] Thanh (2017).

[66] Tung (2018), p. 17.

[67] Moshirian et al. (2019), p. 15.

[68] The Economist (2017).

3 The Use of Fintech to Facilitate Socio-economic Development

In Vietnam, the Communist Party and Government have promulgated Strategies for the country's socio-economic development. According to Section IV Orientation in development, innovation model, and restructuring of the economy of Vietnam's socio-economic development strategy for the period of 2011–2020 of the Eleventh Congress of Vietnam Communist Party, Vietnam should effectively mobilize and use all resources to facilitate the socio-economic development through some main ways as follows: implementing money policies in the way that extends forms of non-cash payment, developing financial market with risk management, fostering the application of science and technology and the development of services on science, technology, and ensuring social security.[69]

Besides, the Prime Minister issued Decision no. 450/QD-TTg dated April 18, 2012, approving the Financial Strategy until 2020 with a focus on the following issues: finance plays an important role in boosting rapid and sustainable development; national finance must be efficiently, comprehensively, reasonably, and equitably developed; and, financial discipline, uniformity, transparency and modernization of national finance need to be ensured.

In addition, Vietnam is among the 25 priority countries on which the World Bank is focusing its financial inclusion efforts through the 'Universal Financial Access (UFA) by 2020' initiative, which seeks to bring two billion unbanked people into the formal financial system.[70]

In the current context of the country, fintech developments could give rise to exciting opportunities to facilitate the socio-economic development.

At first, fintech is the key driver for financial inclusion[71], which enhances the allocation of existing resources and involves the expansion of financial resources. Then it can, in turn, support sustainable development.[72]

It is a fact that around 61% of the population in Vietnam have no access to banking services, especially the poor and rural inhabitants. This is because they currently have problems in terms of identity verification and credit checking due to the inadequacies of credit information systems, leading to the challenge of assessing

[69]See Xay Dung Dang (2011).

[70]Vietnam Investment Review (2018).

[71]Financial inclusion involves delivering financial services at affordable cost to all parts of society. It enables people to manage their financial obligations efficiently, reduce poverty and supports wider economic growth. First, it reduces individual's unlnerability. For instance, facilitating saving allows people to weather shocks and invest in their education, health and micro-business. Second, it increase the efficiency of daily life: bills can be paid electronically without time off work. Third, it allows the socialization and diversification of people's financial risks through the financial system. Fourth, it supports economic growth through increasing financial resources to support real economic activity. FATF (2013), p. 12; Buckley, Arner, Zetzsche and Veidt (2019), p. 8.

[72]See Buckley, Arner, Zetzsche and Veidt (2019), p. 13.

creditworthiness.[73] In addition, the financial needs of low-income people, where deposits or loans, tend to involve small amounts, leading to higher operating costs for the providers. From the perspective of financial institutions, providing loans, credit cards, and other banking services such as deposits and money transfers to these people is both difficult and expensive. Reasons for this include poor access to physical banking facilities such as branches and ATMs, a lack of spare money to deposit in accounts because of low incomes, and failure to use banking services due to low financial literacy rates.[74] Consequently, those who do not have bank accounts or credit cards must carry out money transactions in cash. These transactions involve high handling costs and are an impediment to economic efficiency. Moreover, the difficulty of tracking cash transactions in a cash-centered society encourages the formation of underground economies and tends to have a negative impact on economic monitoring and tax collection.

However, with the development of fintech, it provides various financial services such as digital payment, crowdfunding, P2P lending, personal finance management, and information comparison for millions of users, including non-banked and unbanked groups with significant transaction value. Through business models and incentives, fintech helps to redirect financial resources to provide finance. For instance, by providing unique forms of capital mobilization from the community such as crowdfunding and P2P lending, fintech companies create a credit assessment mechanism to help underserved borrowers, who are often turned down by traditional financial intermediaries, obtain credit or help start-ups mobilize capital to run their business.

Besides, fintech has transformed mobile devices, such as smartphones, into portable ATMs, allowing users to access basic financial services without the need to go to bank branches or ATMs. In addition, it is now possible to use mobile devices to make payments, both online and face-to-face. The funds that can be used for these mobile payments is no longer limited to money tied up in bank accounts and credit cards, thanks to the emergence of electronic money, which can be used even by people who do not have bank accounts or credit cards. Moreover, with QR code payment, accepting electronic payments has become possible at low costs, making this method attractive to retailers that handle small-ticket items. Fintech, if rightly designed and applied, could come to the account holder's assistance.[75] Thus, through promoting financial inclusion and increase the amount of financial resources available, by which saving, investment increases, fintech can contribute to sustainable development.

At the same time, fintech has made it possible for financial service providers to acquire customer information more easily and at a lower cost than in the past. Identity verification processes can be completed more quickly and no longer need to be carried

---

[73]The percentage of people with bank accounts in Vietnam is just around 30%. See Iwasaki (2018), Pacific Business and Industries, Vol. XVIII, No. 68, p. 6.

[74]Financial literacy means the ability to manage one's finance independently, without a financial advisor. See Klapper et al. (2015), p. 16.

[75]Buckley, Arner, Zetzsche and Veidt (2019), p. 10.

out at specific locations, thanks to new methods such as image capturing of documents. The use of new biometric identification mechanisms (such as fingerprint and iris scanning, voice or heartbeat recognition)[76] is also leading to faster processing and cost reduction. Thus, through providing services with modern technologies, lower costs, and simpler procedures, fintech helps to save financial resources and enhance the effectiveness of financial services, then promote socio-economic development.

Furthermore, it can be seen that fintech is a way to create a cashless environment (specifically, the reduction of the percentage of payments made in cash), then it can increase collaboration across sectoral boundaries. Using fintech could help businesses take less time handling cash, increase convenience and safety benefits, including a reduced need for consumers and foreign tourists to withdraw cash. Besides, government administration processes involving the receipt of levies or the payment of benefits can be more efficient. While the crime rate is quite high in Vietnam[77], the handling or transportation of cash involves greater risk for financial institutions, businesses, and consumers, and the costs are substantial.

4 Current Regulations on Fintech in Vietnam

Fintech has been considered as a new business sector, constantly developing and innovating; therefore, the policy and regulatory framework for fintech in Vietnam is generally insufficient and unclear.

Vietnam's current regulations on fintech relating to several different legal areas, which can be divided into two groups including regulations on science, information technology, intellectual property and regulations on financial technology services. First, the operation of fintech companies is associated with disruptive technologies and is based on internet applications, mobile phones, cloud computing, and open-source software. Hence, the issue of intellectual property rights and information security is essential. Currently, regulations on science, information technology, intellectual property include Law on cyber information security (2015), Law on information technology (2006), Law on e-transactions (2005), Law on science and technology (2013), Law on high technologies (2008), Law on intellectual property (2005, amended in 2009), and guiding documents regulating the research, application, and development of science and information technology, the conduct of e-transactions, the protection of intellectual property right related to disruptive innovation, and cyber information security. These regulations have contributed to ensuring the research, application, and development of science and information technology, to encourage e-transactions, to protect intellectual property rights which is related to disruptive innovation, and to ensure cyber information security in order for the entry into the financial market and the development of fintech companies.

[76] Arner et al. (2016), p. 32.

[77] TTXVN (2018); OSAC (2019).

Second, current regulations on financial technology services mainly regulate the payment sector and are generally stipulated in some legal documents, including Law on the State Bank of Vietnam (2010), Decree No. 101/2012/ND-CP dated November 22, 2012, and Decree No. 80/2016/ND-CP dated July 1, 2016, on non-cash payment, Circular No. 39/2014/TT-NHNN dated December 11, 2014, Circular No. 20/2016/TT-NHNN dated June 30, 2016, and Circular No. 30/2016/TT-NHNN dated October 14, 2016, on intermediate payment services.

Accordingly, the payment service of fintech companies is licensed by the State Bank[78] and it includes electronic payment gateway[79] and e-wallet[80]. Besides, conditions on intermediate payment services of fintech companies include (i) conditions of establishment license/enterprise registration certificate; (ii) business plan conditions; (iii) legal capital requirement (at least VND 50 billion); (iv) conditions on the legal representative, the general director (director) have professional qualifications and practical experience; (v) conditions of material facilities, technical infrastructure, information technology systems, appropriate technology solutions; (vi) conditions of the management accounting information system to ensure the separate monitoring of the capital and assets and to determine the results of business activities.[81]

In addition, the regulations on procedures, application dossiers for granting, withdrawing and reissuing licenses to provide intermediate payment services for fintech are stipulated in Decree 101/2012/ND-CP, Decree 80/2016/ND-CP, and Circular No. 39/2014/TT-NHNN, and the regulations on security solutions and settlement of complaints when providing financial intermediary services in Circular 30/2016/TT-NHNN have created the legal basis for setting up fintech companies and for fintech to provide payment services with modern technology to users, and at the same time for ensuring the safety and security of the financial system in the economy.

For the e-wallet service, according to Article 9 of Circular No. 39/2014/TT-NHNN: (i) The organization providing e-wallet service is not allowed to issue more than one e-wallet for a customer's payment account at a bank and grant credit to the customers who use that e-wallet service, pay interest on the balance of an e-wallet, or any other action that may increase the monetary value of an e-wallet; (ii) organizations providing e-wallet services must allow the State Bank to check and supervise in real-time the total amount of money of e-wallets of customers and the total amount on the payment guarantee account of organizations providing e-wallet services at banks; and (iii) the recharge of e-wallets, withdrawals from e-wallets of customers must be made via the customer's payment account at banks.

Up to now, the Vietnamese Government has issued many policies, programs, and projects related to the development of fintech, which focuses on creating a favorable environment for the development of diversified fintech products and services, and developing the infrastructure, business models, and electronic payment systems.

---

[78] See Law on the State Bank of Vietnam (2010), Article 4 and Article 6.

[79] See Circular 39/2014/TT-NHNN (2014), Article 3.

[80] See Decree 80/2016/ND-CP (2016), Article 4.

[81] See Decree 101/2012/ND-CP and Decree 80/2016/ND-CP.

No.	Policy, Program, Project	Main Content
1	National Program on E-commerce development for the period from 2014 to 2020 promulgated with Decision No. 689/QD-TTg dated May 11, 2014	To build and develop e-commerce infrastructure; To propagate and raise the public awareness on e-commerce; To provide training and develop human resources for e-commerce; To develop e-commerce products and solutions; To give consultancy on the establishment of e-commerce application plan; To enhance management and organizing capacity for e-commerce development activities
2	Assistance policies on national innovative start-up ecosystem to 2025 promulgated with Decision No. 844/QD-TTg dated May 18, 2016	To build information portal and start-ups support centers; To develop technical facilities and infrastructures; To support innovative start-ups through the support of the establishment of communications programs, start-up networks, and venture capital; To encourage the use of scientific and technological development funds; To issue new regulations or improve current regulations to promote the innovative start-up ecosystem
3	Project on the increase of accessibility to banking services for the economy promulgated with Decision No.1726/QD-TTg dated September 5, 2016	To create a legal framework to support the design and development of banking service products, especially non-credit ones, creating conditions for the population and enterprises, especially policy beneficiaries, to have sustainable access to banking services; To encourage the involvement of various types of institutions to provide banking services for rural, deep-lying and remote areas and support small- and medium- sized enterprises; To step up the application of information technology in the modernization and development of diverse banking products and services toward simplicity, convenience, high accessibility; To expand the accessibility to banking services along with protecting legitimate interests of banking service customers and raise financial knowledge for the population

(continued)

(continued)

No.	Policy, Program, Project	Main Content
4	Project on the development of non-cash payments in Vietnam during 2016-2020 promulgated with Decision No. 2545/QD-TTg dated December 30, 2016	To improve the legal framework and policies by reviewing the laws related to non-cash payment to ensure uniform management of payment systems of Vietnam's economy on the basis of international practice and standards; To upgrade and expand the Internet Banking Payment System (IBPS) to meet the needs of the economy and serve international economic integration; To develop retail payment services; To enhance electronic payment in the public sector; To innovate securities clearing and settlement system; To innovate payment system on the interbank monetary and foreign exchange market; To enhance management and supervision of international payment and money transfer; To supervise and apply international criteria and standards to payment systems; To enhance propagation, provision of guidance and protection of consumers in non-cash payment; To intensify the cooperation in non-cash payments
5	Project on the science and technology application in the process of restructuring the industry and trade sector up to 2025, with a vision to 2030 promulgated with Decision No. 754/QD-TTg dated May 31, 2017	To improve the mechanism, policies, and regulations to prioritize the application of science and technology; To apply science, technology, and technical solutions to synchronize and modernize the commercial infrastructure system; To development e-commerce and modern business models; To support enterprises in enhancing the capacity of doing research, development, application, reception and transferring technologies

(continued)

(continued)

No.	Policy, Program, Project	Main Content
6	Establishment of Steering Committee on Fintech under State Bank of Vietnam (SBV) according to Decision No. 328/QD-NHNN dated March 16, 2017	Steering Committee on Fintech is responsible for: Formulating and submitting to SBV Governor the annual action plan of the Committee; Advising Governor solutions to complete the ecosystem including a legal framework to facilitate the performance and the development of fintech companies in Vietnam; Discussing and submitting to SBV Governor several crucial substances relating to strategy and plan for accelerating the development of fintech in Vietnam
7	Project on the improvement of legal framework on the management of virtual assets, digital currencies and virtual currencies promulgated with Decision No. 1255/QD-TTg dated August 21, 2017	To review and evaluate the current legal framework for virtual assets, digital currencies, and virtual currencies in Vietnam and do research about related international experiences; To review, research, and propose amendments and new legislative documents on digital currencies; To prepare to issue legislative documents on virtual assets and currencies; To consider proposing amendments to and promulgation of new legal documents on taxes on virtual assets and currencies; To consider proposing measures for violations related to virtual assets and currencies; To do research to amend laws in order to improve the legal framework for management and handling of virtual assets and currencies

The above policies, programs, and projects are an essential basis for the establishment of the regulatory framework for fintech and facilitating the development of modern and effective financial and banking services in the future. Notably, the establishment of the Steering Committee on fintech under the State Bank of Vietnam is evidence for the determination of the Government to create a favorable environment to encourage the development of fintech as well as to the focus on solutions to improve the fintech ecosystem in Vietnam.

In practice, the State Bank has proactively approached and organized talks with fintech start-ups to facilitate its entry into the market. Since 2008, the State Bank has allowed many non-bank financial institutions to provide payment services in Vietnam. Most of them have provided services related to an electronic payment gateway and an electronic wallet.[82] Since Circular No. 39/2014/TT-NHNN came

[82] See Thang (2018).

into effect, non-bank financial institutions have been officially licensed to provide intermediate payment services in order to promote non-cash payments in the country. Payment intermediaries could become involved in providing four services, including electronic payments, electronic wallets, collection and payment, and electronic money transfer so far. In addition, there are five innovative areas that have been identified as critical areas for development by the State bank of Vietnam, including API, Digital Payment, P2P lending, Blockchain, and e-KYC.[83]

It can be seen that the absence of an appropriate regulatory framework for fintech in Vietnam currently has led to some problems. As for fintech start-ups having innovative ideas for business, there is no legal protection for their legitimate rights and interests. Thus they hesitate to introduce new products and services to customers. Besides, without a sufficient regulatory framework, consumers are not willing to use new financial products and services of fintech companies because of the concern about the security of products and services that are provided by fintech companies, especially the services offered via the internet and electronic devices, and the risks they might not avoid in the future. Moreover, operating without a proper regulatory framework, the operation of fintech start-ups might not be under the supervision of competent authorities, financial crimes related to fintech, therefore, could hardly be controlled.

For instance, regarding the online payment and remittance sector, the absence of regulations on standards for online payment application, technical standards, infrastructure, risk prevention, and customer protection might be a hindrance to the access mobile payment service and the legitimate protection of the interests of customers. Besides, financial crimes might be committed easily, such as illegal money transferring activities via Chinese points of sale (POS) installed in a local store in Vietnam.[84]

Regarding crowdfunding, there is no specific provision on the rights and responsibilities of each participant; therefore, it will be problematic when disputes among participants arise. As for the project initiator who proposes the idea or project to be funded, there is a risk that his idea might be stolen or copied, especially in the case of unsuccessful calling for capital. As for the crowdfunding platform, it is risky when the platform verifies the information of projects that need to be funded or when the project initiator fails to fulfill its commitments. As for investors, there is a risk that their money might not reach the project initiator because the crowdfunding platform violates its obligations.

Regarding P2P lending, Vietnam has no existing regulations to regulate P2P lending leading to the challenge for consumer protection. In fact, P2P platforms operating in Vietnam are usually registered as investment consultancy firms instead of a financial institution.[85] This means P2P platforms are not under the banking laws, and they do not fall under the supervision of the State Bank of Vietnam. Therefore, this lending model would be a fertile ground for high-tech crimes and fraud, such as

[83] See Linh (2018).

[84] An (2018).

[85] Tan (2019).

tax evasion, money laundering, terrorist financing and theft of personal information, which may cause socio-economic instability. In some cases, the platforms falsely advertised profits, provided inaccurate information related to loan risks, or charged exorbitant interest rates, reaching up to 70% per annum and far exceeding the interest rate cap of 20% per year legally allowed by the country.[86]

5 An Appropriate Regulatory Framework for Fintech in Vietnam

Fintech has been considered as an irreversible development trend, and its dramatic development is beyond the existing regulatory framework in the financial market. This situation has put regulators under pressure to take appropriate approaches in order to enhance financial inclusion and economic growth as well as to prevent potential risks. Designing a regulatory framework that ensures the safety of users and the public, whilst facilitating the commercial use and consumer enjoyment of innovation in general, of fintech, in particular, is by no means easy.[87]

It is crucial for regulators to select relevant facts to look at and make the decision on what, when and how they should make a regulatory intervention.[88] The 'what question' is related to identifying the disruptive technology that must be regulated.[89] The 'when question' concerns the timing of any regulatory intervention.[90] The 'how question' is about the form and substance of the regulation.[91] Based on the fact-based approach, the answers for those questions will be diversified as regulators must opt for either reckless action (regulation without sufficient facts) or paralysis (doing nothing).[92] There are some main possible regulatory approaches including doing nothing (which spans being permissive to highly restrictive, depending on context), cautious permissiveness (on a case-by-case basis, or through special charters), structured experimentalism (such as sandboxes or piloting), and development of specific new regulatory frameworks.[93] First, 'doing nothing' approach involves simply not regulating fintech, and the result can be either permissive or laissez-faire depending upon whether current banking regulation applies to the sector. This approach may well protect against risk but at the cost of stifling innovation.[94] Second, the cautious experimentation approach helps regulators to acquire knowledge of business models and identify regulatory perimeters of modern technologies. However, this approach

[86]See Bao Thanh Nien (2019).

[87]See Buteno and Larouche (2015), p. 72.

[88]See Fenwick et al. (2017), p. 571.

[89]See Alemanno et al. (2013), p. 287.

[90]See Moses (2011), pp. 768–769; see also Shah et al. (2015), p. 3.

[91]See Black (2008).

[92]See Fenwick et al. (2017), p. 561.

[93]See Zetzsche et al. (2017), p. 1.

[94]See Zetzsche et al. (2017), pp. 11–12.

should only be a temporary tool as it isn't suitable for market-wide use, and fails to provide long-term legal certainty for business development.[95] Third, a structured experimentalism approach with regulatory sandboxes to support competitive innovation in financial markets. Eligibility to enter a sandbox is standardized and publicized. This approach is cost-effective for participants and resource-effective for regulators, allowing easier comparison among potential entrants to the sandbox. However, sandboxes, while providing transparency in entry criteria and processes, are very much human-driven and analog in their monitoring.[96] They might have a propensity for regulatory bias, regulatory capture, or competition distortion.[97] Therefore, they are only suitable for being a process-driven application method for entry, typically for a limited time.[98] Fourth, a formal approach could be adopted, in which existing regulations are reformed, or new regulations are developed in order to provide a more appropriate and balanced framework for new entrants and new activities.[99]

In the context of many different views on the management of fintech and the diversity of regulatory approaches, Vietnam has been cautious and has been drafting a regulatory sandbox for fintech to pilot fintech products under the supervision of the State Bank in order to foster innovation while containing risks of constantly changing technology. The regulatory sandbox is expected to at least provide criteria and requirements to be met by participants and control mechanisms to be employed by the government to manage the participants' activities.[100]

At present, the draft of a regulatory sandbox for fintech prepared by the State Bank has been sent to related ministries and some international financial institutions for comments. Accordingly, the State Bank will be the focal point to receive applications for joining the sandbox. Fintech solutions, products and services participating in the testing mechanism must be innovative and can contribute positively to innovation and modernization of banking operation in particular and the economy in general. In addition, the approved fintech solution, products, or services must be the first innovative ones applied in Vietnam or be applied to new and highly innovative services that could be beneficial for customers in Vietnam. Moreover, the approved fintech solution, products or services must meet the requirements of risk management, without or less likely to cause adverse impacts on financial institutions, in particular, and the financial system in general. Also, they must be designed to include KYC solutions, suspicious transaction identification, and prevention, payment acceptance units authentication in accordance with anti-money laundering and terrorist financing regulations.[101]

However, because of the differences in the nature, potential impacts, and related risks of each fintech product, there is no uniform regulatory model for all fintech

[95] See Zetzsche et al. (2017), p. 26.

[96] See Zetzsche et al. (2017), p. 13.

[97] See Clements (2018), p. 40.

[98] See Zetzsche et al. (2017), p. 13.

[99] See Zetzsche et al. (2017), p. 14.

[100] Bui (2019).

[101] The State Bank of Vietnam (2019b).

products. For example, as for virtual currencies, Vietnam declared that the issuance, supply, and use of virtual currencies as a means of payment is illegal. As for P2P lending, the government recently announced the development of a pilot program for P2P lending, and a set of official rules are expected to follow. As for digital payment, it is quite clear that Vietnam already developed some new regulations to regulate this sector.

Thus, the adoption of a sequential reform process before building an appropriate regulatory regime for fintech products is essential in order to encourage the development of fintech and ensure public interests without stifling innovation.

A reasonable regulatory approach could comprise four sequenced stages: (1) A testing and piloting environment. (2) A regulatory sandbox, which widens the scope of testing and piloting and removes the regulators' disincentive to grant dispensations. (3) A restricted licensing/special charter scheme, under which innovative firms can further develop their client base and financial and operational resources. (4) When the size and income permits, the full regulatory regime will be applied.[102]

6 Conclusion

This chapter has presented the current situation of fintech in Vietnam and has illustrated that fintech plays an important role in spurring financial inclusion, which underlines the sustainable balance of the socio-economic development.

Vietnam has been considered as a strong market for fintech because of its young and tech-savvy population, high mobile phone and internet penetration rates, and relatively low financial inclusion rates. The fintech market is still fledgling, with more than 150 companies have joined with increasing transaction volumes and high growth rates. Fintech products are provided, including digital payment, crowdfunding, P2P lending, remittance, blockchain, personal finance management, and information comparison with modern technologies, lower costs, and simpler procedures. The digital payment sector has been witnessed as one of the fastest-growing sectors, and one of the hottest investment trends for start-ups in Vietnam and cashless payments are booming. Along with a fast-growing start-up movement, the Vietnamese market has developed capital mobilization from the community that is often referred to as crowdfunding. P2P lending is one type of crowdfunding, and it is the second-largest fintech segment in Vietnam with around 40 start-ups so far. The development of P2P lending platforms as an alternative financing model in Vietnam makes it easier to mobilize capital from investors for small and medium enterprises and individuals who are unable to get access to bank loans.

In the current context of the country, fintech developments could give rise to exciting opportunities to facilitate socio-economic development by enhancing the allocation of existing resources and involving the expansion of financial resources. Also, through providing services with modern technologies, lower costs, and simpler

[102] See Zetzsche et al. (2017), p. 56.

procedures, fintech helps to save financial resources, enhances the effectiveness of financial services, and increases collaboration across sectoral boundaries, thus promoting the socio-economic development.

However, the policy and regulations on fintech are generally insufficient and unclear, leading to risks for all stakeholders in the fintech space and the obstacle for innovation in the country. In the context of the diversity of regulatory approaches to fintech, Vietnam aims to use regulatory sandbox to pilot fintech products and has been drafting a regulatory sandbox. However, because of the differences in nature, potential impact, and related risks of each fintech product, there is no uniform regulatory model for all fintech products. Thus, the adoption of a sequential reform process before building an appropriate regulatory regime for Fintech products is essential to encourage the development of Fintech and ensure public interests without stifling innovation.

References

Alemanno A, den Butter F, Nijsen A, Torriti J (eds) (2013) Better Business Regulation in A Risk Society. Springer, New York

An T (2018) Vietnamese Currency Security Faces Big Challenges from Technology https://www.vir.com.vn/vietnamese-currency-security-faces-big-challenges-from-technology-59390.html. Accessed 31 March 2020

Arner D, Barberis J, Buckley R (2016) The Evolution of Fintech: A New Post-Crisis Paradigm? https://papers.ssrn.com/sol3/papers.cfm?abstract_id=2676553. Accessed 31 March 2020

Bao Thanh Nien (2019) Bung No Cho Vay Khong Gap Mat [The Boom of Loan without Meeting] https://thanhnien.vn/tai-chinh-kinh-doanh/bung-no-cho-vay-khong-gap-mat-1112577.html. Accessed 31 March 2020

Banking Vietnam (2016) http://banking.org.vn/2016/national-payment-corporation-of-vietnam/. Accessed 31 March 2020

BDA Partners (2017) BDA Advises VMG Media on the Sale of VNPT Epay to UTC Investment http://www.bdapartners.com/transaction/bda-advises-vmg-media-on-the-sale-of-vnpt-epay-to-utc-investment/. Accessed 31 March 2020

Black J (2008) Forms and Paradoxe of Principles Based Regulation. LSE Law, Society and Economy Working Papers 13

British Business Group Vietnam (2019) Vietnam - 2019 Fintech https://bbgv.org/business-center/knowledge/sector-reports-knowledge/vietnam-2019-fintech/. Accessed 31 March 2020

Buckley R, Arner D, Zetzsche D, Veidt R (2019) Sustainability, Fintech and Financial Inclusion https://www.ssrn.com/abstract=3387359. Accessed 31 March 2020

Bui H (2017) Creating A Robust Crowdfunding Ecosystem in Vietnam - The Factors Influencing the Crowdfunding Ecosystem in Vietnam https://pdfs.semanticscholar.org/5711/f5026164c7167fe032f229e0844f385aee86.pdf. Accessed 31 March 2020

Bui H (2019) Regulatory Sandbox for Fintech in Vietnam – Opportunities and Challenges http://www.conventuslaw.com/report/regulatory-sandbox-for-fintech-in-vietnam/. Accessed 31 March 2020

Buteno A, Larouche P (2015) Regulation for Innovation or Regulation of Innovation. Law, Innovation and Technology, Vol. 7, Issue 52

Chi K (2017) Foreign Investors Pouring More Money in Vietnamese Fintech Firms https://english.vietnamnet.vn/fms/science-it/190178/foreign-investors-pouring-more-money-in-vietnamese-fintech-firms.html. Accessed 31 March 2020

Clements R (2018) Regulating Fintech in Canada and the United States: Comparison, Challenges and Opportunities https://papers.ssrn.com/sol3/papers.cfm?abstract_id=3304759. Accessed 31 March 2020

Comicoca (2019) Crowdfunding https://comicola.com/gay-quy-cong-dong/. Accessed 31 March 2020

CSIRO's Data61 (2018) Vietnam Today: First Report of The Vietnam's Future Digital Economy Project https://data61.csiro.au/~/media/D61/Files/FutureVietnameseDigitalEconomy.pdf?la=en&hash=34B6BAD6D690FD6A89FC5BAC75278DF1E6023333. Accessed 31 March 2020

Countryeconomy.com (2018) GDP Improves in Vietnam https://countryeconomy.com/gdp/vietnam. Accessed 31 March 2020

Danso.org (2019) https://danso.org/viet-nam/. Accessed 31 March 2020

Dat N (2019) Vietnam Tops World in Growth of Mobile Payment Users https://e.vnexpress.net/news/business/industries/vietnam-tops-world-in-growth-of-mobile-payment-users-3896920.html. Accessed 31 March 2020

Das K (2018) Growing Market Potential of Fintech in Vietnam https://www.vietnam-briefing.com/news/growing-market-potential-of-fintech-in-vietnam.html/. Accessed 31 March 2020

Duyen H, Mai D (2019) Cho Vay Ngang Hàng Trên Thế Giới Và Thực Tiễn Tại Việt Nam [Global Peer-To-Peer Lending and The Practices in Vietnam] http://tapchitaichinh.vn/ngan-hang/cho-vay-ngang-hang-tren-the-gioi-va-thuc-tien-tai-viet-nam-306106.html. Accessed 31 March 2020

Ernst & Young Vietnam (2018) Fintech Landscape in Vietnam

FATF (2013) FATF Guidance: Anti-Money Laundering and Terrorist Financing Measures and Financial Inclusion https://www.fatf-gafi.org/media/fatf/documents/reports/AML_CFT_Measures_and_Financial_Inclusion_2013.pdf. Accessed 31 March 2020

Fenwick M, Kaal W, Vermeulen E (2017) Regulation Tomorrow: What Happens When Technology Is Faster Than the Law. American University Business Law Review 6(3):561–593

Fintechnews Singapore (2015) Fintech Vietnam: 6 Vietnamese Fintech Startups To Watch http://fintechnews.sg/877/vietnam/vietnam-fintech-startups-watch/. Accessed 31 March 2020

Fintechnews Singapore (2018) Foreign Tech Giants Eye Vietnamese Market with Fintech Solutions http://fintechnews.sg/15846/vietnam/foreign-tech-giants-eye-vietnamese-market-fintech-solutions/. Accessed 31 March 2020

Fintechnews Singapore (2018) Top 15 Most Well-Funded Southeast Asian Fintech Companies http://fintechnews.sg/19325/funding/top-15-most-well-funded-southeast-asian-fintech-companies/. Accessed 31 March 2020

Fintechnews Singapore (2019) Vietnam Fintech Startups https://fintechnews.sg/vietnam-fintech-startups/. Accessed 31 March 2020

Fintechnews Vietnam (2018) Vietnam Fintech Sector Report: All about Digital and Mobile Payments? https://fintechnews.sg/20056/vietnam/vietnam-fintech-sector-report-mobile-payment-digitial/. Accessed 31 March 2020

Fintechnews Vietnam (2019) Overview of Vietnam's Major E-Wallet and Mobile Payment Players https://fintechnews.sg/32843/vietnam/overview-of-vietnams-major-e-wallet-and-mobile-payment-players/. Accessed 31 March 2020

Ha N (2018) Fintech – Is This the New Trend in Vietnam? https://techinsight.com.vn/language/en/fintech-new-trend-vietnam-2/. Accessed 31 March 2020

IntellAsia Finance Vietnam (2017) Fintech The Focal Point for Vietnamese Startups to Attract Foreign Capital https://www.hkbav.org/uploads/Intellasia/140817Intellasia_Finance_Vietnam.pdf. Accessed 31 March 2020

Iwasaki K (2018) Emergence of Fintech Companies in Southeast Asia – Rising Hopes of A Solution to Financial Issues. Pacific Business and Industries, Vol. XVIII, No. 68 https://www.jri.co.jp/file/english/periodical/rim/2018/68.pdf. Accessed 31 March 2020

Klapper L, Lusardi A, van Oudheusden P. (2015) Financial Literacy Around the World: Insights from the Standard & Poor's Ratings Services Global Financial Literacy Survey, GFLEC Working Paper

Linh P (2018) Hợp Tác Fintech - Xu Hướng Phát Triển Tất Yếu Của Ngân Hàng Hiện Đại [Cooperation with Fintech – Development Trend of Modern Banks] https://www.sbv.gov.vn/. Accessed 31 March 2020

Moses Bennett L (2011) Agents of Change: How the Law 'Copes' with Technological Change. Griffit Law Review 20:763–794

Moshirian F, Susantono B, Yu R (2019) Challenges and Opportunities Associated with Financial Technology in the 21st Century https://papers.ssrn.com/sol3/papers.cfm?abstract_id=3337918. Accessed 31 March 2020

Nikkei Asian Review (2017) Vietnam's Momo Payment App on Board with Uber https://asia.nikkei.com/Business/Vietnams-MoMo-partners-with-Uber. Accessed 31 March 2020

OSAC (2019) Vietnam 2019 Crime & Safety Report: Ho Chi Minh City https://www.osac.gov/Content/Report/7c3d6679-458a-42c1-94fd-15f4aec63341. Accessed 31 March 2020

Phan Law Vietnam (2018) Crowdfunding in Vietnam – Realities and Progress https://phan.vn/en/crowdfunding-in-vietnam-realities-and-progress.html. Accessed 31 March 2020

Shah S, Brody R, Olson N (2015) The Regulation of Tomorrow. Deloitte University Press, New York

Tam L, Hanh L (2018) Fintech for Promoting Financial Inclusion in Vietnam: Fact Findings and Policy Implications. Business & Social Sciences Journal 3(1):12–20

Tan Z (2019) Reviving Trust: P 2P Lending in Vietnam https://kr-asia.com/reviving-trust-p2p-lending-in-vietnam. Accessed 31 March 2020

Thang H (2018) Fintech 2018: Nỗ Lực Kết Nối Hiệu Quả Để Phát Triển Thanh Toán Điện Tử Ở Việt Nam [Fintech 2018: An Effort to Develop Electronic Payment in Vietnam] http://baochinhphu.vn/Utilities/PrintView.aspx?distributionid=337838. Accessed 31 March 2020

Thanh L (2018) Ngân Hàng Nhà Nước Tuyên Bố Cấm SửDụng Bitcoin [The State Bank of Vietnam Declared Bitcoin Illegal] https://tuoitre.vn/ngan-hang-nha-nuoc-tuyen-bo-cam-su-dung-bitcoin-20171028102135916.htm. Accessed 28 April 2019

Thao N (2018) E-Wallet Services in Fierce Competition for Vietnamese Consumers http://ven.vn/e-wallet-services-in-fierce-competition-for-vietnamese-consumers-33346.html. Accessed 28 April 2019

The Asian Banker (2018) How Fintech Outgrew Banks in The Mobile Wallet Market in Vietnam http://www.theasianbanker.com/updates-and-articles/how-fintech-outgrew-banks-in-the-mobile-wallet-market-in-vietnam. Accessed 28 April 2019

The Economist (2017) Big Data, Financial Services and Privacy https://www.economist.com/finance-and-economics/2017/02/09/big-data-financial-services-and-privacy. Accessed 28 April 2019

The State Bank of Vietnam (2019) List of Non-Bank Institutions Licensed for Providing Payment Intermediary Service https://www.sbv.gov.vn/webcenter/portal/en/home/sbv/statistic/settleactiv/ulcipss?centerWidth=0%25&leftWidth=20%25&rightWidth=0%25&showFooter=false&showHeader=false&_adf.ctrl-state=7eet5qid_86&_afrLoop=31663122572218095#%40%3F_afrLoop%3D31663122572218095%26centerWidth%3D80%2525%26leftWidth%3D20%2525%26rightWidth%3D0%2525%26showFooter%3Dfalse%26showHeader%3Dfalse%26_adf.ctrl-state%3Dm2f59yytd_4. Accessed 31 March 2020

The State Bank of Vietnam (2019) The Draft of Regulatory Sandbox for Fintech in Vietnam

Thong V (2019) Vietnam Has 154 Fintech Firms https://vnexpress.net/kinh-doanh/viet-nam-co-154-cong-ty-fintech-3993229.html. Accessed 31 March 2020

Thuy N (2017) Crowdfunding in Vietnam: The Impact of Project and Founder Quality on Funding Success https://pdfs.semanticscholar.org/ede8/ee208603002d8db556b2fedaa2e62fc3bad7.pdf. Accessed 31 March 2020

Tima (2017) https://tima.vn/Home/About/. Accessed 31 March 2020

Tung H (2018) Fintech - Làn Sóng Công Nghệ Làm Thay Đổi Tài Chính Thế Giới [Fintech – The Wave of Technology to Change the World Finance] https://khoahocvacongnghevietnam.com.vn/file_pdf/25-1-2A-2019.pdf. Accessed 31 March 2020s

Tung H (2019) Fintech – Technological Wave in Financial and Banking Sector. Vietnam Journal of Science, Technology and Engineering, Vol 1 + 2 (2019):25–27

TTXVN (2018) Tình Hình Tội Phạm Vẫn Ở Mức Độ Nghiêm Trọng, Bạo Lực Gia Tăng [Crime Situation s Still Serious and Violence is on the Rise] http://tuyengiao.vn/thoi-su/tinh-hinh-toi-pham-van-o-muc-do-nghiem-trong-bao-luc-gia-tang-114669. Accessed 31 March 2020

Rake R (2018) Vietnam Mobile Payment Market https://www.alliedmarketresearch.com/vietnam-mobile-payment-market. Accessed 31 March 2020

Retail New Asia (2019) Vietnam Fintech Sector in the Fast Lane https://www.retailnews.asia/vietnam-fintech-sector-in-the-fast-lane/. Accessed 31 March 2020

United Nations Environment Programme (2016) Fintech and Sustainable Development Assessing The Implications

VeriMe (2018) Vietnam's Largest Payment Gateway: Ngan Luong Partners With Verime for Secure Digital Identity https://medium.com/@verime.mobi/vietnams-largest-payment-gateway-nganluong-partners-with-verime-for-secure-digital-identity-8dba170b47a4. Accessed 31 March 2020

Vietnam Investment Review (2018) How Vietnam Will Adapt to The Fintech Revolution https://www.vir.com.vn/how-vietnam-will-adapt-to-the-fintech-revolution-62232.html. Accessed 31 March 2020

Vietnam Investment Review (2019) Bleak Future for E-Wallets https://www.vir.com.vn/bleak-future-for-e-wallets-65602.html. Accessed 31 March 2020

Viet Nam News (2016) Mobile Pay Threatens Banks: Experts https://vietnamnews.vn/economy/282914/mobile-pay-threatens-banks-experts.html#COcC8ZAmkLcHClFP.97. Accessed 31 March 2020

Viet Nam News (2018) Consumer Lending Potential in VN Untapped Experts https://vietnamnews.vn/economy/394600/consumer-lending-potential-in-vn-untapped-experts.html#clWpdViMl01OzFTU.97. Accessed 31 March 2020

Viet Nam News (2018) Poor People Lack Access to Mobile Banking https://vietnamnews.vn/economy/462341/poor-people-lack-access-to-mobile-banking.html#cxilM8U2CcFDWVut.97. Accessed 31 March 2020

Viet Nam News (2019) Government Moves to Legalise P 2P Lending https://vietnamnews.vn/economy/506959/government-moves-to-legalise-p2p-lending.html#rxbZDh4FGFzgFblp.97. Accessed 31 March 2020

Vietnamnet (2019) Mobile Payment Market Booms in Vietnam https://english.vietnamnet.vn/fms/business/219154/mobile-payment-market-booms-in-vietnam.html. Accessed 31 March 2020

VTV News (2018) AI, Big Data Se Thong Tri Thi Truong Cho Vay Ca Nhan Truc Tuyen [AI, Big Data Will Dominate Online Personal Lending Market] https://vtv.vn/cong-nghe/ai-big-data-se-thong-tri-thi-truong-cho-vay-ca-nhan-truc-tuyen-20180509163302194.htm. Accessed 31 March 2020

Worldometers (2019) http://www.worldometers.info/world-population/vietnam-population/. Accessed 31 March 2020

Xay Dung Dang (2011) Chiến Lược Phát Triển Kinh Tế-Xã Hội 2011–2020 [Socio-Economic Development Strategy 2011-2020] http://www.xaydungdang.org.vn/Home/vankientulieu/2011/3511/CHIEN-LUOC-PHAT-TRIEN-KINH-TEXA-HOI-20112020.aspx. Accessed 31 March 2020

Zetzsche D, Buckley R, Arner D, Barberis J (2017) Regulating A Revolution: From Regulatory Sandboxes to Smart Regulation https://papers.ssrn.com/sol3/papers.cfm?abstract_id=3018534. Accessed 31 March 2020

The 'Independence Day' of Payments Law? Fintech's Impact on Financial Regulation in Japan

Akira Tokutsu

Abstract Fintech has been a buzzword in Japan since 2015. The fintech business model in Japan is similar as in other countries: crowdfunding, cryptocurrency, blockchain, AI, Big Data, and cashless payments. What has been the largest impact of fintech in Japan? At first glance, fintech seems to require a change in the financial regulation framework, but this is not the case. In Japan, traditional financial regulation is piecemeal or trident, with a separate legislative framework for banking, insurance, and securities. This framework is not unreasonable because it is designed to respond to different risks. Of course, some other new financial businesses appeared before fintech, and regulation responded to the new risk. Fintech is not a completely new business but just the unbundling of current financial businesses. Especially, payment became more independent from banking today, thanks to the fintech movement. Therefore, regulation just for payment is required more clearly. Currently, the FSA is planning to create a new category of regulation for it. It seems fintech requires a change in the basic framework of financial law. But both in practice and in theory, a pure payment service has attracted attention before fintech. Therefore, fintech, or any other technological innovation, does not require a complete change of regulation but a clarification of current law.

Keywords Fintech · Japan · Payment · Banking · Financial regulation

1 Introduction

FinTech is occurring all over the world. It is the same in Japan. For instance, Nikkei (the most popular business newspaper in Japan: Nihon Keizai Shinbun) had no article about fintech around the end of 2014. However, the number of articles about fintech

---

A. Tokutsu (✉)
Department of Law, Tohoku University, Sendai, Japan
e-mail: tokutsu@law.tohoku.ac.jp

M. Fenwick et al. (eds.), *Regulating FinTech in Asia*, Perspectives in Law, Business and Innovation, https://doi.org/10.1007/978-981-15-5819-1_8

has increased dramatically. It started with an article on January 1, 2015, and Nikkei had 526 articles by 2017.[1]

This chapter introduces how fintech influences financial regulation in Japan. When new technology comes, the same question always arises: what is the impact of innovation in the field of law?[2] It is now the turn of fintech. In Japan, some scholars say fintech makes the current framework of law and regulation out-of-date and requires 'innovation' in the legal framework.[3]

Before addressing this question, this chapter introduces examples of fintech businesses (Sect. 2) and the current framework of financial regulation in Japan (Sect. 3). I would like to argue that fintech businesses are almost the same in Japan as in other countries. In Sect. 4, I sketch the transformation of financial regulation because of the impact of fintech. Then, I explain the transformation of financial regulation with the example of cryptocurrency (Sect. 5).

2 Fintech 2020 in Japan

'Is an ATM (Automated Teller Machine) a part of fintech?' This question is asked often in discussing the definition of 'fintech.'[4] Although an ATM must be a part of the financial technology, generally, Japanese do not think of it as fintech. In Japan, fintech was not defined clearly. Additionally, I do not think it is productive to focus on questions of definition.[5] However, it is necessary to list examples of fintech in Japan in order to evaluate the impact of fintech.

Tentatively, in this chapter, I define fintech as any business relating to finance, providing new services supported by IT (information technology), and launched in the 2010s. However, I do not have any functional or precise definition. I am going to list some fintech businesses in Japan without any formal order or classification scheme. This list is not intended to be comprehensive. On the contrary, some people may think that some items on this list do not belong to fintech. This classification need not be exclusive. Some businesses could be classed in some categories simultaneously. For instance, some robo-advisor businesses can also be classified as AI (2.4), Big Data (2.5), and mobilization (2.6).

---

[1]I surveyed the number of articles with Nikkei telecom. I searched with the key word 'fintech' and excluded articles about 'Fintech Global,' a private investment company established in 1994, which is not related with fintech (Table 1).

[2]In the case of the internet or cyberspace, many scholars discussed about the impact of cyberspace to law. See, Easterbrook (1996) and Lessig (1999).

[3]Yanagawa (2016), p. 1.

[4]This traditional question is also used in the US. *See*, US National Economic Council Report (2017), p. 2.

[5]US National Economic Council Report (2017) p. 2, uses the word 'fintech' broadly to encompass a wide spectrum of technological innovations which impact a broad range of financial activities, including payments, investment management, capital raising, deposits and lending, insurance, regulatory compliance, and other activities in the financial services space.

Table 1 Uses of the Term 'Fintech' in the Nihon Keizai Shinbun

Year	By 2014	2015	2016	2017	2018	2019
Number of Articles	0	116	384	526	467	348

Table 2 Crowdfunding in Japan 2018

Total Value	Lending	Purchase	Donation	Investment (Fund)	Investment (Stock)
204,499 million JPY	90.2%	5.9%	0.4%	3.0%	0.5%

Yano Keizai Kenkyujo, Press Release 2036 (December 3rd, 2018), available at: https://www.yano.co.jp/press-release/show/press_id/2036. Accessed 4 February 2020

This list is the same or very similar to other countries' lists of fintech.

2.1 *Crowdfunding*

I am not sure whether crowdfunding belongs to fintech or not because it became popular before the fintech movement since 2015. However, crowdfunding is thought of as one of the older and typical examples of fintech in Japan.

Crowdfunding are usually classified into four types: Investment, Lending, Purchase, and Donation. Among them, lending crowdfunding is also called P2P lending or social lending. In Japan, the most popular crowdfunding is lending, while equity crowdfunding is less prevalent (Table 2).

2.2 *Cryptocurrency/Virtual Currency*

Bitcoin and other cryptocurrencies are seen as examples of fintech. In February 2014, an unidentified person stole 750,000 bitcoins from the accounts of MTGOX, an exchange for Bitcoin. This scandal triggered the 2016 Reform of Payment Services Act in Japan (see Sect. 5). Just after the MTGOX scandal, the price of Bitcoin fell, but it went up again. Other cryptocurrencies, i.e., Ethereum, NEM, are also popular in Japan. Some news reported that 60% of Bitcoin trading in the world was implemented in Japan in 2017.[6] These cryptocurrencies are bought mainly for investment purposes because it is not common that people use it for payment. Although Japanese are often said not to like risky investments, they invest a lot in risky non-regulated assets. This is interesting for researchers.

[6] Crypto Compare's website, available at: https://www.cryptocompare.com/coins/btc/analysis/JPY. Accessed 4 February 2020.

In January 2018, another scandal happened. Many NEMs were stolen from another cryptocurrencies exchange, CoinCheck. Due to this scandal, prices fell down again, not only in NEM but also in other cryptocurrencies.

However, the causes of these scandals were not the deficits of cryptocurrencies. The lack of cybersecurity of exchanges, MTGOX and CoinCheck, caused these scandals. Therefore, investment in cryptocurrencies possibly is going to be kept in Japan until now.

Additionally, ICOs (Initial Coin Offerings) also attract attention. An ICO is a tool for companies to raise funds offering cryptocurrencies.[7]

2.3 Blockchain and Applications

Blockchain is a distributed ledger used in cryptocurrencies, including Bitcoin. It is a decentralized tool for record-keeping with distributed nodes. Blockchain has two types. One is the open type, which anyone joins, like Bitcoin. The other is a closed type, which is designed to limit the participants of blockchain. Blockchain has a strong point against manipulation. Because it records data in distributed ledgers, it is almost impossible, or at least extremely difficult, to manipulate it. This characteristic made blockchain attract attention for other use cases. Applications of blockchain to other financial businesses are also seen as a part of fintech. Traditional mechanisms for cyber securities are centralized ledgers with heavy safety measures. However, this is an expensive option. Blockchain is thought of as a substitute for centralized ledgers, and it provides security without such substantial costs.

At first, blockchain seems to be applicable to the settlement for financial instruments and bank accounts. In fact, NASDAQ launched NASDAQ Linq, a securities settlement system with blockchain, in the US.[8] In Estonia, LHV Bank launched 'cuber,' which is a system of money transfer using nominal cryptocurrency as a token.[9] In Japan, the Tokyo Stock Exchange has an interest in the settlement with blockchain. It implemented a demonstration of the blockchain-based settlement system in September 2017.[10] However, there is still no news that TSE has started to provide this service to customers.

---

[7]St. Arnaud, a Belgium Beer restaurant in Nagoya, Japan, implemented an ICO and succeeded in funding for the first time in Japan. The restaurant issued SAT, a token, in the consideration of payment of cryptocurrencies. SAT can be used for payment in this restaurant.

[8]Nasdaq Linq Enables First-ever Private Securities Issuance Documented with Blockchain Technology (Dec 30, 2015), available at: http://ir.nasdaq.com/releasedetail.cfm?releaseid=948326. Accessed 4 February 2020.

[9]See, available at: http://www.cuber.ee/en_US/. Accessed 4 February 2020.

[10]JPX website, Proof of Concept Testing for Utilization of Blockchain/DLT in Capital Market Infrastructure, available at: https://www.jpx.co.jp/english/corporate/research-study/dlt/index.html. Accessed 4 February 2020.

In addition, Japanese private companies are trying to utilize blockchain for 'electronic transportation documents.' Blockchain is expected to be a tool to share and record the information about transportation documents amongst many parties.[11]

Finally, 'smart contracts' are attracting a lot of attention. This is another use of blockchain, which is an agreement that is enforced automatically without any human intervention, such as a court or other judicial mechanism. Some people have suggested that the courts would become less important because smart contract provide automatic enforcement without the need for any intervention.

2.4 *AI (Artificial Intelligence)*

New financial services to utilize AI are also seen as a part of fintech. One example is robo-advisors, which is an AI-based automatic investment advisor and management system. Some start-up companies provide 'WealthNavi' and 'THEO,' while traditional brokerage houses also provide robo-advisors to customers, today.

2.5 *Big Data*

The utilization of Big Data is also a part of fintech in Japan. AI, as mentioned in Sect. 2.4, is also a type of utilization of Big Data. Though Japanese Law does not have any specific definition of 'Big Data,' generally speaking, search records in Google and Yahoo, individual information in SNS, like Facebook, and shopping records in online shopping portal websites like Amazon, are typical examples of 'Big Data.' In theory, Big Data can be utilized in financial service businesses.

Today, Big Data has been used in the insurance industry, which is commonly referred to as 'InsurTech.' For instance, a private company, SmartDrive, collects driving record information for insurance companies to evaluate premiums of auto insurance proportionally to the probability of insured events. IBM Watson Health collects medical information to evaluate premiums for life and health insurance.

2.6 *Mobilization (Services Available with Smartphones and Other Mobile Devices)*

As above, many new businesses with innovative technologies like blockchain and AI are at the stage of planning or testing, though some of them have started to be provided to customers. However, businesses with real innovations are not the majority

---

[11] Our research group had some meetings about this topic with the private company. The records of the meetings are published. See, Workshop of Law and Technology about Blockchain (2018).

in Japanese fintech. The majority of start-up companies in the Fintech Association of Japan, an industry group of fintech companies, are providing services for individuals to manage financial assets by themselves with a smartphone or other mobile tools. For instance, some companies provide apps for automatic saving up money to their bank account, apps to manage individual financial assets, and apps to manage accounting and tax documents.

What these businesses have in common is just 'mobilization,' while there are a variety of businesses. Among them, many provide some financial services connecting individual bank accounts, because most Japanese customers keep the majority of their financial assets there.[12] It is necessary for fintech companies to connect a customers' bank account when they are trying to provide the service of a financial advisor or asset management. This could be thought of as a substitute for a part of business traditionally served by banks. It is also referred to as an 'unbundling' of financial industries.

2.7 Cashless/Mobile Payment

The most attractive business among mobilization, or unbundling, fintech, is mobile-cashless payment. Of course, Japan has already had cashless payment like credit cards and prepaid instruments, though cash, legal tender, is the most popular payment still now. For instance, before mobile phones, calling cards were popular in Japan. Now, Suica, a prepaid instrument issued by the largest train company, is one of the most popular payment instruments. People typically use Suica with a card, although Suica also has an app usable with mobile phones.

Today, IT companies also established mobile payment apps. Yahoo and Softbank group issued Pay Pay from a subsidiary. LINE, the most popular communication SNS in Japan, released LINE Pay. Of course, many Japanese also pay attention to Libra. These payment apps can be used among consumers, while Suica and other former payment instruments are used just between consumers and business.

This is one kind of mobilization, but the most attractive field of fintech in Japan.[13]

Judging from the above, Japanese fintech examples are almost the same or very similar to other countries, although there must be some differences. For instance, the ratio of cashless payments is lower than in other developed countries because it is just 20%.[14] Therefore, we can compare with the impact on financial regulation from fintech all over the world.

[12]The largest part of individuals' financial assets is cash and bank deposits in Japan. The Bank of Japan released the statics relating to funds flow reveals that 53.3% of individuals' financial assets are cash and bank deposit in 2018 financial year. See, Bank of Japan website, available at: https://www.boj.or.jp/statistics/sj/index.htm/. Accessed 4 February 2020.

[13]Japanese government set the goal that the ratio of cashless payment increases to about 40% by June 2027. See, Growth Strategy (2017), p. 70.

[14]METI (2018), p. 4.

3 Framework of Financial Law in Japan

3.1 *Piecemeal Regulation: Banking, Insurance, and Securities*

In Japan, the Financial Service Agency (FSA) is in charge of financial regulation, mainly. Different from the US, the FSA is one comprehensive administrator relating to financial law. Traditionally, Japanese financial law can be divided into three categories: banking, insurance, and securities. The FSA Establishment Act, art. 3, states that the purpose of the FSA is to protect deposit holders, insurance policyholders, investors of securities, and any equivalent person. These three categories are the consumers of banking services, insurance, and securities.

In theory, the definition of financial law does not have to follow the jurisdiction of FSA. However, in practice, the jurisdiction must be important. Therefore, traditionally, financial law seemed piecemeal regulations among banking, insurance, and securities.

3.2 *Justification of Trident Regulation*

Japanese financial law adopts so-called trident regulation. The FSA regulates banks with Banking Acts, insurance companies with the Insurance Business Act, and securities business with the former Securities and Exchange Act (reformed into the Financial Instruments and Exchange Act in 2006). For instance, banks and insurance companies are required licenses (Banking Act art. 4 (1) and Insurance Business Act art. 3 (1)), and securities businesses are required to register (Financial Instruments and Exchange Act art. 29). All of them must be under supervision by the FSA. The acts impose financial regulation, including minimum capital requirements and a code and duty of conduct, including the prohibition of other businesses. In particular, the FSA prohibits them from non-financial business strictly. Roughly speaking, these regulations assume that only a stable company can implement financial businesses.

The purpose of these rules is to stabilize the financial systems and maintain the soundness of financial markets.[15] Some questions can arise: why is the financial regulation piecemeal, though the range of 'financial law' is not defined clearly in theory? However, piecemeal regulation can be justified, at least to some extent. Banking, insurance, and securities are different businesses and have different risks, different markets, and different customers, even though all of them belong to 'financial business.'

[15] Banking Act, Art. 1, Insurance Business Act art. 1, and Financial Instruments and Exchange Act, Art. 1.

3.2.1 Banking

The Banking Act art. 2 (2) stipulates that a banking business is (i) both receiving deposits and lending money simultaneously or (ii) exchange transactions. The Japanese Supreme Court judged that 'exchange transactions' mean sending money to someone at a distance.[16] This can be called settlement, in other words.

Banking businesses necessarily contain two deficits: liquidity mismatch and systemic risk.

First, the simultaneous business of receiving deposits and lending money necessarily leads to a mismatch. If you asked, 'how much money do you have?', you would answer the quantity of not only cash (legal tender) but also banking deposits. People think bank deposit is the same as cash, which they can always use. That is because the bank has to pay the deposit (saving accounts and checking accounts) to customers on demand. On the contrary, the bank has to wait for the due date to collect money lent to others. Therefore, if all deposit holders demand payback, the bank would be insolvent and go bankrupt. Of course, in that case, deposit holders must suffer loss because they cannot collect all their money. Demanding payback without any need for cash is unreasonable for deposit holders.

However, in the case where the other deposit holders demand that the bank pay and one deposit holder does not demand, she or he failed to collect the money from the bank. When a deposit holder does not know the activities of the other deposit holders, it must be reasonable for all deposit holders to demand payback, though it must be better for all deposit holders that all of them keep the deposit in fact. If not all deposit holders demand, all of them can collect money when they need cash. It is the prisoners' dilemma in game theory, and this phenomenon is called a 'bank-run.' The cause of a bank-run is the situation where the bank owes the debt to always pay on demand (high-liquidity obligation) and has loan debts to collect just after the due-date (low-liquidity claim). There is a liquidity mismatch in the banking business.[17]

Therefore, the bank has mandatory deposit insurance. Deposit insurance covers up to 10 million JPY in individual saving accounts and all amounts in checking accounts, even in the case of banks' insolvency. This insurance solves the prisoners' dilemma and bank run problem. However, insurance also reduces the incentive for deposit holders to monitor banks' solvency. This is the moral hazard problem. Therefore, the banking act imposes on banks a duty for sound business.[18]

Second, former business, exchange transaction, leads to systemic risk. Today, bank deposits, saving account and checking account, play a role of payment method through bank wire like, or more often than, cash. It is a symptom that, in 2017, the reformed Civil Code art. 477 acknowledged the bank wire as a payment of a debt. If one bank goes bankrupt, many transactions must fail settlement because the bank

---

[16] Saik-ō Saibansho [Sup. Ct.] Mar. 12, 2001, Hei 13, 55 Saik-ō Saibansho keiji hanreishū [Keishū] 97 (Japan)

[17] Macey (2006), pp. 5–6.

[18] Macey (2006), pp. 6–11.

transfer is used as a means of payment. As a result, the bank's insolvency leads not only that all of the deposit holders to the bank lose the money, but also that other parties will fail to collect the money from deposit holders because of the failure of the settlement. One bank's failure has overflow effects and leads to many companies' bankruptcies. This is called systemic risk.

To prevent systemic risk, deposit insurance covers all amounts in checking accounts. In addition, the Banking Act orders the bank to follow stable and sound business principles with low risk and to deter high risk-high return business.

3.2.2 Insurance

In Japan, no statute contains a definition of insurance. Generally speaking, insurance is a means to protect individuals and companies ('insured') from some identified risk. Insurance utilizes the law of large numbers to calculate the possibilities of losses from the risk. Each insured pays the premium to an insurance company. Then, the insurance company pools insured people's risks to make payments in the case when the insured accidents happen. With insurance, the insured can hedge against the risk of a contingent or uncertain loss. Roughly speaking, this description of insurance can be applied to law, though there are some differences among statutes relating to insurance.

Insurance can be divided into two categories: life insurance and damage insurance. Insurance is a tool to diversify and transfer the risk of death or damage.

Because of the nature of insurance mentioned above, the possibilities of insured accidents is important. However, each policyholder cannot calculate it by himself. Insurance is designed to protect the insured from the losses in the future. If the insurance company fails payment on insured accident, insured people fail to diversify or transfer risk. In addition, the law of large numbers requires many policyholders in insurance contracts by definition. In the contract, it is important to keep equality among policyholders. Necessarily, the number of insurance companies is small and can be led to monopoly or oligopoly, and the market mechanism does not work well. Therefore, the FSA and government supervise the insurance companies to prevent them from taking too much risk and to ensure that they sell sound and fair insurance products.[19]

3.2.3 Securities

Even in Japan, securities can be defined, in theory, following the Howey test from US case law. The Howey test requires that 'securities' are (i) the investment of money to (ii) common enterprise (iii) with a reasonable expectation of profits derived from the efforts of others.[20] In US case law, this test is the standard for judges to apply securities

[19]Insurance Business Act, Art. 1.

[20]SEC v. W. J. Howey Co., 328 U.S. 293 (1946) 301.

law. On the contrary, Japanese law lists specific instruments to be applied as security law in advance. Some scholars criticize securities in Japanese law because of the lack of flexibility. However, the context is the discussion relating rules vs standards.[21] A rule defines the range of prohibition and the contents of duties specifically and clearly. On the contrary, a standard is designed to be fulfilled by the adjudicator. Therefore, the creation cost of rules is higher than standards, while the application cost of rules is cheaper than standards. There is clearly a tradeoff. I cannot say one is always superior to the other. Regardless of the form of law, the theoretical concept of 'securities' is accepted universally.

In the field of securities, an investor makes a decision by evaluating the prospective profits derived from the common enterprise. The companies with good prospective profits can raise money with an advantageous condition, while others with bad prospective profits have to accept worse conditions on financing. The latter may face fear by takeover because the price of the share decreases. The capital market mechanism and the principle of survival-of-the-fittest improve social economics. This assumes the investors can get the correct information relating to the prospective profits by the common enterprise, and the capital market works fairly. To fulfill such conditions, the Financial Instruments and Exchange Act stipulates mandatory disclosure and maintains the price formation function of the capital market.[22]

3.2.4 Some Exceptional Cross-Sectional Regulations

As seen above, there are some differences between businesses and the purpose of regulations among financial business. The purpose of banking regulation is to protect the financial system rather than individual deposit holders, while insurance law and securities regulation are designed for the protection of policyholders and investors primarily. The latter two try to secure the reasonable decisions of relevant actors.

Of course, some of the regulations are applied to all financial businesses regardless of classification. For instance, in the phase of selling financial goods to investors, the same regulation to provide enough information to investors covers all three categories. Therefore, the Financial Instruments Sales Act is applied to all financial instruments, including the above three categories.[23]

Similarly, the AML (Anti-money laundering regulation) is the same as the distribution regulation. AML imposes the duty of KYC (Know Your Customer) on all financial companies, including banks, insurance companies, securities brokerages, and any other financial businesses.[24] All financial companies should require customers' identity verification. It is a heavy burden for financial companies, especially for small companies.

---

[21] Kaplow (1992), p. 560.

[22] Financial Instruments and Exchange Act, Art. 1.

[23] Financial Instruments Sales Act, Art. 2 (1).

[24] Act on Prevention of Transfer of Criminal Proceeds, Art. 2.

However, many financial regulations are diverse to be adjusted to each financial business and its risk.

3.3 *Other Financial Businesses*

In Sect. 3.2, I suggested piecemeal financial regulation was reasonable because the three types of financial business were diverse. However, that does not mean all financial business can be classified into these three categories. There is another financial business to be regulated. The trident regulation framework does not work as well at such when dealing with such a financial business.

3.3.1 Money Lending

Money lending is a part of the banking business, but traditionally, money lending has been done by independent companies from banks and regulated heavily because of paternalism. In some or many cases, borrowers may make unreasonable decisions, and lenders can compel to impose strict or unreasonable conditions to borrowers because of the gap of bargaining power. Therefore, the Money Lending Business Act requires registry for money lending business[25] and regulates it with three perspectives: amount limitation, interest rate restriction, and code of conduct. This Act limits the money lending up to one-third of customers' income per year (amount limitation).[26] This act stipulates the maximum interest rate in lending money to consumers.[27] The Interest Rate Restriction Act stipulates the restrictions.[28]

3.3.2 Derivatives

Another example of financial business is derivative instruments, including futures, options, and swaps. The Commodity Derivatives Transaction Act renamed from the Commodity Exchange Act regulates future transactions of red beans, oil, and other goods. In addition, the Financial Instruments and Exchange Act started to regulate futures about financial instruments, FX (foreign currency exchange) trading, on the act was renamed from the Securities and Exchange Act in 2006. Before then, the Financial Futures Transaction Act 1998 regulated such transactions. Today, the Financial Instruments and Exchange Act covers not just securities but also all financial instruments, excluding banking and insurance.

---

[25] Money Lending Business Act, Art. 3 (1).

[26] Money Lending Business Act, Art. 13-2.

[27] Money Lending Business Act, Art. 12–8.

[28] Interest Rate Restriction Act art.1 limits interest rate up to 20%, 18%, and 15% depending on amount of lent money.

3.3.3 Payment

(a) Credit Cards

Exchange transaction means sending money, payment, or settlement. Though it is a part of the banking business, other companies serve it. Today, the most popular payment instrument is a credit card. Credit card payment is usually connected to bank accounts. On the payment with a credit card, the money is wired from the user's bank account, via the card company. In credit card payment, banking regulation can respond to the systemic risk entailed with payment.

Though credit card payment is not regulated by a specific act, the Installment Sales Act regulates the installment payment during longer term than two months with a credit card. This is because the installment payment is the same as lending money until the payment day. Therefore, this regulation is designed for the protection of credit cardholders like borrowers in money lending (at 3.3.1). The Installment Sales Act stipulates installment payment with a credit card as 'Intermediation of Comprehensive Credit Purchases.' [29] The purpose of this act is to keep the fair conditions of the transaction and to deter severe and unreasonable conditions[30] and the excessive amount of sales to elderly people. This act requires Comprehensive Credit Purchase Intermediaries (credit card companies) registries.[31] The intermediaries face code of conduct, including the duty to providing customers document to tell conditions.[32]

(b) Prepaid Payment Instruments

Another act, the Payment Service Act, regulates prepaid payment instruments, including calling cards and Suica (at 2.7). First, this act stipulates the prepaid payment instrument just for issuers (Prepaid Payment Instruments for Own Business). Its examples are calling cards and gift certificates. This act requires issuers just notification.[33] On the contrary, this act stipulates prepaid payment instruments available to others, like Suica, differently from the first type for own business. This act requires the issuers' registries.[34]

Based on this act, of both first type issuers and second ones should make security deposits for issuance. The amount of deposit should not be less than half of unused money on prepaid payment instruments.[35] Users have seniority in this deposit in the case of bankruptcy of issuers.[36] These deposits are the response to systemic risk entailed with payment service.

---

[29] Installment Sales Act, Art. 2 (3).

[30] Installment Sales Act, Art. 1 (1).

[31] Installment Sales Act, Art. 31.

[32] Installment Sales Act, Art. 30.

[33] Payment Service Act, Art. 5.

[34] Payment Service Act, Art. 7.

[35] Payment Service Act, Art. 14.

[36] Payment Service Act, Art. 31 (1).

(c) Fund Transfer Service

The Payment Service Act regulates another payment service, namely a fund transfer service. It is the same service as 'exchange transactions' in the banking business. This act permits a single sending money business with loser conditions and relaxed procedures than a bank. This act requires fund transfer service providers just registries, not banking license.[37] The providers should make a security deposit for providing service. The amount should be more than 10 million JPY and more than the amount of money on sending process added with procedural cost in the case of legal enforcement.[38] Because users have seniority in this security deposit,[39] this deposit is designed to respond to systemic risk. In addition, this provider should follow the amount of limitation. The amount of sending money should not be more than 1 million JPY (a little bit less than 10 thousand USD) with one transaction.[40]

These examples show how new financial businesses are launching. Especially, payment services are in the process of being one independent category from the banking business before the fintech era. The law imposes more relaxed rules than banking regulations, which are designed to respond to systemic risk.

4 A New Framework in a Fintech Era?

4.1 Unbundling/Rebundling

As mentioned in Sect. 2, the majority of fintech business involves the unbundling of traditional financial business, though some of them use new innovative technology like blockchain and AI. In addition, many fintech companies are trying to offer a new package of financial services. This is often called 'rebundling.' Rebundling happens between financial businesses or between financial business and non-financial businesses.

Piecemeal trident regulation does not fit well with unbundling and rebundling because fintech companies are different from pure banking, pure insurance companies, or pure securities brokerages. Therefore, there is a seed to change the current framework of financial law in Japan.

---

[37] Payment Service Act, Art. 37.

[38] Payment Service Act, Art. 43.

[39] Payment Service Act, Art. 59 (1).

[40] Payment Service Act, Art. 2 (2) and Order for Enforcement of the Payment Services Act, Art. 2.

4.2 Promoting or Deterring Unbundling?

At first, should the government permit unbundling of financial services? Should the government permit newcomers (fintech companies) entering into a part of traditional financial businesses served by banks, insurance companies, and securities brokerages?

The FSA had many options to respond to these questions in theory. The FSA could prohibit them completely. It could also promote fintech companies.

Unbundling does not involve launching new financial businesses from scratch. The majority of fintech companies provide new service to customers connecting their banking accounts. These unbundling services are launched in two different ways: the bank's initiative and the customer's initiative.

First, banks choose fintech services to make their services more attractive. From the customers' perspective, the financial services seem provided by a bank. A fintech company is just a tool or an agent ('Kundenberater' in German Civil Law[41]) for the bank. This is the same as the situation where the bank uses a Post Company or email as a tool to communicate with customers before the fintech era. It is just a type of outsourcing. Therefore, the bank's initiative in unbundling is not new at all.

On the contrary, the customers' initiative in prompting unbundling is new phenomena. Customers choose the services by fintech companies by themselves sometimes without the bank's permission. Customers permit the fintech company to connect with 'their' account in the bank. Should the government promote or deter the customer's initiative unbundling?

This question depends on whether a customer of the bank should control to design financial services provided to the customer. Following the law and economics literature,[42] the actor who can design the financial services most efficiently should control it under the assumption that nobody can choose first the best contract with enough credible information (incomplete contract).

On the one hand, the consumer has the largest incentive to improve financial services because she or he gets the benefits from the service. In addition, the customer is in the best position to know her or his needs. Based on these points, we can say consumers should control.

On the other hand, consumers do not have enough information about financial services because they are not specialists. They sometimes—or even often—choose unreasonable or harmful services. One option to respond to this problem is that the government makes a specific code of conduct imposed on fintech companies and other financial companies while consumers hold the control right to design financial services. However, this option does not work well when the government does not have enough information relating to the industry. Then, the second and more practical option arises. Financial companies like banks with enough information and specialties relating to finance design financial services for consumers. This is can

[41] BGB, Art. 278. In German law, the fault and default of Kundenberater seems principal's in the context of contract law.

[42] Hart (1995), pp. 29–33; Grossman and Hart (1986).

be referred to as bank-initiative unbundling. In this case, the improvement of the consumers' interest depends on the market competition amongst banks.

The key to unbundling is the system to connect to the bank to use the data and function held by the bank safely. This connection system is called an API (Application Programming Interface). The EU made Payment Service Directive 2,[43] which imposes the duty to provide API to fintech companies on banks in November 2015. This mandatory API, called open API, is a prominent example of consumer's initiative unbundling.

Japan did not have any specific law relating to API before the 2017 Banking Act Reform. At that time, consumers had to tell their passwords or PINs about their banking account to fintech intermediary companies in order to use fintech services on the initiative of consumers. Fintech intermediaries provided money-sending or other services to consumers in the way that fintech companies access to consumers' banking account with the passwords or PINs. The contract of many banks did not permit consumers to leave agents to manage their banking account. Therefore, consumers' initiative unbundling might constitute the breach of contract. In addition, consumers did not have any other option than leaving full access to fintech intermediary companies because they told passwords or PINs of their banking account.

To respond to these problems, the Banking Act Reform 2017 imposes on fintech intermediary companies the duty of registry as 'Settlement Agents for Electronic Settlement Systems.'[44] This reform imposes on banks the duty to make a policy relating to collaboration with intermediary companies. It prohibits banks from unjustifiable discrimination to intermediaries.[45] This reform makes it possible to design the scope of access to a bank account.

This reform imposes on fintech intermediary companies (settlement agents in this reform) the duty of faith to consumers,[46] and the duty of adequate management of information.[47]

The 2017 Reform is different from an Open API. However, it is evaluated by imposing the duty of the best efforts for Open API. In other words, this reform requests banks to help consumers to design financial services, while the consumer does not have full control to design financial service. In Japan, the control of financial service is shared with banks and consumers.[48] I evaluate this reform as an attempt to promote consumer's initiative unbundling.

[43] Directive (EU) 2015/2366, available at: https://ec.europa.eu/info/law/payment-services-psd-2-directive-eu-2015-2366_en. Accessed 4 February 2020.

[44] Banking Act, Art. 52-61-2.

[45] Banking Act, Art. 52-61-11.

[46] Banking Act, Art. 52-61-9.

[47] Banking Act, Art. 51-61-12.

[48] Of course, this description assumes that fintech companies provides new services before designing financial service package by banks or consumers.

4.3 The Same Principle

Promoting unbundling is different from relaxing the incumbent financial regulation. For instance, a robo-adviser, an investment adviser with AI (see Sect. 2.4 above), is regulated by the current financial regulation for an investment adviser in securities law. In Japanese law, just providing advice requires the registry of an Investment Advisory and Agency Business. Managing investment decision requires the registry of Investment Management Business. Purchasing financial instruments in the exchange requires the registry of type-I Financial Instruments Business Operators (typically, securities brokerages). In addition, financial law imposes a code of conduct, including the duty of loyalty and duty of the best execution.

The same law regulates fintech unbundling business if the business belongs to the financial business regulated by current financial law. Using new technology like AI and blockchain is a small problem in the phase for administrators and adjudicators to apply the law, though they have to know and understand new technology in target financial service at that phase.

On the contrary, unbundling sometimes requires the framework of financial law, because traditional financial regulation assumes just three businesses, i.e., banking, insurance, and securities, in Japan. Especially, as shown at Sect. 2.7, payment business separated from banking attracts the largest attention, today.

4.4 The 'Independence Day' of Payment from Banking

Unbundling by fintech requires a review of the current financial regulation regime constituted by trident regulation in Japan. The FSA launched Study Group of Financial Systems in the Financial Council to respond to this problem. This study group reviewed the current regulatory regime and concluded that current regulation should be reconstructed more functionally and cross-sectionally and set the goal that financial regulation should be the same-risk-same-rule principle.[49]

The Study Group proposed four functions, or sections, of finance: (i) payment, (ii) credit (lending money), (iii) asset management, (iv) risk transfer. [50] Then, it reviewed the regulation to respond to risk of each function. However, it must be noticed that this proposal does not disrupt the current framework completely. This new classification is not far from the current financial regulation. Among the three financial businesses, insurance is almost equal to risk transfer. Securities (original securities excluding derivative transactions[51]) are almost equal to asset management. On the contrary, a banking business contains plural functions in the new regime. A bank provides both

---

[49] Financial Council (2018a), p. 5.

[50] Financial Council (2018a), p. 6.

[51] In current regime, Financial Instruments and Exchange Act regulates derivatives transaction (at 3.3.2), but derivatives are out of traditional definition of securities based on Howey test. In Study Group's framework, derivative should belong to risk transfer.

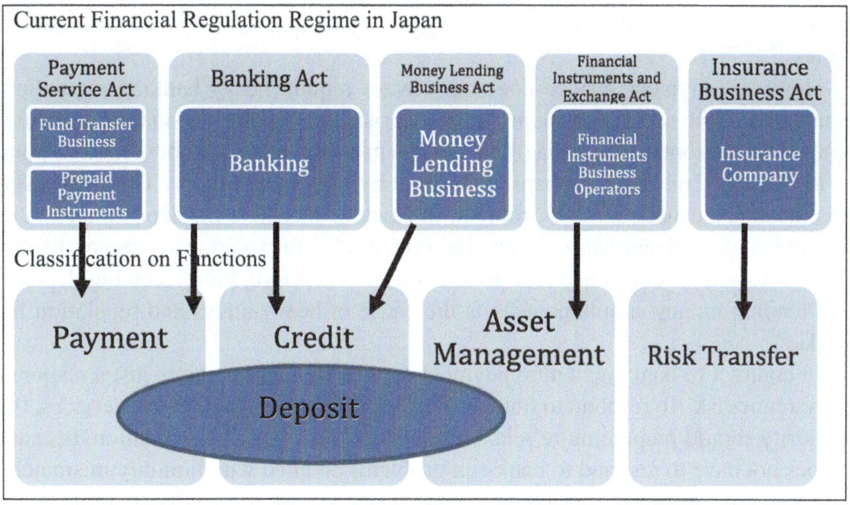

Fig. 1 Functional Section by Study Group of Financial System (Financial Council 2018b)

settlement service and credit (lending money) (see Fig. 1). In addition, the status of the deposit is unclear in this new regime. The Study Group said that deposits could be said to be payments, asset management, and credit. Because consumers can use a money bank deposit account like cash (legal tender), a banking deposit service is a settlement. The Study Group assumes fund transfer business and prepaid payment instrument (at 3.3.3) also belong to payment. Banking contains a lending money business. The saving account has interest, though it is low compared with securities like stock and bond. Therefore, the deposit can be said to be a kind of asset management. A bank uses money in banking deposits for lending money. Therefore, a deposit is deeply related to credit.[52]

Therefore, the difference between the new regime and traditional trident regulation is just banking. In the new regime, the banking business is divided into three categories: payment, money lending, and deposits. In addition, payment service separated from banking had started before the fintech era, as seen in Sect. 3.3.3. From this overview, one general point becomes clear: fintech strengthens the movement of independence of payment from the banking business.

After payment becomes independent from the banking business, the discussion moves to what risk payment service contains and what the adequate regulation is necessary to respond to that risk.

As mentioned in Sect. 3.2.1, the payment system entails systemic risk because the insolvency of one company managing payment system influences not only its consumers but also the partners with which consumers are contracting. This contagion effect can lead to a chain of bankruptcy. The systemic risk is entailed with small

[52]Financial Council (2018a), pp. 10–11.

payment companies like fintech start-ups as well as large payment companies like banks.[53]

However, payment service does not always require heavy banking regulation. Banking has two serious problems: systemic risk and liquidity mismatch. The latter leads to the prisoners' dilemma (the bank-run problem described above). To respond to the liquidity mismatch, a bank is covered by deposit insurance. Then, however, this insurance causes another problem, the lack of incentive for deposit holders to monitor banks and moral hazard. The Banking Act has the solution to these problems. It has a variety of duties and a code of conduct. Therefore, both receiving deposits and lending money simultaneously is the cause of heavy duties and regulation for banks.[54]

In contract to banking, a pure payment service business requires just a response to systemic risk. To respond to fintech start-ups providing just payment services, the authority should prepare more relaxed regulation than banking regulation, because it does not have to respond to bank-run problems entailed with liquidity mismatch.

Today, the FSA has already prepared regulations in the Payment Service Act for the fund transfer service and prepaid payment instruments, while another agent, METI (Ministry of Economy, Trade and Industry), has prepared the law in the Installment Sales Act for credit card (Sect. 3.3.3). However, these rules are evaluated as exceptions from banking. For instance, the fund transfer service has the limitation of the amount of cash within one transaction because of that. There are some gaps among these payment business regulations because of the lack of general idea about the regulation for payment service. For instance, the act requires fund transfer service the same amount as full money on the process of sending in the security deposit, while issuers of prepaid payment instruments are required just half of the amount of unused money. Today, the government is discussing removing unreasonable and unjustifiable limitations from current payment regulation and establishing adequate and efficient regulation for pure payment service. It should be designed to respond to systemic risk, not liquidity mismatch. [55]

Based on this idea, the FSA submitted a bill reforming the Payment Service Act to the Japanese Diet on March 6, 2020.[56] The FSA proposed three classes of fund transfer services.[57] The current fund transfer service, whose limitation of sent money is 1 million JPY, is renamed as a Type-II Fund Transfer Service. In the reform bill, the FSA proposed to launch two new categories of Fund Transfer Service. First, the FSA proposed a large-amount fund transfer service and prepared new regulations to respond to the risk. The bill names this a Type-I Fund Transfer Service, which requires

[53]Financial Council (2018a), p.7, Magnuson (2019), p.1200.

[54]Financial Council (2018a), p.8.

[55]Financial Council (2019); Sangyo Kouzou Shingikai (2019).

[56]FSA website, available at: https://www.fsa.go.jp/common/diet/index.html Accessed 10 March 2020.

[57]2020 Reform Bill of Payment Service Act, Art. 36-2.

the authorization of the FSA,[58] while Type-II only requires registration.[59] To respond to systemic risk originating from a large-amount payment network, the FSA proposed the prohibition of a Type-I fund transfer service operator from holding liquidity mismatch,[60] in addition to inspection procedures and supervision. Moreover, the FSA proposed another category of fund transfer service for a small amount of money (several tens of thousands of JPY [equal to several hundred USD]). This is called a Type-III Fund Transfer Service. Because the systemic risk is small compared to Type-I or Type-II, the FSA thinks that regulation can be more relaxed than with current payment services.[61] For instance, a Type-III operator does not have to make a security deposit if it records the money, and the sending service is separated from the operator's own account.[62]

Adding another category, payment, to financial regulation framework owes to the fintech movement. However, it is noteworthy that the idea relating to new financial regulation to respond to just systemic risk entailed with payment is not new in practice (see Sect. 3.3.3 above) or in theory at all. What the fintech movement has done is just to provide support to the idea.

The idea that banking has two different businesses (the simultaneous operation of deposit and money lending, and exchange transaction) and each business contains different risk (liquidity mismatch or systemic risk) has been known since narrow-banking theory in the 1990s.[63] Pure payment service is the same as the 100% reserve requirement of narrow banking. The fintech movement has not made any new ideas. It draws more attention to the pure payment business separated from banking.

4.5 *Prohibition of Another Business*

Rebundling entailed unbundling has another impact on financial law. In the fintech era, IT companies try to enter into the finance business, while traditional and current financial regulations prohibit financial companies from engaging in other business.[64] Especially, the law prohibits them from the non-financial business even through subsidiaries.

The main purpose of this regulation was to maintain the soundness of the financial business. Financial regulation is trying to separate financial business from non-financial business risk. However, if the financial business is implemented through the subsidiary or parent company, the liability is not applied to another company,

---

58 2020 Reform Bill of Payment Service Act, Art. 40-2.

59 2020 Reform Bill of Payment Service Act, Art. 38.

60 Financial Council (2019), pp.10-11. 2020 Reform Bill of Payment Service Act, Art. 51-2 prohibiting Type-I operators from accepting deposit from customers.

61 Financial Council (2019), pp.11-12; Sangyo Kouzou Shingikai (2019) p.8.

62 2020 Reform Bill of Payment Service Act, Art. 45-2 (1).

63 Dewatripont and Tirole (1994), p. 38. Originally from Tobin (1987) and Friedman (1959), Ch.3.

64 For instance, Banking Act, Art.12; Insurance Business Act, Art.100.

because courts rarely permit piercing corporate veil in Japan. The risk does not matter in the case IT companies manage a financial business through a subsidiary or parent company from the perspective of financial law.

However, recently another problem happens relating to the prohibition of another business. Today, large IT companies, like GAFA (Google, Amazon, Facebook, Apple), are trying to enter into the financial business, like Libra by Facebook. If such a large IT company enters into financial business, their economic power will become even more powerful. One government cannot control or regulate such a large company because of its economic and political power. Therefore, many governments seem to start planning new ideas to regulate such a large IT platform from many perspectives. One candidate is anti-trust law. Japan has a provision relating to too-large economic power in anti-trust law.[65] The provision has been considered unique, even strange, from an academic perspective, and it was called a 'general concentration.'[66] However, recently it has attracted attention relating to the Big Tech problem. Regulating too-large IT companies is one of the largest tasks for the Japanese government and economics now. The prohibition of another business possibly would become another candidate to respond to this problem,[67] though it is not related to a financial regulation perspective.

5 Cryptoassets: An Example of Transformation of Financial Regulation in Fintech Era

I have sketched the impact of fintech on financial regulation in Japan in the previous chapter. Now, I describe a specific example in this section: the regulation relating to crypto-assets or virtual currencies.

5.1 Introduction of Cryptocurrencies Regulation

After the MTGOX scandal (mentioned in Sect. 2.2) in 2014 and its bankruptcy, the Japanese government adopted regulation relating to cryptocurrencies ahead of the other developed countries. Payment Service Act Reform 2016 made provisions relating to cryptocurrencies and exchanges. At that time, the act called cryptocurrency as 'virtual currency' on statute. Originally, the act assumed the electronic data that can be used as a payment tool and is attached with no legal right, because this reform was influenced by Bitcoin scandal. This chapter calls such cryptocurrency as 'payment crypto-asset(s)' for the avoidance of confusion, while someone calls it as a payment token.

---

[65] Act on Prohibition of Private Monopolization and Maintenance of Fair Trade, Art. 9.

[66] Tokutsu (2014), p.210.

[67] Tokutsu (2014), p.215.

This reform regulates not cryptocurrency itself but the exchange for it. According to the act, exchanges for cryptocurrency are required registry.[68] The act imposes the duty of asset separation,[69] financial requirements including minimum legal capital, 10 million JPY,[70] and mandatory audit by a certified public accountant[71] on the exchanges.

The AML was also amended to respond to cryptocurrency. 2016 Reform of Act on Prevention of Transfer of Criminal Proceeds imposed exchanges the duty to require customer's identity verification,[72] to make and keep the record of transactions,[73] to notify suspicious transactions about illegal money laundering to the authority,[74] and to establish the governance system for employee-education and internal self-regulation.[75]

5.2 *Extension of Cryptocurrencies Regulation: From Virtual Currency to Cryptoasset*

Originally, the 2016 Reform was designed to respond to payment crypto-assets. However, it is possible to apply blockchain included in crypto-assets to other usages. The data managed by blockchain can have the record relating to legal right or obligation. It is called a 'token,' and can be sold and bought in the market. For instance, a token is attached to the right to get some services in specific stores or restaurants. It is called 'utility token (utility crypto-asset).' Then, another token is attached with the right to receive profits originated from a specific business. It is a 'security token (security crypto-asset).'

In theory, a utility token is the same as calling cards or gift certificates and can be evaluated prepaid payment instruments. On the contrary, security token belongs to 'securities' in theory. However, it was unclear whether the Japanese Financial Instruments and Exchange Act was applied to security token, because, as mentioned in Sect. 3.2.3, the act is rule-based and list the objects to be applied exclusively.

The FSA could not leave these token unregulated. Therefore, the FSA provided the interpretation of Payment Service Act originally designed for payment crypto-asset, that these rules were applied to all tokens, including utility token and security token. That was because the act says that a crypto-asset includes the data that can be exchanged with another crypto-asset with unspecified people.[76] It was called 'type-II

68 Payment Service Act, Art. 63-2.

69 Payment Service Act, Art. 63-11 (1).

70 Payment Service Act, Art. 63-5 (1) iii.

71 Payment Service Act, Art. 63-11 (2).

72 Act on Prevention of Transfer of Criminal Proceeds, Art. 4.

73 Act on Prevention of Transfer of Criminal Proceeds, Art. 6-7.

74 Act on Prevention of Transfer of Criminal Proceeds, Art. 8.

75 Act on Prevention of Transfer of Criminal Proceeds, Art. 10.

76 Payment Service Act, Art. 2 (5) ii.

crypto-asset.' Most of the utility tokens and security tokens were designed to be paid with payment crypto-asset like Bitcoin and Ethereum in the platform. They could be seen a part of 'type-II crypto-asset' because they were exchanged as another crypto-asset with unspecified people. [77] As a result of this interpretation, the rule originally designed for payment crypto-assets was applied to utility tokens and security tokens.

5.3 Arrangement of Regulation to Respond to Risks

However, based on the basic idea mentioned in Sect. 4.3, this result must be strange and unreasonable. Even if the technology in financial services is the same, the regulation should respond to the nature and risk of financial services. If the nature and risk are different, the rule to be applied should be changed, according to the FSA Study Group report, 2018.

Therefore, the 2019 Reforms of Financial Instruments and Exchange Act and Payment Service Act solved the problem. This reform created a new category of securities, 'Electronic Transferable Recorded Right,'[78] and it was excluded from the range of the Payment Service Act. After this reform, security law in Japan has regulated security tokens.

On the contrary, no reform relating to utility token was done until now. Therefore, it is regulated by the same rule as payment crypto-asset regulation in the Payment Service Act. I think it is better that utility token is regulated by the rule of prepaid payment instruments. However, people are thinking about the difference between prepaid payment instruments regulation and fund transfer service regulation in Japan. The former requires just 50% reserves, while the latter requires a full amount reserve. If the FSA does not think the 50% mandatory reserves for the prepaid payment instrument is reasonable, it makes sense that the FSA has not made the rule for utility tokens and left it regulated with the same rules of payment crypto-assets.

As described above, crypto-asset is a technological concept, not a legal one. Originally, financial law regulated all crypto-asset uniformly, overlooking the differences in risk. After recognizing crypto-asset contains diverse services, however, the reform was done to respond to each risk, and it possibly is on the process still now. On the one hand, this process is to make new regulations to respond to a new phenomenon. On the other hand, it is also to clarify what risk current regulation is responding.

6 Overview of Future Financial Regulation in Fintech Era

Fintech has had an impact on financial regulation. It is important, however, that the fundamental principle behind the legal rules—that regulation should respond to each

[77] Japan Cryptocurrency Business Association (2017), p. 3.

[78] Financial Instruments and Exchanges Act, Art. 2 (3).

risk of diverse financial business—has not been changed.[79] The influence of fintech is just an adjustment to the legal rules.

From a practical perspective, understanding the new financial businesses served by new technology and its risk is more important than discussing the framework of financial law, at first. Then, we find the deficits to be responded when we apply incumbent law to new businesses.

Therefore, it is important to collect information about new businesses. It is useful to establish the structure to let business companies tell the authority information. One example is the 'FinTech Demonstration Test Hub' [80] launched in 2017 by the FSA in Japan. In this 'Hub,' companies apply a new business plan to FSA, and if the FSA permitted, the companies would implement the plan under relaxed regulation than prior application. It is an 'experiment,' and, if it works well, the FSA will employ a new, relaxed interpretation. It is an example of a regulatory sandbox, which is also implemented in the UK, Korea, and many countries. This is not just deregulation or loosening regulation. This Hub contains the process the companies submit information to the authority. [81]

The authority has another candidate to respond to new technology. It leaves the companies to make the rules because they have much more information about new business and technology than the authority. One is self-regulation.[82] Of course, it is necessary to set incentives for companies to make adequate rules by themselves.

In addition, international collaboration will be more important,[83] because IT makes it easier to provide financial services across borders. Not just the harmonization of rules but also the international collaboration of enforcement will become much more important.

However, I would like to emphasize that the largest impact of new technology is the opportunity for us to confirm and clarify why the incumbent financial regulation has current form, what risk it responds to, and why the government imposes special regulation on financial services.

Acknowledgements This work was supported by JSPS KAKENHI Grant Numbers JP19K01362, JP18H00808, JP18H03611.

[79] Morishita (2017), pp. 776–777.

[80] Available at http://www.fsa.go.jp/news/29/sonota/20170921/20170921.html. Accessed 30 June 2020.

[81] Magnuson (2019), pp. 1215–1216.

[82] Magnuson (2019), p. 1219; Morishita (2017) p.779.

[83] Magnuson (2019), p.1206, pp.1222-1224; Morishita (2017), pp. 782–786.

References

Blockchain ni kansuru hou to gijutsu kenkyukai (Workshop of Law and Technology about Blockchain) (2018) The possibilities and difficulties of blockchain—the discussion between law and technology. Kinyuhomujijo 2082: 26–36 (in Japanese)

Easterbrook FH (1996) Cyberspace and the law of the horse. University of Chicago Legal Forum 1996:207–216

Dewatripont M, Tirole J (1994) The prudential regulation of banks. Massachusetts Institute of Technology, Cambridge, Massachusetts

Friedman M (1959) A program for monetary stability. Fordham University Press, New York

Grossman SJ, Hart OD (1986) The costs and benefits of ownership: a theory of vertical and lateral integration. Journal of Political Economics 94:691–719

Growth Strategy 2017 (Initiatives and Program). https://www.kantei.go.jp/jp/singi/keizaisaisei/pdf/miraitousi2017_inttv_prgrm.pdf. Accessed 31 March 2020

Hart Oliver (1995) Firms, contracts and financial structure. Oxford University Press, Oxford

Japan Cryptocurrency Business Association (2017) Initial coin offering he no taiou ni tsuite (About response to the initial coin offering). https://cryptocurrency-association.org/cms2017/wp-content/uploads/2017/12/20171208_01.pdf. Accessed 31 March 2020 (in Japanese)

Kaplow L (1992) Rules versus standards: an economic analysis. Duke Law Journal 42:557–629

Kinnyu Shingikai (Financial Council) (2018a) Kinnyuseido study group chukan seiri—kinoubetsu oudanteki na kinyu taikei ni mukete (Intermediate summary of study group of financial system—towards the functional and cross-sectional framework of financial regulation) (June 9)

Kinnyu Shingikai (Financial Council) (2018b) Kinnyuseido study group chukan seiri—kinoubetsu oudanteki na kinyu taikei ni mukete—no gaiyo (Outline of intermediate summary of study group of financial system—towards the functional and cross-sectional framework of financial regulation) (June 9)

Kinnyu Shingikai (Financial Council) (2019) Kessai hoseui oyobi kinnyu service chukai housei ni kansuru working group houkoku (Report of working group relating to legal infrastructures of settlement and financial intermediaries) (December 20)

Lessig L (1999) The law of the horse: what cyberlaw might teach. 113 Harvard Law Review

Macey JR (2006) Commercial banking and democracy: the illusive quest for deregulation. Yale J Regulation 23:1–27

Magnuson W (2019) Regulating fintech. Vanderbilt Law Review 71:1167–1226

METI (Ministry of Economy, Trade and Industry) (2018) Cashless vision. https://www.meti.go.jp/press/2018/04/20180411001/20180411001-1.pdf. Accessed 31 March 2020 (in Japanese)

Morishita T (2017) FinTech jidai no kinnyuho no arikata ni kansuru josetsuteki kento (Introductory review of financial law in fintech era). In Kuronuma E, Fujita T (eds) Kighoho no shinro (Direction of enterprise law) [Festschrift for prof. Kenjiro Egashira's 70 Years]. Yuhikaku, Tokyo, pp 771–825

Sangyo Kouzou Shingikai (Chamber of Industrial Structure), Shomu Ryutsu Johou Bunkakai (Subcommittee of Commercial Distribution Information), Kappy Hanbai Sho-iinkai (Panel of Installment Sales) (2019) Toumen no seidoka ni muketa seiri to kongo no kadai -technology shakai ni okeru kappuhanbai-housei no arikata- (Immediate summary for installing infrasturucture and future tasks-the future of installment sales legal infrastructure at technology society-) (December 20)

Tobin J (1987) The case for preserving regulatory distinctions. Challenge 30(5):167–183

Tokutsu A (2014) Regulation of bank shareholding: a functional and historical analysis. In: Zenichi Sh (ed) Enterprise law-contracts, markets, and laws in the US and Japan. Edward Elgar, Cheltenham, pp 205–221

US National Economic Council Report (2017) A framework for fintech. https://obamawhitehouse.archives.gov/sites/obamawhitehouse.archives.gov/files/documents/A%20Framework%20for%20FinTech%20_FINAL.pdf. Accessed 31 March 2020

Yanagawa N (2016) FinTech and legal system. NBL 1076:1–1 (in Japanese)

Legislative Development on Crypto-Assets in Japan: Revisions to the Payment Services Act, etc.

Ren Yatsunami

Abstract Japanese law began to regulate transactions on virtual currencies when revisions to the Payment Services Act and revisions to the Act on Prevention of Transfer of Criminal Proceeds were put into effect in April 2017. However, considering the recent hacking incidents and social problems on crypto-assets, the Financial Services Agency in Japan established the 'Research Group on Virtual Currency Exchange Business, etc.' in March 2018. Then, legislative efforts mainly based on the report by the Research Group resulted in the revisions of the Payment Services Act, etc. On March 15, 2019, the 'Bill to Revise the Payment Services Act, etc. in Response to Diversification of Financial Transactions Associated with the Development of Information Communication Technology' was approved at a Cabinet meeting. On the same day, the bill was submitted to the Diet by the Financial Services Agency. Through the proceedings of the Diet, the Act to Revise the Payment Services Act, etc. was enacted on May 31, 2019, and promulgated on June 7, 2019. By this legislation, which will enter into force soon in 2020, revisions to the Payment Services Act, revisions to the Financial Instruments and Exchange Act, and revisions to the Act on Sales, etc. of Financial Instruments are made in efforts to develop regulation for crypto-asset transactions.

Keywords Crypto-asset · Japan · Payment Services Act

1 Introduction: Background of Revisions to the Payment Services Act, etc.

This chapter aims to introduce the recent legislative development on crypto-assets in Japan. Japanese law began to regulate transactions on virtual currencies when revisions to the Payment Services Act (Act No. 59 of June 24, 2009) and revisions to the Act on Prevention of Transfer of Criminal Proceeds (Law No. 22 of March 31, 2007)

R. Yatsunami (✉)
Faculty of Law, Kyushu University, Fukuoka, Japan
e-mail: yatsunami@law.kyushu-u.ac.jp

M. Fenwick et al. (eds.), *Regulating FinTech in Asia*, Perspectives in Law, Business and Innovation, https://doi.org/10.1007/978-981-15-5819-1_9

were put into effect in April 2017. These revisions introduced a registration system for 'Virtual Currency Exchange Service Providers [*Kaso-tsuka Kokan-gyosha*]' for the purpose of protecting users by imposing requirements on minimum capital, separate management on assets, information management and disclosure, etc. Also, for the registration system, the Cabinet Office Ordinance on Virtual Currency Exchange Service Providers (Cabinet Office Order No. 7 of March 24, 2017) supplemented rules on such requirements. In addition to the role of protecting users, these revisions intended to prevent criminal use of virtual currencies, including money laundering or terrorism financing.[1]

However, even after the introduction of the registration system of Virtual Currency Exchange Service Providers, considerable incidents, and social problems in respect of crypto-assets have still been reported on several occasions. For instance, Coincheck, a bitcoin exchange service provider, suffered malicious hacking (cracking), and this incident resulted in a leakage of users' cryptocurrencies (NEM) in January 2018. Through the on-site inspections of the hacking incident, the Financial Services Agency has recognized there is still a lack of regulation on the management of users' crypto-assets by such service providers.[2]

Thus, the Financial Services Agency established the 'Research Group on Virtual Currency Exchange Business, etc. [*Kaso-tsuka Kokangyo To Ni Kansuru Kenkyukai*]' in March 2018. The Research Group was chaired by Prof. Hideki Kanda, a professor at Gakushuin University, and it organized 11 research meetings for discussing appropriate regulatory measures for virtual currency exchange businesses. As a summary documentation of their discussions, they published the 'Report of the Research Group on Virtual Currency Exchange Service, etc.' on December 21, 2018.[3] Then, legislative efforts mainly based on the report by the Research Group resulted in the revisions of the Payment Services Act, etc.

On March 15, 2019, the 'Bill to Revise the Payment Services Act, etc. in Response to Diversification of Financial Transactions Associated with the Development of Information Communication Technology' was approved at a Cabinet meeting. On the same day, the bill was submitted to the Diet by the Financial Services Agency. Through the proceedings of the Diet, the Act to Revise the Payment Services Act, etc. was enacted on May 31, 2019, and promulgated on June 7, 2019 as the Act No. 28 of June 7, 2019. By this legislation, which will enter into force soon in 2020, revisions to the Payment Services Act, revisions to the Financial Instruments and Exchange Act (Act No. 25 of April 13, 1948), and revisions to the Act on Sales, etc. of Financial Instruments (Act No. 101 of May 31, 2000) are made in efforts to develop regulation for crypto-asset transactions.

In this chapter, Sect. 2 will introduce the main points of the revisions to the Financial Services Act. In Sect. 2, for the convenience of comparison, the current version of the Payment Services Act will be called the '2016 Payment Services Act,' and the revised version is referred to as the '2019 Payment Services Act.' Then,

---

[1]Watanabe and Kasai (2019), p. 27.

[2]Matsuo (2019), p. 6.

[3]Research Group on Virtual Currency Exchange Service, etc. (2018), pp.1 et seq.

Sects. 3 and 4 will summarize the main points of revisions to the Financial Instruments and Exchange Act and those to the Act on Sales, etc. of Financial Instruments, respectively.

2 Revisions to the Payment Services Act

2.1 Change in Terminology: 'Virtual Currency' to 'Crypto-Asset'

When Japan introduced the registration system for Virtual Currency Exchange Service Providers [*Kaso-tsuka Kokan-gyosha*] in April of 2017, the 2016 Payment Services Act has adopted the term 'virtual currency [*Kaso-tsuka*].' At that time, the term 'virtual currency' has been generally popular, and especially it was the term used by the Financial Action Task Force (FATF).[4]

However, it is recognized that in recent years the usage of the term 'crypto-asset' has been increasing internationally.[5] In addition, it has been pointed out that the term 'virtual currency' would give a false impression in respect of the distinction between it and the legal currency.[6]

For considering the recent international trend and discussion on terminology, the 2019 Payment Services Act adopts the usage of the term 'crypto-asset' instead of 'virtual currency' (Article 2 (2) of the 2019 payment Services Act).

2.2 Crypto-Asset Custody Services

Under the 2016 Payment Services Act, according to its Article 2 (7) (iii), the 'management of users' money or virtual currency' in connection with '(i) purchase and sale of a virtual currency or exchange with another virtual currency,' or '(ii) intermediary, brokerage or agency services for the Act set forth in the preceding item' [the acts listed in Article 2 (7) (i) and (ii)] falls into the scope of 'Virtual Currency Exchange Service.' Thus, a 'crypto-asset custody service,' a service only for managing or transferring users' crypto-asset to designated addresses, does not meet the definition of the Virtual Currency Exchange Service as used in the 2016 Payment Services Act, unless any act listed in the items (i) and (ii) shown above is not performed.[7]

However, it is recognized that, as well as the Virtual Currency Exchange Services under the 2016 Payment Services Act, the Crypto Asset Custody Services are at the

[4]Financial Action Task Force (2014), p. 4.

[5]Ishizono (2019), p. 13.

[6]Watanabe and Kasai (2019), p. 28.

[7]Ishizono et al. (2019), p. 13.

similar risks, including the risk on leakage of users' crypto-assets and the risk on money laundering or terrorism financing.[8] Considering these risks, the 2019 Payment Services Act categorizes the act of 'managing crypto-assets for another person' as a form of Crypto Asset Exchange Service, except for the cases where any other law provides special provisions (Article 2 (7) (iii) of the 2019 Payment Services Act).[9] Therefore, under the 2019 Payment Services Act, irrespective of whether or not acts listed in (i) or (ii) above are performed, a Crypto Asset Custody Service would fall within the scope of Crypto Asset Exchange Service.

2.3 *Registration of Crypto Asset Exchange Provider*

In the 2016 Payment Services Act, Chapter V (Article 87–98) provides the rules on 'Certified Associations for Payment Service Providers.' However, to be a member of the Certified Association for Payment Service Providers is not compulsory under the 2016 Payment Services Act for registration to be a Crypto Asset Exchange Service Provider.

In contrast, under the 2019 Payment Services Act, an application for registration to be a Crypto Asset Exchange Service Provider may be rejected, in case that the applicant is neither a member of the Certified Association for Payment Service Providers nor a corporation making (i) its internal regulations which are equivalent to the self-regulatory rules of the Certified Association for Payment Service Providers and (ii) its compliance system for such internal regulations (Article 63-5 (6) of the 2019 Payment Services Act).[10]

2.4 *Notification for Change in Name of the Relevant Crypto Asset, etc*

So far, when a Crypto Asset Exchange Service Provider makes any change in items indicated in its registration application, such a change must be ex-post facto notified to the Financial Services Agency (Article 63-6 (1) of the 2016 Payment Services Act).

Under the revised Act, an ex-ante notification to the Financial Services Agency is required for changes in information of the registration application in respect of (i) name of the relevant crypto-asset, (ii) terms of the crypto-asset exchange services, and (iii) means of the crypto-asset exchange services (Article 63-6 (1) of the 2019 Payment Services Act). As to changes that are unlikely to have an impact on the

---

[8] Ishizono et al. (2019), p. 13.
[9] Matsuo (2019), p. 8.
[10] Ishizono et al. (2019), p. 16.

protection of users, ex-post facto notification is still adopted under the revised Act (Article 63-6 (2) of the 2019 Payment Services Act).[11]

2.5 *Advertisement or Solicitation*

Considering that crypto-asset exchange services are used for speculative reasons in many recent cases, under the 2016 Payment Services Act, the lack of regulations with respect to advertisement or solicitation of such services was identified as a legislative challenge.[12] Thus, the 2019 Payment Services Act introduced regulations on advertisement and solicitation of crypto-asset exchange services.

Firstly, Article 63-9-2 of the 2019 Payment Services Act introduced regulation of information disclosure. By this article of the 2019 Payment Services Act, information disclosure is made obligatory with regard to specific items, including (i) Crypto Asset Exchange Service Provider's trade name, (ii) information that the provider is a Crypto Asset Exchange Service Provider and its registration number, (iii) information that the crypto-asset is not Japanese or foreign legal currency, and (iv) the characteristics of the relevant crypto-asset which are specified by the relevant Cabinet Office Ordinance as important for users' decisions.[13]

Secondly, Article 63-9-3 of the 2019 Payment Services Act prohibits Crypto Asset Exchange Provides and their officers to conduct specific acts including (i) any act to make a misrepresentation or misleading representation, at the conclusion or solicitation of a Crypto Asset Exchange Contract, concerning the characteristics of the crypto-asset or any other items of crypto-asset specified by the relevant Cabinet Office Ordinance, (ii) any act to make a misrepresentation or misleading representation, in advertisements on a Crypto Asset Exchange Service, concerning the characteristics of the crypto-asset or any other items of crypto-asset specified by the relevant Cabinet Office Ordinance, (iii) any act to make a representation, at the conclusion or solicitation of a Crypto Asset Exchange Contract or in advertisements on a Crypto Asset Exchange Service, to induce the sale, purchase, or exchange of a crypto-asset not for payment purposes but for the purposes of promoting interests, and (iv) any other acts specified by Cabinet Office Ordinance which are likely to spoil the protection of users or endanger appropriate and secure performance of Crypto Asset Exchange Service.[14]

---

[11] Harigai et al. (2019), p. 39.

[12] Watanabe and Kasai (2019), p. 28.

[13] Takeuchi and Yamane (2019) p. 28.

[14] Takeuchi and Yamane (2019), p. 28.

2.6 *Information Disclosure in Case of Crypto Asset Exchange, etc.*

When a Crypto Asset Exchange Provider conducts an exchange of a crypto-asset or similar act by granting credit to users, the provider must to take appropriate measures for protecting users such as information disclosure on the relevant crypto-asset exchange contracts (Article 63-10 (2) of the 2019 Payment Services Act).[15]

2.7 *Obligations for Preservation of User's Assets*

The revisions of the Payment Services Act in 2019 enhanced the protection of users' assets in three ways as explained below.

Firstly, the 2019 Payment Services Act adds an obligation on a Crypto Asset Exchange Service Provider to entrust users' money.[16] Currently, there is an obligation for a Crypto Asset Exchange Service Provider to separately manage users' money and the provider's money (Article 63-11 of the 2016 Payment Services Act). As a relative rule on this obligation, Article 20 (1) of the Cabinet Office Ordinance on Virtual Currency Exchange Service Providers elaborate detailed means for such obligation of separate management.

As a newly introduced rule, under the 2019 Payment Services Act, the Crypto Asset Exchange Service Provider has an obligation not only to manage users' money separately from its own money but also to entrust users' money to a trust bank, trust company, or other similar entity in accordance with the relevant Cabinet Office Ordinance (Article 63-11 (1) of the 2019 Payment Services Act).

Secondly, there is a regulation on separate management for the protection of users' assets. On this point, the 2016 Payment Services Act had already established a requirement that a Crypto Asset Exchange Service Provider to manage a user's crypto-assets separately from crypto-assets of the other users' crypto-assets, with the means by which it is possible to promptly identify the user's assets from the others' assets (Article 63-11 (1) of the 2016 Payment Services Act). This requirement on separate management remains under the revised Act (Article 63-11 (2) [first sentence] of the 2019 Payment Services Act). In addition, the revised Act requires a Crypto Asset Exchange Service Provider to manage a user's crypto-assets separately from the other users' crypto-assets by the reliable methods specified in the relevant Cabinet Office Ordinance (Article 63-11 (2) [second sentence] of the 2019 Payment Services Act).[17] The relevant rules in the Cabinet Office Ordinance are in the process of

[15] Kawai et al. (2019), p. 7.

[16] Ishizono et al. (2019), p. 15.

[17] Takeuchi and Yamane (2019), p. 29.

preparation, but it has been generally explained that the reliable methods include the management of crypto-assets with 'cold wallets.'[18]

Thirdly, regulation on performance guarantee crypto-assets is introduced by the 2019 Payment Services Act.[19] A Crypto Asset Exchange Service Provider must hold, for its own account, crypto-assets of the same type and same quantity as the users' crypto-assets which are subject to 'requirements specified by the relevant Cabinet Office Ordinance as being necessary for ensuring users' convenience and smooth performance of crypto-asset exchange services' (Article 63-11-2 of Payment Services Act). Such performance guarantee crypto-assets shall be managed separately from the other crypto-assets in the providers' own account (Article 63-11-2 of Payment Services Act).

2.8 *Preferential Payment in Case of Claims for the Return of Crypto Assets*

Under the 2016 Payment Services Act, even though there is a regulation on separate management of users' crypto-assets (see Sect. 2.7 shown above), such users' crypto-assets still constitute the assets of the Crypto Asset Exchange Service Provider in the sense of private law. As a result, if there is a bankruptcy of the Crypto Asset Exchange Service Provider, users cannot claim the return of their crypto-assets, and their claims remain as general unsecured claims.

On the contrary, under the 2019 Payment Services Act, if a Crypto Asset Exchange Service Provider goes into bankruptcy, users who delegated the management of their crypto-assets to the Crypto Asset Exchange Service Provider have the right to receive payment in priority to general creditors, except for the case in which such preferential right will be subordinate to claim on the provider's estate (Article 63-19-3 of the 2019 Payment Services Act).[20]

---

[18] Watanabe and Kasai (2019), p. 29.

[19] Watanabe and Kasai (2019), p. 29.

[20] Matsuo (2019), p. 7. See also Takeuchi and Yamane (2019), p. 29.

3 Revisions to the Financial Instruments and Exchange Act

3.1 Electronically Recorded Transferable Rights

3.1.1 Definition

As to the question on whether an 'Initial Coin Offerings (ICO)' or 'Security Token Offerings (STO)' is governed by the Payment Services Act, by the Financial Instruments and Exchange Act, or by both of them, it has not been clarified by any official authority so far. In this sense, one of the aims of the bill in 2019 was to propose revisions to the Financial Instruments and Exchange Act to resolve this uncertainty on applicable rules in respect of ICO or STO and to prepare adequate rules on these businesses.[21]

For the purpose of clearly demarcating the scope of tokens to which the revised Financial Instruments and Exchange Act is applicable, the revised Act introduced a new legal concept, namely 'Electronically Recorded Transferable Rights.' To be categorized as the Electronically Recorded Transferable Rights, (i) such rights should be listed in Article 2 (2) of the Financial Instruments and Exchange Act and at the same time (ii) such rights should be represented by proprietary value transferable through electronic data processing system; however, (iii) rights specified in the relevant Cabinet Office Ordinance considering their liquidity or other circumstances are excluded from the category of Electronically Recorded Transferable Rights (Article 2 (3) of the revised Financial Instruments and Exchange Act).[22]

3.1.2 Regulation on Information Disclosure

Under the revised Financial Instruments and Exchange Act, disclosure requirements are applicable to the Electronically Recorded Transferable Rights (Article 3 (iii) (b) of the revised Financial Instruments and Exchange Act). Accordingly, when an issuer of the Electronically Recorded Transferable Rights makes a public offering or secondary offering, in principle, the issuer must submit a 'securities registration statement' (Article 4 (1) and Article 5 (1) of the Financial Instruments and Exchange Act) and also prepare a 'prospectus' (Article 13 (1) of the Financial Instruments and Exchange Act).[23] Details on entries to be included in the securities registration statement and the prospectus is expected to be specified by the relevant Cabinet Office Ordinance in the near future.

Also, after the issuer of the Electronically Recorded Transferable Rights has submitted the securities registration statement, the issuer is obliged to submit both annual securities reports and semi-annual securities reports (Article 24 (1) item 3

[21] Masuda et al. (2019), p. 30.

[22] Masuda et al. (2019), p. 31.

[23] Matsuo (2019), p. 10.

and Article 24-5 (1) of the Financial Instruments and Exchange Act). Entries to be included in annual or semi-annual securities reports are expected to be specified by the relevant Cabinet Office Ordinance too.

3.1.3 Regulation on Licensing

Under the revised Financial Instruments and Exchange Act, the Electronically Recorded Transferable Rights constitute the so-called 'Paragraph 1 Securities,' which stand for securities specified by Article 2 (1) of Financial Instruments and Exchange Act (Article 2 (3) of the revised Financial Instruments and Exchange Act). Accordingly, in order to make a sales contract or a public offering on such securities in the course of a business, registration as a Type 1 Financial Instruments Business Operator is compulsory (Article 28 (1) (i) and Article 29 of the revised Financial Instruments and Exchange Act).[24]

3.2 Crypto Asset Derivatives Transactions

3.2.1 Definition

In addition to the purpose of preparing regulations on the Electronically Recorded Transferable Rights, the revisions to the Financial Instruments and Exchange Act also aim at preparing regulations on Crypto Asset Derivative Transactions.[25] Under the Financial Instruments and Exchange Act, 'derivatives transactions' include Market Transactions of Derivatives, Over-the-Counter Transactions of Derivatives, and Foreign Market Derivatives Transactions (Article 2 (20) of the Financial Instruments and Exchange Act).

Under the revised Financial Instruments and Exchange Act, crypto-asset derivatives transactions, in any type of derivatives transactions above, are governed by the revised Act as the revised Act specifies that 'crypto-assets' fall into the scope of 'Financial Instruments' (Article 2 (24) (iii)-2 of the revised Financial Instruments and Exchange Act).[26]

3.2.2 Regulation on Licensing

As mentioned above, crypto-assets constitute Financial Instruments under the revised Financial Instruments and Exchange Act, which results in that acts to make a transaction, intermediary, brokerage, or agency of crypto-asset derivative transactions in

---

[24] Matsuo (2019), p. 10.

[25] Harigai et al. (2019), pp. 38 et seq.

[26] Masuda et al. (2019), p. 28.

the course of a business constitute Financial Instruments Businesses (Article 2 (8) of the Financial Instruments and Exchange Act).[27] Then, as a regulation of licensing, it is stipulated that any 'Financial Instruments Business shall be conducted only by persons registered by the Prime Minister' (Article 29 of the Financial Instruments and Exchange Act). In relation to such registration, Article 29-2 specifies matters to be indicated in the written application for registration, and Article 29-4 specifies cases on the refusal of registration.

4 Revisions to the Act on Sales, etc. of Financial Instruments

4.1 Role of the Act on Sales, etc. of Financial Instruments

The Act on Sales, etc. of Financial Instruments aims 'to protect customers by specifying matters which financial instrument providers, etc. should explain at the time of the sale, etc. of financial instruments and imposing liability on financial instrument providers, etc. for damages where a customer incurs any loss due to the failure of a financial instrument provider, etc. to explain said matters at the time of the sale, etc. of financial instruments, and by establishing measures to ensure the appropriateness of solicitations of sales, etc. of financial instruments by financial instrument providers, etc.' (Article 1 of the Act on Sales, etc. of Financial Instruments). Speaking of cases on crypto-assets exchange services, as any violation of rules in the Payment Services Act does not automatically constitute any civil liability, if there is not such special Act, a user, who makes a claim against the Crypto Asset Exchange Service Provider, needs to bear the burden of proof under the general tort law in Japan (See Article 709 of the Civil Code). Then, with the intention of alleviating such a burden, the revised Act on Sales, etc. of Financial Instruments specifies the rules on accountability that the Crypto Asset Exchange Service Provider shall bear.[28]

According to the 2019 revisions to the Act on Sales, etc. of Financial Instruments, any act making a user acquire crypto-assets, that are prescribed in Article 2 (5) of the Payment Services Act, constitutes a sale of a financial instrument (Article 2 (1) (vi) (c) of the revised Act on Sales, etc. of Financial Instruments). Moreover, agency or intermediary services resulting in the acquisition of crypto-assets are governed by the Act on Sales, etc. of Financial Instruments (Article 2 (2) of the revised Act on Sales, etc. of Financial Instruments).

---

[27] Kawai et al. (2019), p. 15.

[28] Kawai et al. (2019), pp. 21–22.

4.2 Accountability

According to Article 3 of the Act on Sales, etc. of Financial Instruments, 'financial instrument providers,' that includes a person conducting sales of crypto-assets or conducting agency or intermediary service for such sales in the course of business, are obliged to explain to users 'Important Matters' elaborated below. As to what constitutes the 'Important Matters,' Paragraph (1) of this Article specifies as follows (Article 3 (1) of the Act on Sales, etc. of Financial Instruments). Firstly, if there is the risk of loss of principal or the risk of exceeding the initial principal in the relevant sales of financial instruments, because of fluctuations in interest rates, currency values, quotations on a Financial Instruments Market, or any other indicator, (a) the fact that there is such risk, (b) the relevant indicators, and (c) significant parts of the transaction scheme shall be explained as 'Important Matters.' Secondly, if there is the risk of loss of principal or the risk of exceeding the initial principal in relevant sales of financial instruments, because of changes in the situation of the business service or property of the seller of financial instruments or changes in the situation of other person, (a) the fact that there is such risk, (b) the relevant person, (c) significant parts of the transaction scheme shall be explained as 'Important Matters.'

In relation to the accountability rules, the Act requires that explanations of sales of financial instruments shall be provided in the necessary manner and to the necessary extent for facilitating users to understand the explained matters (Article 3 (2) of the Act on Sales, etc. of Financial Instruments). Clarifications of the interpretation of 'necessary manner' or 'necessary extent,' especially in cases on crypto-assets, would be desirable through the accumulation of discussions and judicial precedents.[29]

5 Conclusion

As introduced through this chapter, the recent legislation for making revisions to the Payment Services Act, the Financial Instruments and Exchange Act, and the Act on Sales, etc. of Financial Instruments, aims at developing regulations on crypto-asset businesses in Japan. However, it should be noted that this chapter does not provide an exhaustive enumeration of the Japanese rules on crypto-asset businesses, as the relative rulemaking process is on-going. For instance, the Financial Services Agency held a public comment period for the bill on the relevant Cabinet Office Ordinance in February 2020. Paying attention to the ongoing legislative process, further detailed reviews would be desirable hereafter for a deeper analysis and understanding of Japanese regulations on crypto-assets.

[29] Kawai et al. (2019), p. 23.

References

Aoki S (2019) *Ango-shisan (bitcoin) to kyosei-shikko, tosan* (Court enforcement and bankruptcy in relation to crypto assets (bitcoin)). Kinyu Homu Jijo 2119:18–25

Arai T, Honma A, Masahira H, Noguchi Y, Suehiro K, Komiyama K (2019) *Joho-tsushin-gijutsu no Shinten Ni Tomonau Kinyu-torihiki No Tayoka Ni Taio Surutameno Shikinkessai Ni Kansuru Horitsu To No Ichibu Wo Kaisei Suru Horitsu' No Kaisetsu (3)* (Explanation on the Bill to Revise the Payment Services Act, etc. in Response to Diversification of Financial Transactions Associated with the Development of Information Communication Technology (3)). NBL (New Business Law) 1153:25–31

Arai T, Honma A, Masahira H, Noguchi Y, Suehiro K, Komiyama K (2019b) *Shikinkessai-ho to no kaisei-ho no kaisetsu (ge)* (Explanation on law to revise the Payment Service Act, etc. (2)). Shukan Kinyu Zaisei Jijo 16:32–37

Arai T, Noguchi Y, Honma A, Suehiro K, Masahira H, Komiyama K (2019c) *'Joho-tsushin-gijutsu no shinten ni tomonau kinyu-torihiki no tayoka ni taio surutameno shikinkessai ni kansuru horitsu to no ichibu wo kaisei suru horitsu' no kaisetsu: joho data no ri-katsuyo no syakaiteki na shinten wo fumaeta seido seibi* (Explanation on the bill to revise the Payment Services Act, etc. in response to diversification of financial transactions associated with the development of information communication technology: Development of institutions based on the social progress on application of information data). Kinyu Homu Jijo 2122:43–49

Financial Action Task Force (2014) Virtual currencies: Key definitions and potential AML/CFT risks (June). http://www.fatf-gafi.org/media/fatf/documents/reports/Virtual-currency-key-definitions-and-potential-aml-cft-risks.pdf. Accessed 31 March 2020

Harigai M, Arai E, Kataoka M (2019) *Shikinkessai-ho to no kaisei-ho no kaisetsu (chu)* (Explanation on law to revise Payment Service Act, etc. (2)). Shukan Kinyu Zaisei Jijo 9:38–42

Honda K (2019) *Kaso-tsuka henkan seikyuken no sashiosae wo meguru jitsumu-jo no shomondai* (Practical problems on the seizure of right to claim for return virtual currency). Kinyu Homu Jijo 2111:6–14

Ishizono T, Ohno Y, Takeuchi H, Omote D, Suzuki Y, Yamane A (2019) *'Joho-tsushin-gijutsu no shinten ni tomonau kinyu-torihiki no tayoka ni taio surutameno shikinkessai ni kansuru horitsu to no ichibu wo kaisei suru horitsu' no kaisetsu (1)* (Explanation on the bill to revise the Payment Services Act, etc. in response to diversification of financial transactions associated with the development of information communication technology (1)). NBL (New Business Law) 1150:11–19

Kawai K (2019) *Ango-shisan ni kansuru jitsumu-jo no hoteki kadai* (Legal challenges on practices in relation to crypto assets). Kinyu Homu Jijo 2119:11–17

Kawai K, Miyake A, Aoki S, Tanaka T, Nagase T, Hayashi K (2019) Revisions to Payment Services Act provisions, etc. on crypto assets (Anderson Mori and Tomotsune Financial Services and Transactions Group Newsletter, May 23). https://www.amt-law.com/asset/pdf/bulletins2_pdf/190523.pdf. Accessed 31 March 2020

Komori T, Okada H, Inoue T (2020) *Chikujo-kaisetsu: 2019-nen shikinkessai-ho to kaisei* (Commentary: 2019 revisions to the Payment Services Act, etc). Shoji Homu, Tokyo

Masuda M, Sawai T, Okuda M, Sadamori T, Chujo S (2019) *'Joho-tsushin-gijutsu no shinten ni tomonau kinyu-torihiki no tayoka ni taio surutameno shikinkessai ni kansuru horitsu to no ichibu wo kaisei suru horitsu' no kaisetsu* (Explanation on the bill to revise the Payment Services Act, etc. in response to diversification of financial transactions associated with the development of information communication technology (2)). NBL (New Business Law) 1151:27–34

Matsuo M (2019) *Ango-shisan ni kansuru Shikinkessai-ho, Kinyushohin-torihiki-ho To No Kaisei: 'Joho-tsushin-gijutsu no shinten ni tomonau kinyu-torihiki no tayoka ni taio surutameno shikinkessai ni kansuru horitsu to no ichibu wo kaisei suru horitsu' no gaiyo* (Revisions to the Payment Services Act, the Financial Instruments and Exchange Act, etc.: Summary of the Act to revise the Payment Services Act, etc. in response to diversification of financial transactions associated with the development of information communication technology). Kinyu Homu Jijo 2119:6–10

Research Group on Virtual Currency Exchange Service, etc. (2018) *Kaso-tsuka-kokangyo-to ni kansuru kenkyukai hokokusho* (Report of the research group on virtual currency exchange service, etc) (December 21). https://www.fsa.go.jp/news/30/singi/20181221.html. Accessed 31 March 2020

Suzuki Y, Ochiai T (2019) 2019 Amendments to the Payment Services Act, etc.: new legislation for crypto-assets and more (Atsumi and Sakai Newsletter, March 27). https://www.aplaw.jp/Newsletter_AS_006.pdf. Accessed 31 March 2020

Takeuchi H, Yamane A (2019) *Shikinkessai-ho to no kaisei-ho no kaisetsu (jo)* (Explanation on law to revise the Payment Services Act, etc. (1)). Shukan Kinyu Zaisei Jijo 2:27–31

Watanabe M, Kasai S (2019) *Ango-shisan (kaso-tsuka) wo meguru seido seibi: shikinkessai-ho to kaisei an no gaiyo oyobi syutaru ronten* (Development in legal institutions on crypto-assets (virtual currency): overview and main discussions in the proposal on the revision of the Payment Services Act and so on). Rippo To Chosa 412:26–40

Watanabe M, Matsuzaki T (2020) *Shikinkessai-ho to no kaisei to ango-shisan* (Revisions to the Payment Services Act, etc. and crypto-assets). Ginko-homu-21 64(1):26–31

Horizontal Shareholding Among Fintech Firms in Asia: A Preliminary Competition Law Assessment

Steven Van Uytsel

Abstract This chapter introduces the problem of horizontal shareholding in the fintech sector in Asia. A great deal of the fintech debate surrounds Grab and Go-Jek, two ridesharing platforms that are aggressively expanding their business geographically and product-wise. To finance the expansion, these firms rely on various investors. These investors do often not limit their interest in these two firms but also become shareholders in firms offering the same products. This form of shareholding, also known as horizontal shareholding, is increasingly characterizing the fintech scene in Asia. This triggers the question on how this phenomenon should be approached from a competition law perspective. Horizontal shareholding indeed facilitates the flow of information between competitors or enables control over the executives of competing firms. The issue is still controversial as there is disagreement on the effects of horizontal shareholding and on how competition law should be applied to the issue. However, there is an understanding that further research is warranted. Part of this research, this chapter argues, should not be on direct price increase due to horizontal shareholding. The international character of the horizontal shareholding in the Asian fintech sector requires a rethinking of the possible anticompetitive effects. This chapter claims that such an effect may be market division. Enforcement may be a difficult issue. However, when a merger occurs in this sector, enforcement authorities should pay close attention to the issue of horizontal shareholding.

Keywords Fintech · Competition law · Horizontal shareholding · Price increase · Market division · Asia · Grab · Go-Jek

1 Introduction

South-East Asia is in the spell of fierce competition. Grab and Go-Jek are challenging each other to become the region's super-platform for online services. This rivalry

S. Van Uytsel (✉)
Faculty of Law, Kyushu University, Fukuoka, Japan
e-mail: uytsel@law.kyushu-u.ac.jp

M. Fenwick et al. (eds.), *Regulating FinTech in Asia*, Perspectives in Law, Business and Innovation, https://doi.org/10.1007/978-981-15-5819-1_10

has been reported in various news channels around the world. Fortune, an American business magazine, has headlined the competition as follows: *Grab vs. Go-Jek: Inside Asia's Battle of the 'Super Apps'*.[1] The Financial Times published an article titled *Grab v. Gojek: Inside the Tech Battle for South-East Asia.*[2] Kr-Asia, a digital media company focusing on the most promising technology-driven businesses and trends across the Asia-Pacific region and located in China, has reported the news as *The Many Battlefronts of Grab Versus Gojek in Southeast Asia.*[3]

People familiar with South-East Asia know that Grab and Go-Jek offer services similar to Uber or Lyft. Grab originated in 2012 as a ridesharing service in Malaysia,[4] while Go-Jek developed a motorbike hailing app around 2015 in Indonesia.[5] Without looking into the full history of both companies, both Grab and Go-Jek expanded their countries of operation. Grab moved to Singapore and then expanded its ridesharing business Cambodia, Indonesia, Myanmar, the Philippines, Thailand, and Vietnam.[6] Go-Jek introduced its business model in Vietnam, Singapore, Thailand, and the Philippines.[7] It is evident that, whereas the companies were not competing with each other at the time of the inception, the expansion into South-East Asia made them direct competitors.

Why is this news important for fintech? The answer to this question can be found in the newspaper articles cited above. One of the titles refers to the 'many battlefronts.'[8] Clay Chandler, writing for the Fortune, gave content to what this could mean. He gave his article the subtitle *The rival ride-sharing services are now dueling to deliver everything from groceries to mortgages to Southeast Asia's middle class.*[9] The word 'mortgages' says everything. The two platforms 'have grown well beyond their original range of offerings to cover services including lifestyle, entertainment, and financial needs.'[10]

The competition of Grab and Go-Jek extends beyond the ridesharing economy. It also includes the other sectors they are active in. The question is how long will this competition persist? Various newspapers have recently reported that Grab and Go-Jek have been negotiating a merger. The Nikkei Asian Review mentions that there have been casual discussions.[11] Techcrunch formulates the news of a merger

[1]Chandler and Barret (2019).

[2]Ruehl (2019).

[3]Mulia (2019a).

[4]Available at: https://www.grab.com/sg/brand-story/. Accessed 31 March 2020.

[5]Available at: https://www.gojek.com/about/. Accessed 31 March 2020. Note that Go-Jek was established in 2010. However, at that time, the firm operated as a call-center.

[6]Available at: https://www.grab.com/sg/locations/. Accessed 31 March 2020.

[7]Available at: https://www.gojek.com/about/. Accessed 31 March 2020.

[8]Mulia (2019b).

[9]Chandler and Barret (2018).

[10]Mulia (2019b).

[11]Available at: https://asia.nikkei.com/Business/Startups/Gojek-Grab-merger-makes-sense-but-hurdles-mar-its-path. Accessed 31 March 2020.

as a rumor and equally mentions that both firms are denying any such move.[12] The Financial Times hints that the shareholders of the Softbank Group urge for a merger between the two firms.[13] The Strait Times accounts that Go-Jek denies any talks with Grab to merge.

Whether or not Grab and Go-Jek merge, there Grab and Go-Jek may already be moving in a direction that is diminishing competition. A merger may only aggregate the result of the rising competition law problem. The problem is that, if we look at the shareholding structure of the leading Asian fintech firms, these firms are increasingly controlled by the same shareholders. This issue is called horizontal shareholding.[14] Horizontal shareholding exists when 'the leading shareholders of horizontal competitors overlap.'[15] Even though still contested, Azar, assisted by Martin Schmalz and Isabel Tecu, has signaled that such type of ownership may have anti-competitive effects.[16] It is the aim of this chapter to further contribute to this literature on horizontal shareholding by showing the prevalence of this type of shareholding in the fintech sector. On the one hand, empirical evidence of the horizontal shareholding will be introduced. On the other hand, the possible effects of this horizontal shareholding will be highlighted. A merger may aggregate these effects, but also facilitates enforcement of competition law principles.

This chapter will be structured as follows. In Sect. 2, after providing a short general overview of fintech, this Chapter will introduce how Grab and Go-Jek are challenging fintech in South-East Asia. The way of financing the transformation from a ridesharing platform to a firm also involved in fintech will be highlighted in Sect. 3. The general premise that fintech is being financed by small groups of wealthy investors will be tested in relation to the Asian fintech oriented ridesharing firms. As this exercise will indicate that there is horizontal shareholding, Sect. 4 will elaborate on the insights how horizontal shareholding could impact competition law. Before concluding in Sect. 6, the findings of Sects. 3 and 4 will be combined in Sect. 5. Section 5 will elucidate the possible effects of the horizontal shareholding among several of the main Asian fintech firms.

---

[12] Available at: https://techcrunch.com/2020/02/25/grab-and-gojek-began-discussing-a-potential-merger-more-than-three-months-ago/. Accessed 31 March 2020.

[13] Available at: https://www.ft.com/content/075162ba-5dff-11ea-b0ab-339c2307bcd4. Accessed 31 March 2020.

[14] This phenomenon is called horizontal shareholding. Horizontal shareholding will be the term used in this Chapter. However, the literature uses different terminology to refer to a situation in which the leading shareholders of horizontal competing firms overlap. Some literature uses the terminology of common ownership. See Azar (2019); Azar et al. (2018); Patel (2018). Other literature mentions mutual fund holding. See Solomon (2016). Still other literature refers to the issue as common shareholding. See Campell (2018). Interlocking shareholding is frequently used by Ittai Paldor. Paldor (2019), p. 6. Elhauge points out that not all uses are interchangeable. Hence, some papers cover broader relations than only horizontal shareholding.

[15] Elhauge (2018).

[16] Azar et al. (2018).

2 Fintech in South-East Asia, Driven by Ridesharing Platforms

2.1 Fintech, Fintech Products and Fintech Firms

Fintech is 'the delivery of financial products and services via the marriage of technological platforms and innovative business models.'[17] The products and services can be of various kinds. Fintech products and services can 'be broken down into those offering credit, processing payments, giving advice, managing assets, issuing currencies, and helping with legal compliance.'[18] To be a fintech firm, it is not required that all these products and services are offered as a combined package. It is even possible that the fintech firm does not hold any money from consumers. Advisory fintech firms, for example, provide recommendations to consumers based upon financial information provided by the same consumer.[19]

Fintech products and services can also be distinguished based on the institution offering them. Traditional financial institutions—institutions that have obtained a bank, insurer, broker, or a similar license—are known for pursuing a digitalization track. Any traditional financial institution can offer the possibility to execute payments or, within certain limits, obtain loans online. Interdisciplinary teams of data scientists and computer engineers are offering new technologies to their respective traditional financial institutions.[20] Fintech are also developed by start-ups. These firms are offering a novel business idea. One of the earliest, and novel, business ideas that has been put into practice is, according to Rory Van Loo, peer-to-peer lending.[21] This business format links 'individuals who have money to those who want it.'[22] These start-ups will, if successful, grow and potentially adjust their fintech products and services to the needs and opportunities of the market. Technology firms, such as Google and Facebook, or retail companies, such as Amazon or Rakuten, can move

---

[17] Buckely and Webster (2016), p. 5.

[18] Van Loo (2018), p. 238. Different studies refer to different classifications of FinTech services. In a European study, a reference is made to a study of IOSCO, Price Waterhouse Coopers, and Ernst and Young. The International Organization of Securities Commissions (IOSCO) categorizes payments, lending and crowdfunding, planning, trading and investment, insurance, data and analytics, blockchain, and security. PricewaterhouseCoopers has less categories and divides FinTech into transaction and payments systems, banking, investment and wealth management, and insurance. Ernst and Young uses the following typology: money transfer and payments, borrowing, borrowing, financial planning, saving and investments, and insurance. To conclude, the European Study classifies FinTech products and services into (1) banking (deposits and lending and equity), (2) payments, transfers, and forex, (3) digital currencies, (4) wealth and asset management, (5) personal financial management, (6) InsurTech, and (7) enabling technologies and infrastructure. See Fraile Carmona et al. (2018), pp. 21–22.

[19] Van Loo (2018), pp. 239–340.

[20] Van Loo (2018), pp. 239.

[21] Van Loo (2018), p. 239.

[22] Van Loo (2018), p. 239.

into financial services. [23] Advanced start-ups with mixed ownership,[24] such a Grab and Go-Jek, could also be firms that start to offer financial services.

2.2 *Grab and Go-Jek Challenging Fintech in South-East Asia*

The initial steps towards fintech of Grab and Go-Jek was the development of payment apps. Grab developed GrabPay in January 2016. Go-Jek launched its online payment system, Go-Pay, in 2018. Both of these payment systems were internally developed. However, the ambition of these ride-hailing platforms was unstoppable. To expand their fintech business, both platforms evolved towards acquisitions and partnering with other firms.

The roll-out of Grab's financial unit took off when Grab entered into a joint venture with the Japanese firm Credit Saison to offer credit to the 'unbanked' in South-East Asia. A partnership with Malaysia's Maybank allowed Grab to launch GrabPay. Strategic partnerships with mobile wallets apps in other Asian countries, allowed Grab to offer GrabPay in Indonesia and Vietnam.[25] Grab has recently decided to bring all its financial services together in a separate entity, called Grab Financial.[26] Grab Financial now offers payment services, lending services, and insurance services.

A similar evolution can be witnessed with Go-Jek. To guarantee Go-Jek's omnipresence in Indonesia, bought local fintech firms like Kartuku (a leaning offline payment processing firm), Midtrans (Indonesia's top online payment gateway), and Mapan (a community bases savings and lending network).[27] The overseas expansion was made possible with a similar business strategy. Through acquiring Coins.ph, an online payment wallet in the Philippines, Go-Jek has secured its presence in the Philippines.[28] Through partnerships with Boku Inc., Go-Jek made GoPay available to the Indonesian merchants connected to the Boku Inc.'s network. To enable the provision of loans to its Go-Jek drivers, strategic partnerships with peer-to-peer lending platforms, Findaya, Dana Cita, and Aktivaku.[29] After receiving an investment of Allianz X, the digital investment arm of the German insurance firm Allianz, Go-Jek was able to offer insurance protection to its customers. Just like Grab, Go-Jek has announced it will bring its financial arm into an independent entity, called Digital Katalis or Dkatalis for short.[30]

[23] Van Loo (2018), p. 239.

[24] Nicoletti (2017), p. 47.

[25] Zhang (2019).

[26] Zhang (2019).

[27] Balea (2017).

[28] Russel (2019).

[29] Ellis (2018).

[30] Mulia (2019b).

2.3 The Fintech Turn of Other Ridesharing Platforms Active in Asia

The turn to fintech by Grab and Go-Jek has been described as a masterstroke. A business plan purely based on ride-hailing has been proven unprofitable. Uber has been around for a decade in 2018, and it was still in the red. The unprofitability of Uber has affected its initial public offering. Uber was only able to raise a bit more than half of what it was expecting: 76 billion dollars instead of 120 billion dollars. 'Could fintech save Go-Jek and Grab from Uber's fate?' has been a question raised by Kapronasia, a leading financial technology market research and consulting firm.[31] The answer is given by Go-Jek chief executive officer Naidem Makarim. 'The most powerful asset of Go-Jek [is] that we don't need four-wheel ride-hailing to be profitable,' and he continued that '[p]ayments and food delivery account for a much larger share of the company's gross merchandise value than ride-hailing's 25%.'

The continuous struggle of Uber to reach profitability, made the firm shift its strategy also to fintech. The firm announced in October 2019 that it would push, with Uber Money, into financial services. Yet, unlike Grab and Go-Jek, Uber Money's business model is 'providing a wide range of services to a relatively narrow segment of consumers—first to its drivers and then to other gig economy workers.'[32]

Didi Chuxing, a Chinese ride-sharing firm is deploying a similar strategy. After announcing that it would start reorganizing in December 2018, Didi Chuxing 'rolled out of a suite of financial and insurance services in its mobile app for its drivers and users. The services include health insurance, car insurance, credit and lending, wealth management, and auto-financing options. The offerings have been integrated within Didi's app, but they can also be accessed via a separate app, called Didi Finance.'[33] The step towards fintech seems also be inspired by losses accumulated by just offering a ride-hailing app.

Ola, the Indian ride-sharing firm, entered fintech already in 2015 under the brand name of Ola Money. Ola Money is offering, amongst other services, short-term credit, mobile wallet, and insurance. ANI Technologies, the parent company of Ola, has transferred its financial services business Ola Money into a separate entity: Ola Financial Services.[34] Over a period of 4 years, Ola, with Ola Money, has been able to place itself in the Fintech 100—Top 10, as composed by KPMG in 2019.[35]

---

[31] Fulco (2019).

[32] Shevlin (2019).

[33] Singh (2019).

[34] Ganguly (2019).

[35] Available at: https://home.kpmg/xx/en/home/insights/2019/11/2019-fintech100-leading-global-fintech-innovators-fs.html. Accessed 31 March 2020.

3 Financing Fintech in Asia

3.1 Small Groups of Wealthy Investors

In his paper, *Making Innovation More Competitive: The Case of Fintech*, Van Loo indicates that fintech start-ups are heavily funded by a 'small group of wealthy investors—often individuals, but also venture capitalists, private equity firms, and hedge funds.'[36] Mark Fenwick, Joseph A. McCahery and Erik E. P. Vermeulen show in their paper, *Fintech and the Financing of Entrepreneurs: From Crowdfunding to Marketplace Lending*, that the surge of investments of venture capitalists in fintech firms started around 2010.[37] Further research reveals that the tendency has continued. After a dip in investment in 2016, the amount invested in fintech doubled in 2018 compared to 2017.[38] Additionally, financial institutions have taken a stake in the fintech firms. John L. Douglas and Reuben Grinberg, summarizing a set of newspaper articles and KPMG reports, account that 'banking organizations alone have invested $7 billion in fintech start-ups over the past seven years, and in 2015, 35% of investments in fintech were in collaborative technologies for financial institutions.'[39] JP Morgan Chase, in 2016 the largest bank in assets, had even invested in fintech start-ups providing competing products.[40]

The example of JP Morgan Chase is not an exception. Shifting to Europe, where 20% of all venture capital is being invested in fintech between 2017 and 2019 and so surpassing any other sector, we can observe that several investments are made by the same investor in firms offering competing products. In a report by Finch Capital and dealroom.co,[41] it is reported that Seedcamp has, since 2013, invested in 31 fintech start-up firms offering banking and payment services. In 2019, Seedcamp still held investments in 43 fintech firms, which it qualifies under the term fintech on its website.[42] Moving to fintech firms that have called for Series A/B funding,[43] a similar evolution is noticeable. Finch Capital, since 2013, has invested in 18 fintech firms active in the area of banking and payment services.[44] In 2019, Finch Capital still has 14 investments in firms with competing products.[45] Among the investors providing funding at a late stage, Goldman Sachs is related to six banking and

[36]Van Loo (2018), p. 246.

[37]Fenwick, McCahery and Vermeulen (2017), p. 8.

[38]Trulioo (2019); Blackman (2019).

[39]Douglas and Grinsberg (2016–2017), p. 671.

[40]Van Loo (2018), p. 246.

[41]Finch Capital and dealroom.co (2019), p. 9.

[42]Seedcamp (2020).

[43]Series A, Series B, and Series C funding rounds occur when the start-ups are moving towards outside investment.

[44]Finch Capital and dealroom.co (2019), p. 10.

[45]Finch Capital (2020).

payment fintech firms since 2013.[46] Goldman Sachs' website does not allow for giving updated information. The given examples are just a small selection. Finch Capital and dealroom.com's report, for instance, mentions ten investors at the seed funding stage and the stage of Series A/B funding that all hold investments in more than one competitor in the banking and payment services sector.[47] In addition to the banking and payment services sector, this phenomenon is also detectable in Insurtech and Proptech. However, the number of competing firms receiving investments from the same venture capitalists is lower.[48]

The flocking together of several wealthy investors has also occurred in relation to Grab and Go-Jek. The more capital is required for the expansion of these platforms, the more investors have joined an initial small group of investors.

3.2 *The Investment Structure Behind Grab and Go-Jek*

Grab and Go-Jek have been able to grow so much so they could attain the status of a unicorn, a start-up firm valued at above 1 billion US dollars. To achieve this position, but also to finance the expansion to other sectors, both Grab and Go-Jek have attracted quite a number of strategic and financial investors. Unraveling the investor structure of the Grab and Go-Jek teaches us that both unicorns have different investors.

The three main shareholders of Grab are Softbank, Uber, and Didi Chuxing.[49] Other important investors in Grab are SK Holdings, Tiger Global Management Fund, and GGV Capital. Car and motorbike manufacturers, such as Honda, Toyota, Kia, Hyundai, and Yamaha, are relatively new investors in Grab.[50] Toyota made the investment after its trading firm, Toyota Tsusho Corp., had already done so in 2017.[51] Booking Holdings is another recent investor.[52] So is the investment of the technology multinational, Microsoft.[53]

Initial investors in Go-Jek were Sequoia, Northstar, and Warburg Pincus.[54] Among the current strong holders, and thus major investors in Go-Jek, are Tencent Holdings,

[46]Finch Capital and dealroom.co (2019), p. 11.

[47]Finch Capital and dealroom.co (2019), pp. 9–10.

[48]Finch Capital and dealroom.co (2019), pp. 9–10.

[49]Available at: https://thelowdown.momentum.asia/who-are-the-investors-behind-grab/. Accessed 31 March 2020.

[50]Available at: https://thelowdown.momentum.asia/who-are-the-investors-behind-grab/. Accessed 31 March 2020.

[51]Available at: https://thelowdown.momentum.asia/who-are-the-investors-behind-grab/. Accessed 31 March 2020.

[52]Available at: https://thelowdown.momentum.asia/who-are-the-investors-behind-grab/. Accessed 31 March 2020.

[53]Available at: https://thelowdown.momentum.asia/who-are-the-investors-behind-grab/. Accessed 31 March 2020.

[54]Ruehl (2019)

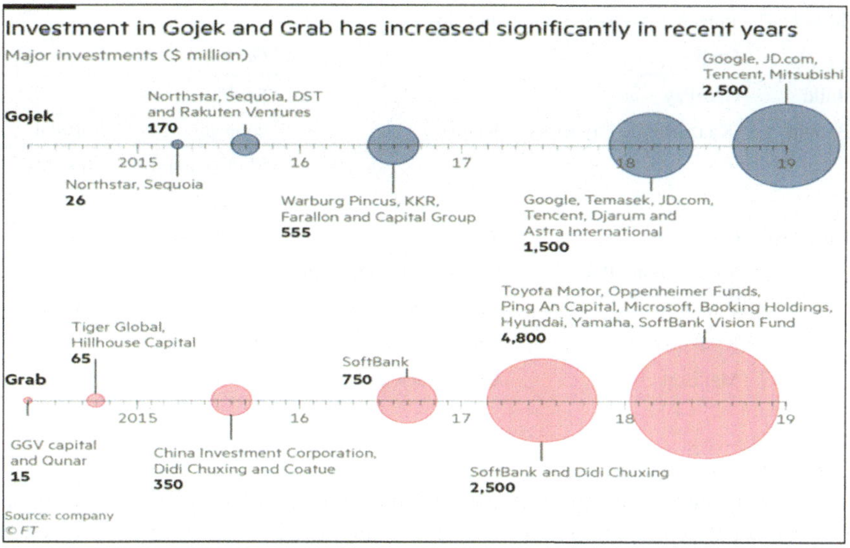

Fig. 1 Investments in Grab and Go-Jek (Available at: https://www.ft.com/content/04e0523c-2256-11ea-b8a1-584213ee7b2b. Accessed 31 March 2020)

JD.com, and Temasek Holdings.[55] The car and motorbike related investors in Go-Jek are Mitsubishi and Astra International.[56] Google is the technology multinational investing in Go-Jek.[57]

Presented on a timeline, Fig. 1 shows when the above-mentioned investors took a stake in Grab and Go-Jek respectively.

At present, Grab and Go-Jek have no overlapping shareholders. However, this is not the case for all ridesharing platforms in Asia.

3.3 Investment Clusters Among the Fintech Oriented Ridesharing Firms in Asia

Tiger Global Management ignored an unwritten rule of venture capital in 2015. During that year, Tiger Global Management made an investment in Uber, while one year earlier it had made an investment in Grab, Uber's competitor. It sparked fierce reactions. In a blog managed by Momentum Works, a firm consulting on venture financing, reported that 'it's understood that investors cannot back its competitors

[55] Ruehl (2019)
[56] Ruehl (2019)
[57] Ruehl (2019)

Table 1 The fintech ecosystem of Grab and Go-Jek

	Grab		Go-Jek	
Build	GrabPay		Go-Pay	
Bought	iKaaz Mobile Payments	Kudo	coins.ph	Kartuku
			MVCommerce	Midtrans
			Mapan	
Partnered	Ovo	ZA Tech	PasarPolis	Dana Cita
	Moca Mobile Payments	Income made Different		
	Citi	Mastercard	Findaya	Aktivaku
	Kasikornbank	Chubb	Boku	
	Maybank	Credit Saison		

(Table 1).'[58] Another investor commented that '[w]hilst it's ok to invest in a few similar companies on the public market, it's different on the private market. Companies share confidential metrics and financial numbers with its investors–and this will tarnish their brand and trustworthiness.'[59]

What Momentum Works highlights, especially in the last statement, relates to the problem of horizontal shareholding. The question now is, considering that all the other ridesharing firms have set up fintech services, whether the presence of horizontal shareholding has diminished?

Table 2 provides a comparison of some of the main shareholders of the different ridesharing platforms in Asia. A short list of top investors into the respective ridesharing platforms has been chosen. Investments made by car manufacturers and cross-shareholding by other ridesharing platforms have not been taken into consideration. it should be noted that Softbank Vision Fund is owned by the Softbank Group. The same applies to Softbank Capital, which is acquired by Foxconn Technologies. Alibaba Group Holdings and Softbank Group have an asterisk behind their name to indicate that the latter is a shareholder of the former.

Based on a short list of investors, it is possible to state that each of these firms have shareholders that are also supporting competitors. This is especially observable if we visualize the shareholding structure with arrows. In Fig. 2, arrows are drawn from the different investors to the firms in which they hold shares. There is no direct connection between Grab and Go-Jek in terms of shareholding. Go-Jek is, through a common shareholder, connected with Ola, while Grab has shareholders in common with Uber and Didi Chuxing. Shareholding in Didi Chuxing seems to bring the shareholder structure around Go-Jek and Ola in contact with the shareholders around Grab and Uber.

[58] Available at: https://thelowdown.momentum.asia/who-are-the-investors-behind-grab/. Accessed 31 March 2020

[59] Available at: https://thelowdown.momentum.asia/who-are-the-investors-behind-grab/. Accessed 31 March 2020.

Table 2 The main investors in the main Fintech oriented ridesharing platforms operating in Asia

Grab	Go-Jek	Uber	Didi Chuxing	Ola
GGV Capital	Tencent Holdings	Softbank Vision Fund	Temasek Holdings	Tencent Holdings
Tiger Global Management Fund	KKR	Tiger Global Management Fund	Tencent Holdings	Tiger Global Management Fund
Vertex Ventures	Aphabet (Google)	Travis Kalanickt	Softbank Group*	Sequoia Capital India
Softbank Capital	JD.com	Garrett Camp	Foxconn Technologies	Softbank Capital
Softbank Group*	Temasek Holdings	Saudi Arabia PIF	Softbank Capital	Temasek Holdings
China Investment Corporation	Warburg Pincus	Aphabet (Google)	Alibaba Group Holdings*	
Microsoft		China Life Insurance	GGV Capital	
		Benchmark Capital	China Investment Corporations	
			China Life Insurance	

Available at: https://www.cbinsights.com/. Accessed 31 March 2020

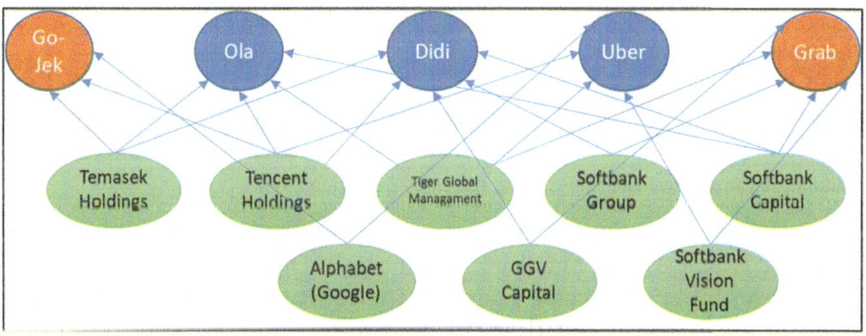

Fig. 2 Visualization of Horizontal Shareholding in Ridesharing Platforms Active in Asia

3.4 *Horizontal Shareholding Across the Main Asian Fintech Firms* Pur Sang

Fintech offering ridesharing firms are only one aspect of the fintech sector in Asia. More and more firms are developing fintech services. If we look at KPMG Fintech 100 list, the 2019 top ten of fintech firms is mainly composed of Asian firms. Besides Grab and Go-Jek, which respectively hold the second and fourth position in the top 10

Table 3 The Main Asian Fintech Firms *Pur Sang*

Ant Financial	JD Digits	Paytm	Policy Bazaar	MoMo
China	China	India	India	Vietnam
KPMG No. 1	KPMG No. 3	KPMG No. 5	KPMG No. 21	KPMG No. 36
Alibaba Holdings Group	JD.com	Alibaba Holdings Group	Tencent Holdings	Warburg Pincus
China Post Capital	Sequoia Capital China	Ant Financials	Tiger Global Management Fund	Goldman Sachs Investment Partners
General Atlantic	China Creation Ventures	Berkshire Hathaway	Wellington Management	Standard Chartered Bank
Sequoia Capital China	China Harvest Investments	Softbank Group	Softbank Vision Fund	
Temasek Holdings	China Taiping Insurance Holdings	Softbank Vision Fund		
China Life Insurance	China International Investment Corporation			
The Carlyle Group	BOCGI			
Warburg Pincus	CITIC Capital			
China Development Bank Capital				
China Investment Corporation				

Available at: https://www.cbinsights.com/. Accessed 31 March 2020

list, the list is composed of Ant Financial (China), JD Digits (China), Paytm (India), Du Xiaoman Financial (China), Compass (United States), Ola (India), Opendoor (United States), and OakNorth (United Kingdom).[60]

Grab, Go-Jek and Ola are all listed in the top 10 of KPMG's 2019 Top 100 Fintech listing.[61] The shareholding structure of these firms has been provided in Table 2 and Fig. 2. If we compose a new table, Table 3, with the two highest listed Chinese fintech firms, the two highest listed Indian fintech firms and the highest listed Vietnamese fintech firm, a rough comparison can be made on which shareholders are shared with Grab, Go-Jek and Ola. Table 3 provides information on the name of these firms, the

[60] Available at: https://h2.vc/wp-content/uploads/2020/02/2019Fintech100.pdf. Accessed 31 March 2020.

[61] Available at: https://h2.vc/wp-content/uploads/2020/02/2019Fintech100.pdf. Accessed 31 March 2020.

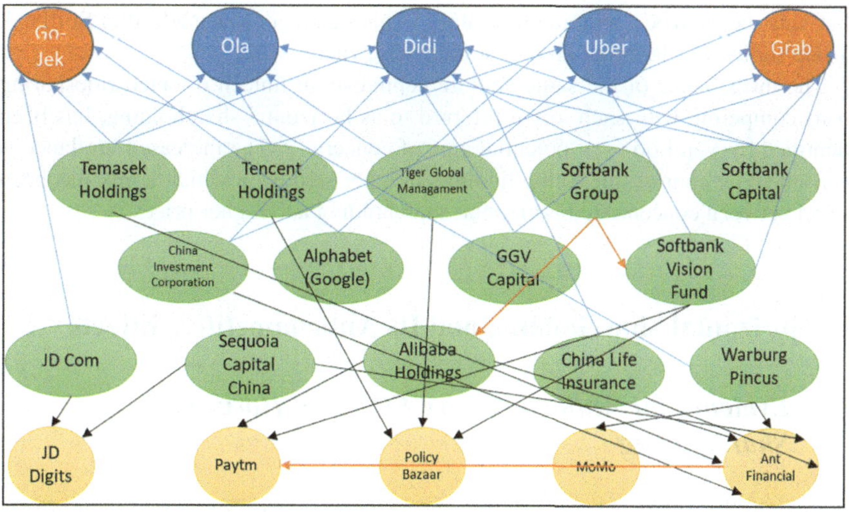

Fig. 3 A simplified shareholding structure of the Main Asian Fintech Firms and Fintech Oriented Ridesharing Firms

country in which the headquarter is located, the ranking within the KMPG 2019 Top 100 Fintech listing, and some of their respective shareholders.

The shareholding of the fintech firms is slightly different than the one of the ridesharing firms that have turned to fintech. This can be explained by the presence of two Chinese firms in the list. These Chinese firms have been able to attract funding from various other Chinese firms that are not investing abroad. Only Alibaba Holdings Group has also invested in the Indian fintech firm Paytm. The Softbank Group, its investment vehicle, Softbank Vision Fund, and Warburg Pincus also invest across the different Asian fintech firms. However, it is noticeable that there is less horizontal shareholding across the discussed fintech firms. Figure 3 visualizes the shareholding structure between the ridesharing platforms that are also active as fintech firms and some of the main fintech firms in Asia.

If there are conclusions to be drawn from Fig. 3, two statements can be made. First, the apparent division in the shareholding structure of Grab and Go-Jek seems to further dampen when bringing in other firms that are active in the fintech sector. Temasek Holdings and Tencent Holdings link with Softbank Group in Didi Chuxing. Indirectly, the same happens in Policy Bazaar and Ant Financial. Through their shareholding in these firms, Softbank Group is linked with Tencent Holdings and Temasek Holdings, respectively. Second, Tiger Global Management Fund has been a maverick by directly investing in competing fintech firms. Whereas this has attracted some negative statements about the firm crossing the line, now statements are made that 'this seems to be a winning formula.'[62] This statement was made after Softbank Group started to adopt that kind of strategy elsewhere.

The investments of the same venture capitalists in fintech oriented ridesharing firms competing with each, often referred to as horizontal shareholding, has been identified by Van Loo as a 'potential area of concern.'[63] The increased vigilance is warranted, he claims, due to the findings in other studies in which a link has been found between concentrated horizontal shareholding and higher prices.[64]

4 Horizontal Shareholding and Its Anticompetitive Effects

4.1 Evidence for Anticompetitive Effects of Horizontal Shareholding

Van Loo discusses the potential anticompetitive effects of horizontal shareholding in the Fintech sector that under the section of 'anticompetitive prices'.[65] Leaving aside for a moment whether an anticompetitive price could be a consequence of horizontal shareholding, a crucial part of the debate centers on the whether the shareholders could at all create an anticompetitive effect. The reason? The studies originating the debate envisioned a particular form of shareholding.[66] First, the shareholding is horizontal, meaning that the investors invest in firms offering competing products.[67] Second, the horizontal shareholding is, in principle, floating around 5%.[68] Third, the

---

[62] Available at: https://thelowdown.momentum.asia/who-are-the-investors-behind-grab/. 31 March 2020.

[63] Van Loo (2018), p. 247.

[64] Van Loo (2018), p. 247. It should be noted that Rory Van Loo admits that it is too early to draw definite conclusions on whether such a harm is present in the FinTech sector. Seen the fact that such shareholding could provide 'crucial funding, economies of scale, and geographic reach to new products,' Van Loo opines that, for the moment at least, an opposite conclusion is more likely. Van Loo (2018), p.247.

[65] Van Loo (2018), p. 246.

[66] José Azar, a Spanish economist, has shown in 2012 that, over a period of ten years, institutional investors have increased their ownership in companies that are horizontally competing with each other. His Ph.D. study, *A New Look at Oligopoly: Implicit Collusion Through Portfolio Diversification* (See Azar (2012)), indicated that such horizontal shareholding of publicly traded companies, which exists when 'the leading shareholders of horizontal competitors overlap,' has more than doubled. See Elhauge (2018); Azar (2012), p. 50. In a paper preceding the publication of the doctoral thesis, Azar gives a concrete number. He mentions that the network density rose from 4% to 14%. Azar (2011), p. 3. The benchmark Azar used for considering companies to be connected by horizontal shareholding was that institutional investors owned 5% in each respective company. See Azar (2012), p. 50. In a paper preceding the publication of the doctoral thesis, Azar gives a concrete number. He mentions that the network density rose from 4% to 14%. Azar (2011), p. 3.

[67] Elhauge (2018); Azar (2012), p. 50.

[68] Azar (2011), p. 3.

minority horizontal shareholding is held in a concentrated market.[69] These premises were proposed by José Azar.

Azar, observing that institutional investors progressively increased their shareholding over the first ten years of the 21st century, planned to provide extend the theoretical insights developed by Daniel P. O'Brien and Steven C. Salop on the *Competitive Effects of Partial Ownership*[70] in relation to cross-shareholding to horizontal shareholding.[71] Building on the insight that a merger, thus the acquisition of all shares, would likely be anticompetitive when it causes an increase of the Herfindahl-Hirschman Index (HHI) above a certain number (200 in the case of the United States),[72] O'Brien and Salop developed a theory that a slight modification to the HHI should also enable a prediction on the anticompetitive effects of only partial share acquisition. The context in which O'Brien and Salop operate, however, is one of cross-ownership, a situation in which competitors own shares in each other, and joint ventures. In this situation, it is likely that 'the interlocking shareholdings diminish each individual firm's incentives to cut prices or expand output by increasing the costs of taking away sales from rivals'[73] if there exists high 'profit or influence interest between the firms.'[74] Azar's contributed to this literature by theoretically extending these findings to horizontal shareholding.

The next step was to provide empirical evidence for Azar's theoretical holding. Together with his colleagues Martin Schmalz and Isabel Tecu, Azar studied the airline industry in the United States (US).[75] The purpose of that study was to calculate the HHI, the modified HHI, and then the difference between these two. Any of these calculations led them to the conclusion that an outcome would be achieved that is much higher than what the US considers as problematic in the case of mergers. The validity of the application of the modified HHI to horizontal shareholding in the airline industry was double-checked by statistically proving that the price of the airline tickets where higher on routes where airlines operated that were connected to each other through horizontal shareholding.[76] On average, the conclusion was, the prices were 3 to 5% higher on routes with horizontal shareholding.

---

69 Azar (2011).

70 It should be noted that the study on the *Competitive Effects of Partial Ownership* was preceded by another study *Quantifying the Competitive Effects of Production Joint Ventures*, which was conducted by Timothy Bresnahan and Steven Salop. They investigated the impact of a joint venture on the competitive price setting. Bresnahan and Salop (1986).

71 O'Brian and Salop (2000).

72 The Herfindahl-Hirschman Index is measured based upon squaring the market share of each firm competing in a market and then summing the resulting numbers. See https://www.justice.gov/atr/herfindahl-hirschman-index. Accessed 31 March 2020.

73 Elhauge (2018), p. 1274.

74 Elhauge (2018), p. 1274.

75 Azar et al. (2018).

76 United States' airline industry, for which it is held that 'seven shareholders who controlled 60.0% of United Airlines also controlled big chunks of United's major rivals, including 27.5% of Delta Airlines, 27.3% of JetBlue Airlines, and 23.3% of Southwest Airlines.' Elhauge (2018), p. 1267.

The theory and the empirical evidence of Azar et al. have been challenged.[77] Part of the critique focuses on whether the portfolio managers, as representatives from the institutional investors, could influence the managers of the firms in which they have invested. It is held that only through explicit communications organized by the institutional investor that the competitive process could be disturbed. Any other pressure, for example, negative voting on management compensation or steering corporate strategy through shareholder voting, is considered unlikely to occur. [78] Another part of the critique questions the methodology. The HHI and the modified HHI as a method for predicting anticompetitive effects leaves too much room for interpretation. To make this statement valid, reference is made to another study using a different method and coming to the conclusion that there is no anti-competitive effect in the airlines sector.[79] Still another critique is the choice of the airline industry in the US There were too many changes in the industry during the time frame covering the period in which Azar et al. collected their data for the empirical test. These changes, among which the mergers between several of the US airlines resulting in, for example, better quality, could also explain the increase in price on various routes.[80]

Recognizing that there is valid criticism towards the theory developed by Azar et al.,[81] Harvard Law School professor, Einer Elhauge has sought to substantiate the existing scholarship. While holding that the existing scholarship's assumption that 'shareholders' influence turns on their shares of stock relative to other shareholders'[82] is intuitive and not resting on economic proof, Elhauge posits that executive compensation and shareholder voting can actually show that the horizontal investors influence the firms in which they take a share. For each of these two elements, Elhauge sees a shift compared to the period before institutional investors were significant shareholders across various firms.[83] Therefore, Elhauge opines that influence by the institutional investors on the policy followed by the firms in which they invest is not as imaginable as is held by more critical studies towards the issue of horizontal shareholding.[84] For executive compensation, Elhauge observes that:

---

[77] Scholars proposing to be careful with competition law enforcement against horizontal shareholding often laud the scholars that have introduced the debate. Thomas A. Lambert and Michael E. Sykuta have been very explicit on this by asserting that '[t]he authors of the common ownership studies have helpfully drawn attention to a potential competitive problem that merits further study. The antitrust scholars who have proposed policy solutions to that purported problem have also made a valuable contribution by showing how existing law might be used to address anticompetitive harms from investors' common ownership of small stakes in competing firms, should such harms prove grave enough to warrant additional antitrust intervention.' See Lambert and Sykuta (2018), p. 55. Other criticism has been formulated by Rock and Rubinfeld (2017); Patel (2018); Ginsburg (2018); Paldor (2019).

[78] Hemphill and Kahan (2019).

[79] Patel (2018), pp. 53-56.

[80] Rock and Rubinfeld (2017), p. 21.

[81] The MHHI does not inform us what other impact of ownership could be expected or what the influence of communication may be.

[82] Elhauge (2018), p. 11.

[83] Elhauge (2018).

[84] Elhauge (2018), pp12-13.

> (1) in less competitive markets, executive compensation was based more on industry performance and less on firm performance; (2) executive compensation had become increasingly based on market performance since the 1990s, which coincides with a dramatic rise in horizontal shareholding; and (3) large institutional investors voted against proposals to make executive compensation based more on individual corporate performance.[85]

The shift that has occurred in shareholder is described by Elhauge as follows:

> (1) before the 1990s explosion in horizontal shareholding, managers were ousted based on individual corporate performance, with industry performance filtered out; (2) since the 1990s explosion in horizontal shareholding, decisions to oust managers have been driven almost as much by industry performance as by individual corporate performance; (3) the influence of industry performance on ouster decisions does not vary with the length of executive tenure or degree of executive power; and (4) 53% of institutional investors admitted in a survey that they tried to influence managers by voting against them.[86]

Despite the contradicting academic debate, the enforcement and policy advisory authorities have not been idle on the issue. The US enforcement authorities have organized a hearing investigating whether their enforcement policy should shift to include enforcement against horizontal shareholding. Several observations were made. First, the US enforcement authorities expressed that they are aware horizontal shareholding is characterizing our contemporary economy. Second, they acknowledged that the research on the impact of this horizontal shareholding on the economy is still in an embryonic phase. This kind of message has been clearly stated in the US Statement to the Organization for Economic Cooperation and Development. The US Statement to the OECD contained the following message: '[g]iven the ongoing academic and research debate, and its early stage of development, the US antitrust agencies are not prepared at this time to make any changes to their policies or practices with respect to common ownership by institutional investors.'[87] This stance has been confirmed by several people attached to the various US enforcement agencies, be it the Federal Trade Commission (FTC) or the Department of Justice. FTC Commissioner Noah Phillips, for example, has indicated that 'the empirics remain unsettled'[88] and that he believes that horizontal shareholding does 'not appear to be at the apex of a massive antitrust conspiracy.'[89] Following these statements, there has been a hearing at the FTC on the issue. Besides a confirmation that horizontal shareholding characterizes our economy, the conclusion was still that much more research would be required to make a policy shift.

The German Monopolies Commission, an independent commission to advise the German government and legislator on competition-related issues, has published a report on minority shareholding by institutional investors.[90] This Commission stressed in the report that 'it would be welcome if indirect minority shareholdings

---

[85] Elhauge (2017), p. 3.

[86] Elhauge (2017), p. 4.

[87] OECD (2017), par. 15.

[88] Phillips (2018), p.6.

[89] Phillips (2018), p.5.

[90] Monopolies Commission (2016).

through institutional investors received more attention on the European level, not least in the framework of a possible further development of the European Merger Control Regulation. Nevertheless, the Monopolies Commission sees a further need for clarification in the sense of economic-policy recommendations.'[91]

Despite the disagreement in the literature and the cautious wording of other enforcement and policy-setting agencies, the European Union has made reference to the phenomenon in two enforcement actions: Dow/DuPont[92] and Bayer/Monsanto.[93]

4.2 Despite Disagreement in the Literature, Initial Enforcement Action in Europe

The former European Commissioner for Competition, Margrethe Vestager, after admitting that 'it's becoming more common for the same investors to hold shares in different companies in the same industry,'[94] has explicitly acknowledged that the horizontal shareholding could lead to a situation in which 'it can be better if those companies don't compete too hard.'[95] Therefore, it is required for the European Commission to follow the issue of horizontal shareholding with close attention. In doing so, the European Commission is building on the position it has taken in the merger of Dow/DuPont[96] and Bayer/Monsanto.[97]

In these merger decisions, the European Commission made several observations regarding the horizontal shareholding. First, all firms involved had a high degree of horizontal shareholding. The European Commission detected that there are '106 shareholders common to BASF, Bayer, DowDuPont, and Monsanto…which collectively account for a significant equity share in each of the four firms: 23.09% for BASF, 28.04% for Bayer, 40.83% for DowDuPont and 35.25% for Monsanto. Importantly, 18 common shareholders are enough to reach, collectively, between 18% and 34% shares in all of these firms, and in particular 34.81% of DowDuPont and 29.28% of Monsanto.'[98]

Second, the European Commission referred to anecdotal evidence to indicate that the horizontal shareholders are actively involved in the strategy setting of the firms

[91] Monopolies Commission (2016), p.13

[92] Case M.7932 – Dow/DuPont, Commission Decision of 27 March 2017, available at: https://ec.europa.eu/competition/mergers/cases/decisions/m7932_13668_3.pdf. Accessed 31 March 2020.

[93] Case M.8084 – Bayer/Monsanto, Commission Decision of 21 March 2018, available at: https://ec.europa.eu/competition/mergers/cases/decisions/m8084_13335_3.pdf. Accessed 31 March 2020.

[94] Vestager (2018). Also quoted by Bostoen (2020).

[95] Vestager (2018). Also quoted by Bostoen (2020).

[96] Available at: https://ec.europa.eu/competition/mergers/cases/decisions/m7932_13668_3.pdf. Accessed 31 March 2020.

[97] Available at: https://ec.europa.eu/competition/mergers/cases/decisions/m8084_13335_3.pdf. Accessed 31 March 2020.

[98] Case M.7932 – Dow/DuPont, par. 218.

in which they participate. Among the many quotes of the investment fund managers, the following can be referred to in order to illustrate their active role:

Vanguard's chairman and chief executive F. William McNabb III stated that Vanguard, one of the largest mutual funds holdings that manages approximately USD 3.6 trillion in assets, will seek active interactions with firms they invest in: '[i]n the past, some have mistakenly assumed that our predominantly passive management style suggests a passive attitude with respect to corporate governance. Nothing could be further from the truth…Glenn H. Booraem, controller of the Vanguard Group's funds and a Vanguard principal, complemented that view: '[w]e believe that engagement is where the action is. We have found through hundreds of direct discussions every year that we are frequently able to accomplish as much—or more—through dialogue as we are through voting. Importantly, through engagement, we are able to put issues on the table for discussion that aren't on the proxy ballot.[99]

The anecdotal evidence is further supported by references to academic literature. The European Commission refers to the study of Azar et al. on the airline industry and of Anton et al. on 'common ownership and management incentives'[100] in the Dow/DuPont merger decision to indicate that

recent empirical studies provide indications that the presence of significant common shareholding in an industry is likely to have material consequences on the behaviour of the firms in such industries, in particular that prices are likely to be higher and that common shareholders tend to shape the monetary incentives of firms' executives in order to align them with industry performance, and not only their firm's specific performance.[101]

The academic studies are contested by Bayer and Monsanto. However, there is no indication that the European Commission is not convinced about the validity of these studies. This can be deducted from the European Commission's observation that neither Bayer nor Monsanto come with evidence to argue the opposite.[102]

Third, the horizontal shareholders have, the European Commission has further noticed, different interests than non-horizontal shareholders. While the latter seems to focus on achieving higher profits for the individual firm, the former aims more at maximizing the profits of the entire industry. The maximization of the profits of the entire industry is easier if the competition in the industry is suppressed. The European Commission exemplifies the divergent interest by referring to a proxy fight within DuPont. In this proxy fight, some of the main horizontal shareholders supported the firm against the request for more revenue growth.[103]

Fourth, the European Commission held that the theory of competitive harm as developed for cross-shareholding and horizontal shareholding, i.e., reduced-price competition, could extend to innovation competition. The main idea is that investments in innovation will reduce not only the current profit of the investing firm, but

[99] Case M.7932 – Dow/DuPont, annex par. 23.

[100] Anton et al. (2018).

[101] Case M.7932 – Dow/DuPont, par. 2349.

[102] Case M.8084 – Bayer/Monsanto, par. 223.

[103] Case M.7932 – Dow/DuPont, annex par. 46-52.

also the future general profits of the industry. Therefore, horizontal shareholding may have a negative impact on competition in general.[104]

Without giving much consideration to the benefits of horizontal shareholding and thus giving more weight to the negative effects of horizontal shareholding, the European Commission order divestures for both mergers to be cleared. When issuing the divesture decision in Bayer/Monsanto, the Commission did not have a problem to state that the divesture to BASF would not create issues with horizontal shareholding because 'the debate regarding common shareholdings is relatively recent and not yet entirely settled.'[105]

4.3 At Least Agreement on the Potential Seriousness of Horizontal Shareholding

The academic literature is divided on what the legal approach should be towards horizontal shareholding. So are the enforcement authorities. However, there is one element they all agree on. Horizontal shareholding needs further research. This message has been expressed in different ways. Ittai Paldor eloquently summarizes that message with references to several other scholars:

The empirical findings are controversial and this controversy has attracted quite some attention, resulting in 'diametrically opposed results.' Ultimately, while there is indeed empirical support for the argument pressed in this Paper, it seems that at present the most compelling conclusion regarding the empirical results is Rock and Rubinfeld's conclusion that 'there is more work to be done,' echoed by Hemphill and Kahan's call for more calibrated empirical research.[106]

That this research can focus on fintech has been pointed out above. Many of the fintech firms are receiving their funding from institutional investors, opening the possibility of horizontal shareholding. When Van Loo makes these observations, he is, without doubt, thinking of the situation in the United States. To open new frontiers, this study has looked at the situation in Asia. Asia's situation is peculiar. The fintech scene in Asia is mainly controlled by ride-sharing platforms, Grab and

---

[104]Case M.7932 – Dow/DuPont, paras. 131 and 2350.

[105]Case M.7932 – Dow/DuPont, par. 3304.

[106]Paldor (2019), p. 45 (footnotes omitted). Plador refers to Hemphill and Kahan, and they write 'The conclusion is that most proposed mechanisms either lack significant empirical support or else are implausible. Uncovering such evidence, if it exists, should be a focus of future work and governmental investigations.' Hemphill and Kahan (2019), pp. 1 and 58. Rock and Rubinfeld express this as 'Moving forward, it is appropriate for scholars, practitioners, institutional investors, and regulators to think about antitrust guidelines for diversified shareholders. We have sketched out and defended a first cut, but more work needs to be done'. Rock and Rubinfeld (2017), p. 48. Acknowledging that there is no ''yes or no' answer to the question whether common ownership will generate substantial competitive harm in a particular market,' Patel holds that 'because of the *a priory* indeterminacy of common ownerships effect on competition and because economic understanding of the nature and extent of those competitive effect continues to evolve, common ownership should be evaluated on a case-by-case basis.' Patel (2018), p. 59.

Go-Jek, in particular. The capital financing the expansion towards fintech (and other areas) is largely derived from institutional investors. These institutional investors are not refraining from investing in competing firms. The investments are being made in other ridesharing platforms, also offering fintech services and in fintech firms *pur sang*. This could raise problems, which may be aggregated through a merger between Grab and Go-Jek.

5 Asian Fintech Firms, Horizontal Shareholding, and Competition Law

5.1 Horizontal Shareholding and Theories of Harm in Competition Law

The intuitively contradictory statement of the European Commission in the Bayer/Monsanto decision shows the current problem with horizontal shareholding. There are different views on whether anticompetitive effects could be generated and how these potential effects should be connected with a theory of harm in competition law.

The most conservative position towards horizontal shareholding, which of course, rejects the findings of the empirical studies, holds that, in principle, there will be no competitive harm. The cautious formulation relates to the possibility that the institutional investors could function as a hub of information, which is shared with the firms in which they invest. The institutional investor could thus act as the ringleader in a price-fixing scheme, where the investor is collecting and distributing information between the different competitors and thus engages in communication. This horizontal coordination represents the theory of harm that the conservative position towards horizontal shareholding is willing to accept.[107] The coordination can also be reached without explicit communication, and this by means of repeated interactions among firms. It is well-known that this form of tacit collusion falls outside the scope of most competition laws.[108]

On the opposite site of the spectrum, horizontal shareholding is considered to have the potential to change the management incentives. In the absence of horizontal shareholding, the managers' incentive is to maximize the profit of the firm and so the return for its shareholders. When horizontal competitors have, to a certain extent, the same shareholders, this incentive will disappear. The idea that the horizontal shareholders could try to voice their preferences at the shareholders meeting will force the executives to act in the interest of the investors.[109] This interest could be to increase the value of the investors' portfolio rather than that of their respective

[107] Paldor (2019), pp. 46-48.

[108] Lianos et al. (2019), p. 19.

[109] Lianos et al. (2019), pp. 14-18.

individual firms. It is said that this action of the managers is unilateral horizontal conduct and does not require any form of coordination.[110] As the basis for competition law enforcement against this theory of harm, reference is made to rules on mergers and acquisition of stock.[111]

In line with the idea that horizontal shareholding could create a shift in the managers' incentive to pursue profits for their respective firms is a reduction in the incentives for innovation. If increased competition is not favored by horizontal shareholders, a decision could be made to reduce the investment in research and development (R&D).[112] R&D could indeed make a firm more efficient and so displace competitors. If investors of the potentially more efficient firm have also invested in these potentially displaced competitors, they risk losing more than when a status quo would have been maintained. The status quo would be maintained by less R&D spending. This finding, it has been held, will not make sense if the R&D spending leads to spillover effects. In such a case, the horizontal shareholding could mitigate the spillover effects by, for example, insinuating that special collaboration, such as joint ventures or strategic alliances, should be created. The basis for potential enforcement would be similar as described in relation to the previous theory of harm.

Since there is a lot of uncertainty in relation to the applicable competition law provisions, suggestions have been made to indicate when horizontal shareholding would be problematic. Edward B. Rock and Daniel L. Rubinfeld suggest creating a safe harbor. Their proposal is that all horizontal shareholding under 15% should not lead to any competition law scrutiny.[113] More radical is the suggestion of Eric Posner, Scott Morton, and Glen Weyl, who suggest that ownership of shares in multiple firms in an oligopolistic industry should be limited to 1%.[114]

5.2 *Possible Anticompetitive Effects Among Asian Fintech Firms*

The vivid discussion on horizontal shareholding that started after Azar's research mainly focused on anticompetitive price setting. Azar, in the end, posited that the average airline ticket prices were three to ten% higher than they would have been if there was no horizontal shareholding. Subsequent studies have revealed that such

[110] Lianos et al. (2019), p. 34.

[111] The literature most often refers to Sect. 7 of the Clayton Antitrust Act (as amended by the Celler-Kefauver Anti-Merger Act of 1950 and then again in 1980). The discussion on the applicability of this Section is mostly academic. The main discussion is whether the Section can be applied to cases of horizontal shareholding in which the shareholders are not active and thus hold the shares 'solely for investment.' In Europe, it has been mentioned that, besides the provisions of the European Union Merger Regulation, also Article 101 of the Treaty of the Functioning of the European Union could apply. Elhauge (2019), pp. 37-61.

[112] Lianos et al. (2019), pp. 33-34.

[113] Rock and Rubinfeld (2017), p. 42-43.

[114] Posner, Morton, Weyl (2017), p. 34.

a price effect is also present in the seed sector and the food sector.[115] A different kind of effect has been presented by Melissa Newham, Jo Seldeslachts, and Albert Banal-Estañol. Their study on the pharmaceutical sector suggests that horizontal shareholding can also influence product-market outcome. Horizontal shareholding could prevent a generic medicine from entering the market if it threatens the position of a medicine of an incumbent firm.[116]

Presuming that any of these anticompetitive effects could be attached to horizontal shareholding, and that requires most likely a case-by-case investigation, the circumstances of the Asian fintech sector has to be taken into consideration to see what is most likely.

The fintech oriented ridesharing firms have developed their fintech business in relation to their original activity, enabling payments for the ridesharing or providing financial support for their drivers. As a consequence, the fintech business of these firms is locally situated. The fintech firms *pur sang* are also operating within geographically determined boundaries. It may be that these boundaries are not necessarily limited to one country. A possible consequence of such a division is that there will be less price competition between the different fintech firms. Hence, the horizontal shareholding will not have any effect on how the prices are being set.

The absence of influence on direct price-setting does not mean that the attention should be shed away from horizontal shareholding. Competition could also be potential. Incumbent firms could switch their business model, or foreign incumbents could enter lucrative markets abroad. It is known that this kind of potential competition also controls the price setting. Potential competition could come from any of the foreign fintech firms. Especially the firms that have grown substantially in their domestic market could be looking for geographical expansion.[117] The question is whether such an expansion is benefitting the investors.

Horizontal shareholders may not favor geographical expansion. Such an expansion could lead to fierce competition that cannot be compensated by the profits the new entrant would be generated. To temper this potential competition, horizontal shareholders could exercise their influence on the executives of the firms in which they have invested. The likely result? The managers of the fintech firms could understand this message in such a way as to divide the relevant fintech product markets geographically among the competitors. Market division, as is well-known, is an indirect way to increase the prices above a competitive level. If it is not through a changed incentive structure for managers, this outcome could also be achieved by increased information transparency between the firms through the horizontal shareholding.

The effects of a market division are currently still mitigated by the existence of two major clusters: one around Grab and one around Go-Jek. The cluster around Grab is

[115]Newham, Seldeslachts and Banal-Estañol (2018).

[116]Lianos et al. (2019), p. 16 n. 60 and 61.

[117]These firms are often called unicorns. 'A unicorn start-up or unicorn company is a private company with a valuation over $1 billion. As of March 2020, there are more than 400 unicorns around the world. Variants include a decacorn, valued at over $10 billion, and a hectocorn, valued at over $100 billion.' Available at: https://www.cbinsights.com/research-unicorn-companies. Accessed 31 March 2020.

being supported by Didi Chixung, Softbank Group, Softbank Group's subsidiaries, Alibaba, and Ant Financial. The cluster surrounding Go-Jek is made of Tencent Holdings, Alphabet, and Temasek Holdings. That these respective firms are respectively supporting Grab and Go-Jek is not a surprise. Alibaba and Tencent are, for example, also fiercely competing in the Chinese domestic market.[118] With their investment in rival firms in South-East Asia, these respective firms are exporting their domestic competition to South-East Asia.[119]

The problem is to prove that market division is being practiced, not so much that a competition law provisions are available for enforcing the law. The situation may change when a merger is being contemplated. If Grab and Go-Jek would merge into a new entity, the competition tempering the negative effects of horizontal shareholding will disappear. Since the new entity will also integrate the shareholding structure of the merging firms, there will be no change about the security that potential competition has not to be feared. The backing of the new entity with stakes in even more fintech firms elsewhere should aggregate the secured feeling that new entrants will not appear in the markets of the new entity. Hence, the new entity will be able to behave as a monopolist. Prices may be adjusted upwards; service quality may be frozen or lowered.

Unlike with market division, a merger would allow an assessment of how the market structure would be affected by the creation of a new entity and how that would lessen competition. In that exercise, it would be possible to also look at the issue of horizontal shareholding. As mentioned, the merger of two competing clusters would create an entity in which there is no element anymore that would provide any temper on the horizontal shareholding structure.

Finally, it is not inconceivable that a new entrant would appear. These new entrants may also receive backing of the shareholders of the new entity. If such a new form of horizontal shareholding would unfold, close attention should be paid to whether price competition would be negatively influenced due to the existence of horizontal shareholding.

6 Conclusion

This chapter has shown that horizontal shareholding, which exists if the same group of investors hold minority shares in competing firms, is increasing in the fintech sector in Asia. The horizontal shareholding does not only exist among the fintech firms that originally started out as ridesharing firms. It is also possible to see this horizontal shareholding between the fintech oriented ridesharing firms and the fintech firms *pur sang*.

Horizontal shareholding is an issue more and more discussed the competition law literature. However, it is a highly controversial issue mainly due to the difficulty of

[118]Xiao (2017); Lashinsky (2018).

[119]Chandler and Barrett (2018).

measuring the influence by these shareholders and the uncertainty which competition law provision should apply to it. Despite the controversy, an increasing number of competition law studies claiming that horizontal shareholding increases prices, lowers innovation or prevents market access.

The composition of the fintech market in Asia may require a rethinking of the anticompetitive effects. Since the horizontal shareholding crosses borders, the influence that could be exerted on the executives of these fintech firms is not necessarily to directly adjust the prices to reflect the profit maximization of the portfolio investments. Instead, the claim is that in such a situation, the influence on the price may be indirect by coordinating in which geographical markets the respective fintech firms should be active.

References

Anton et al. (2018) Common Ownership, Competition, and Top Management Incentives (Ross School of Business Paper No. 1328). https://papers.ssrn.com/sol3/papers.cfm?abstract_id=2802332. Accessed 31 March 2020

Azar J (2019) The common ownership trilemma. https://papers.ssrn.com/sol3/papers.cfm?abstract_id=3451462. Accessed 4 February 2020

Azar J (2012) A new look at oligopoly: implicit collusion through portfolio diversification. Phd Thesis, Princeton University. https://pqdtopen.proquest.com/doc/1239709452.html?FMT=AI. Accessed 4 February 2020

Azar J (2011) A new look at oligopoly: implicit collusion through portfolio diversification. https://papers.ssrn.com/sol3/papers.cfm?abstract_id=1993364. Accessed 4 February 2020

Azar J et al. (2018) The anticompetitive effects of common ownership. Journal of Finance 73(4):1513–1565

Balea J (2017) Go-Jek buys 3 fintech firms to conquer Indonesia payments (15 December). https://www.techinasia.com/grab-transforming-finance-payments-southeast-asia. Accessed 31 March 2020

Blackman Ph (2019) Global fintech investment rockets to a record $111.8B in 2018, driven by mega deals: KPMG pulse of fintech. https://home.kpmg/xx/en/home/media/press-releases/2019/02/global-fintech-investment-hits-record-in-2018.html. Accessed 4 February 2020

Bostoen F (2020) The Uber-Grab merger and the potentially anti-competitive consequences of the battle for ride-hailing dominance. CoRe 64–68

Bresnahan TF, Salop SC (1986) Quantifying the Competitive Effects of Production Joint Ventures. Int J Ind Organ 4(2):155–175

Buckley R P and Webster S (2016) Fintech in developing countries: charting new customer journeys. UNSW Law Research Paper No. 2016–73. https://papers.ssrn.com/sol3/papers.cfm?abstract_id=2850091. Accessed 4 February 2020

Campell N (2018) A Competition Law Analysis of Common Shareholdings. CPI Antitrust Chronicle. https://www.mcmillan.ca/Files/212213_CPI-Antitrust-Chronicle-Neil-Campbell.pdf. Accessed 4 February 2020

Chandler C, Barrett E (2018) Alibaba v. Tencent: Taking the Fight to Southeast Asia. https://fortune.com/2018/06/21/alibaba-tencent-southeast-asia/. Accessed 31 March 2020

Chandler C (2019) Grab vs. Go-Jek: Inside Asia's battle of the 'Super Apps'. https://fortune.com/longform/grab-gojek-super-apps/. Accessed 31 March 2020

Douglas J L, Grinsberg R (2016–2017) Old wine in new bottles: bank investments in FinTech companies. Review of Banking & Financial Law 36: 667-711

Elhauge E (2019) How horizontal shareholding harms our economy – and why antitrust law can fix it. https://papers.ssrn.com/sol3/papers.cfm?abstract_id=3293822. Accessed 4 February 2020

Elhauge E (2018) New evidence, proofs, and legal theories on horizontal shareholding. https://corpgov.law.harvard.edu/2018/02/14/new-evidence-proofs-and-legal-theories-on-horizontal-shareholding/. Accessed 4 February 2020

Elhauge E (2017) The growing problem of horizontal shareholding. Competition Policy International. https://pdfs.semanticscholar.org/2e02/b763929faed5a3d99c65a874fc5951a4e208.pdf. Accessed 4 February 2020

Ellis J (2018) In brief: Go-Jek expands financial services offering with P2P lender partnerships (5 September) https://www.techinasia.com/gojek-findaya-danacita-aktivaku. Accessed 31 March 2020

Fenwick M, McCahery JA, Vermeulen EEP (2017) Fintech and the financing of entrepreneurs: from crowdfunding to marketplace lending. ECGI - Law Working Paper No. 369/2017. https://papers.ssrn.com/sol3/papers.cfm?abstract_id=2967891##. Accessed 4 February 2020

Finch Capital (2020) Portfolio – fintech. https://www.finchcapital.com/fintech. Accessed 4 February 2020

Finch Capital and dealroom.co (2019) The state of European fintech. https://blog.dealroom.co/wp-content/uploads/2019/10/The-State-of-European-Fintech-2019.pdf. Accessed 4 February 2020

Fulco M (2019) Will fintech save Go-Jek and Grab from Uber's fate? (14 June). https://www.kapronasia.com/asia-payments-research-category/will-fintech-save-go-jek-and-grab-from-uber-s-fate.html. Accessed 31 March 2020

Fraile Carmona A et al. (2018) Competition issues in the area of financial technology (FinTech). https://www.europarl.europa.eu/RegData/etudes/STUD/2018/619027/IPOL_STU(2018)619027_EN.pdf. Accessed 4 February 2020

Ganguly S (2019) Here's Ola's plan to diversify its offerings to strengthen footprint in Fintech. https://www.entrepreneur.com/article/343025. Accessed 31 March 2020

Ginsburg D H (2018) Why common ownership is not an antitrust problem. https://corpgov.law.harvard.edu/2018/12/04/why-common-ownership-is-not-an-antitrust-problem/. Accessed 4 February 2020

Hemphill C S, Kahan M (2018) The Strategies of Anticompetitive Common Ownership (NYU Law and Economics Research Paper No. 18–29). https://papers.ssrn.com/sol3/papers.cfm?abstract_id=3210373. Accessed 31 March 2020

Lashinsky A (2018) Alibaba v. Tencent: The battle for supremacy in China. https://fortune.com/longform/alibaba-tencent-china-internet/. Accessed 31 March 2020

Lambert Th A, Sykuta M A (2018) The case for doing nothing about institutional Investors' common ownership of small stakes in competing firms (University of Missouri School of Law Legal Studies Research Paper No. 2018–21). https://papers.ssrn.com/sol3/papers.cfm?abstract_id=3173787. Accessed 31 March 2020

Lianos et al. (2019) Financialisation of the food value chain, common ownership and competition law (Centre for law, economics and society—research paper series: 4/2019). https://www.ucl.ac.uk/cles/sites/cles/files/cles-4-2019_final.pdf. Accessed 31 March 2020

Monopolies Commission (2016) Competitive significance of institutional investors' minority shareholdings. https://www.monopolkommission.de/images/HG21/Main_Report_XXI_Institutional_investors.pdf. Accessed 31 March 2020

Mulia K (2019a) The many battlefronts of Grab versus Gojek in Southeast Asia (31 July). https://kr-asia.com/the-many-battlefronts-of-grab-versus-gojek-in-southeast-asia. Accessed 31 March 2020

Mulia K (2019b) Indonesian lender Bank Artos officially acquired by Gojek investor and BTPN director (27 December). https://kr-asia.com/indonesian-lender-bank-artos-officially-acquired-by-gojeks-investor-and-btpn-director. Accessed 31 March 2020

Newham M, Seldeslachts J, Banal-Estañol A (2018) Common Ownership and Market Entry: Evidence from Pharmaceutical Industry (DIW Berlin Discussion Paper No. 1738). https://papers.ssrn.com/sol3/papers.cfm?abstract_id=3194394. Accessed 31 March 2020

Nicoletti B (2017) The future of FinTech: Integrating finance and technology in financial services. Palgrave Macmillan, London

O'Brien DP, Salop SC (2000) Competitive Effects of Partial Ownership: Financial Interest and Corporate Control. Antitrust Law Journal 67:559–614

OECD (2017) Hearing on Common Ownership by institutional investors and its impact on competition—Note by the United States (DAF/COMP/WD(2017)86). https://one.oecd.org/document/DAF/COMP/WD(2017)86/en/pdf. Accessed 31 March 2020

Paldor I (2019) The perils of institutional investors' diversification: Defying the myth. Hebrew University of Jerusalem Legal Studies Research Paper Series No. 19-06. https://papers.ssrn.com/sol3/papers.cfm?abstract_id=3316111. Accessed 4 February 2020

Patel MS (2018) Common ownership, institutional investors, and antitrust. Antitrust Law Journal 82(1):279–334

Phillips N J (2018) Taking stock: Assessing common ownership. https://www.ftc.gov/system/files/documents/public_statements/1382461/phillips_-_taking_stock_6-1-18_0.pdf. Accessed 31 March 2020

Posner E A, Scott Morton F M, Weyl E G (2017) A Proposal to Limit the Anti-Competitive Power of Institutional Investors. https://papers.ssrn.com/sol3/papers.cfm?abstract_id=2872754. 31 March 2020

Rock E B, Rubinfeld D L (2017) Antitrust for institutional investors. Law and economics research paper series working paper No. 17–23. https://papers.ssrn.com/sol3/papers.cfm?abstract_id=2998296. Accessed 4 February 2020

Ruehl M (2019) Grab v Gojek: inside the tech battle for south-east Asia (26 December). https://www.ft.com/content/04e0523c-2256-11ea-b8a1-584213ee7b2b. Accessed 31 March 2020

Russel J (2019) Go-Jek buys fintech startup Coins.ph for $72 M ahead of Philippines expansion (19 January). https://techcrunch.com/2019/01/18/gojek-coins-ph-philippines/. Accessed 31 March 2020

Seedcamp (2020) Our startups. https://seedcamp.com/our-startups/fin-tech/. Accessed 4 February 2020

Shevlin R (2019) Uber's Fintech Strategy: A Conversation With Peter Hazlehurst (4 November). https://www.forbes.com/sites/ronshevlin/2019/11/04/a-peek-into-ubers-fintech-strategy-a-conversation-with-peter-hazlehurst-head-of-uber-money/#2351e0f512f4. Accessed 31 March 2020

Singh P (2019) Why China's Didi is trying to become a fintech Giant. https://www.entrepreneur.com/article/325822. Accessed 31 March 2020

Solomon D (2016) Rational shareholder indifference: how to awake investors? Iyunei Mishpat 39:317

Trulioo (2019) The year of Unicorns: VC investments in Fintech more than doubled in 2018. https://www.trulioo.com/blog/vc-investments-fintech-2018/. Accessed 4 February 2020

Van Loo R (2018) Making innovation more competitive: the case of fintech. UCLA Law Review 65:232–279

Vestager M (2018) Competition in changing times (FIW Symposium, Innsbruck, 16 February)

Xiao E (2017) How WeChat Pay became Alipay's largest rival. https://www.techinasia.com/wechat-pay-vs-alipay. Accessed 31 March 2020

Zhang W (2019) How Grab is transforming finance and payments in Southeast Asia (19 Augustus). https://www.techinasia.com/grab-transforming-finance-payments-southeast-asia. Accessed 31 March 2020

Fintech, Overcoming Friction and New Models of Financial Regulation

Mark Fenwick and Erik P. M. Vermeulen

Abstract The development of new technologies by financial service providers is not new; banks, for instance, have always utilized technology to improve front- and back-office operations. The historical significance of fintech does not derive from the use of technology per se, but the leveraging of the distinct properties of digital technologies by non-traditional actors to offer consumers a better experience of financial services. More specifically, the goal of overcoming 'friction' in the user experience is here identified as the core feature driving many recent developments in a fintech context. This chapter explores the implications of such an account for incumbent financial institutions and regulators. From the perspective of incumbents, this new emphasis on the consumer experience requires banks and other financial institutions to organize-for-innovation. New capacities and a shift in mindset are needed to deliver a different kind of user experience, and two effective strategies for incumbents are explored. First, adopting more decentralized forms of organization and governance—what we refer to as 'decentralized ecosystems'—that are better placed to innovate and overcome friction. Second, adopting a more strategic approach to venturing, i.e., purchasing start-ups from the fintech sector and integrating their innovations into incumbent operations. From a regulatory perspective, this requires a greater willingness on the part of regulators and other policymakers to foster experimentation in financial services. As such, the goal of regulation needs to shift from a traditional focus on managing systemic risk to more dynamic models that seek to facilitate responsible innovation and the delivery of a better-quality user experience. This can be achieved, for example, by state regulators working together—partnering—with incumbents and start-ups in the financial service ecosystems of the future via regulatory sandboxes and other similar schemes. Regulatory developments in Asia and

M. Fenwick (✉)
Faculty of Law, Kyushu University, Fukuoka, Japan
e-mail: mdf0911@gmail.com

E. P. M. Vermeulen
Tilburg Law School, Tilburg, The Netherlands
e-mail: erikvermeulen@me.com

Senior Legal Counsel Corporate Structure, Signify (formerly known as Philips Lighting), Eindhoven, The Netherlands

M. Fenwick et al. (eds.), *Regulating FinTech in Asia*, Perspectives in Law, Business and Innovation, https://doi.org/10.1007/978-981-15-5819-1_11

Europe provide some evidence that policymakers recognize the need for such a shift in emphasis. However, doubts remain about whether they have gone far enough in pursuing this goal and that the full benefits of the fintech revolution have been realized.

Keywords Fintech · Financial regulation · Friction · Legal design · Regulatory experimentation

1 Introduction

The development and deployment of new technologies by financial service providers is nothing new. Banks, for example, have always had to be aware of the latest developments in security to protect or advance their interests and those of their customers. The development of more sophisticated safes and locking mechanisms over the nineteenth century was driven by the banking sector and the need to mitigate the risk of robbery.[1] In 1950, Diners Club introduced the first universal credit card, a portable payment solution that could be used at numerous member establishments.[2] And automated teller machines (ATMs), first developed and introduced in the late 1960s, offered customers the opportunity to perform financial transactions, such as deposits or withdrawals, without the need to interact with bank staff.[3]

So, technology and financial services have always been interlinked. The historical significance of fintech does not derive from the use of new technology, as such. One could argue that all advances in banking over the last two centuries owe their existence to some development in new technology.

Nevertheless, post-2000, and particularly after the 2008 financial crisis, banks have found themselves confronted with an unprecedented combination of new pressures that all involve technology at some level. These new challenges include developing more customer-friendly services to attract more customers and deepen relationships with existing customers to retain them; rethinking distribution models and internal organization; responding to disruptive competition from challenger banks and new entrants to the market (both start-ups but also corporations from other sectors, most obviously the technology sector); rebuilding trust with all stakeholders, especially customers; and managing new regulatory, capital, and security risks.[4] The crucial point here is that all of these challenges require engagement with disruptive new digital technologies, either directly or indirectly. Technology both facilitates the delivery of better performance and is a crucial infrastructure for managing costs and risks.

As such, digital technologies have now become the primary driver of change in banking. And as banking increasingly switches to online platforms and cash

[1] See Erroll and Erroll (2005).

[2] See Manning (2000).

[3] See Batiz-Lazo (2015).

[4] For an overview of these challenges, see Price Waterhouse Coopers (2014).

'disappears,' traditional branch-based banking is gradually being displaced by direct banking. When most banking operations are done online, technological performance becomes vital. Consequently, many issues facing banks are now, ultimately, IT problems; for example, customer authentication, fraud checking systems, payment processing, basic account infrastructure, and KYC assessments. Finally, in an age of online banking, image, and branding matter more than location and place in distinguishing different providers.[5] In short, every bank is now obliged to reinvent itself, to some degree, as a tech company to succeed as a financial service provider in a digital age. And this can be very hard for incumbents.

Here, we would like to explore the thought that much of the distinctiveness of fintech derives from *the leveraging of the unique properties of digital technologies by non-traditional actors to overcome friction in the user experience of banking and other financial services*. From the start, it is worth emphasizing that this definition is not meant to capture every aspect of the fintech revolution. Rather it is intended as a framework that can help us identify more precisely the challenges created for incumbents and to explore some key elements of what is happening in financial services that have implications for regulatory approaches.

Section 2 describes these unique properties, non-traditional actors, and new user experience. Our emphasis is on how much of what is described as fintech leverages the unique features of digital technologies—the intuitive user interfaces of powerful, networked devices, for example—to overcome friction, i.e., to offer consumers a different and better experience of financial services that makes their lives easier. We argue that this type of account of fintech has important implications for incumbents and regulators, which are then explored in the remainder of the chapter.

Section 3 argues that from the perspective of incumbents, any re-design of the user experience requires banks and other financial institutions to reinvent themselves and to organize-for-innovation. There needs to be a shift in mindset to meet the challenge of digital technologies. Two effective strategies to achieve this goal are outlined. Firstly, adopting more decentralized forms of organization and governance—what we refer to as decentralized ecosystems. A defining feature of such ecosystems is that engagement with consumers—and delivering a frictionless experience—is given much higher priority than in traditional closed and hierarchical models of organizing a business. Secondly, adopting a more strategic approach to venturing, i.e., purchasing start-ups from the fintech sector and performing the delicate task of benefiting from the 'start-up genie's magic' by integrating their innovations into incumbent operations.

Finally, Sect. 4 explores the regulatory implications of this account. From a regulatory perspective, this requires a greater willingness to foster experimentation in financial services. As such, the goal of regulation needs to shift away from a traditional focus on managing systemic risk to more dynamic models that seek to facilitate responsible innovation by working together with incumbents in the decentralized financial service ecosystems of the future via regulatory sandboxes and other similar schemes. We argue that the Open Banking movement in the UK, which informed

[5] On the 'attention economy,' more generally, see Wu (2016).

regulatory developments in the EU (specifically the Payment Services Directive 2) and, more recently, events in Asia described elsewhere in this book, are motivated, at least in part, by the demand to deliver a different type of user experience while ensuring that end-users are protected. Regulatory developments provide some evidence that policymakers recognize the need for such a shift. However, doubts remain about whether they have gone far enough in pursuing this goal and that the full benefits of the fintech revolution have yet been realized.

2 Fintech and the Consumer Experience

Over the last decade, fintech—broadly understood as the use of new technology and innovation to compete in the marketplace of financial institutions and intermediaries—has disrupted the financial services sector and created a new challenge for regulators.[6] Here, we would like to explore the thought that much of the historical distinctiveness of fintech derives from the leveraging of the unique properties of digital technologies to offer consumers a frictionless user experience of banking and other financial services. In this sense, a proper understanding of fintech needs to begin by situating these developments in the context of the so-called digital transformation.

The process of the 'digitization of everything' began in earnest with the launch of the Intel microprocessor in California in the early 1970s and has been driven by an ongoing series of technological developments. Consider the following:

- The shrinking size, increased power, and diverse applications of personal computers and, more recently, smartphones.
- The global reach of communication networks—notably, the internet—and the new forms of economic exchange and social interaction that these networks have made possible.
- The cheap availability of cloud-based databases capable of storing vast amounts of information—Big Data—that can be quickly processed by software algorithms and machine learning for use across multiple social settings.

Powerful digital devices (especially smartphones), global networks, and the 'cloud' form the underlying architecture of the digital age. The crucial shift that has occurred is the worldwide reach of these technologies. There are approximately five and a half billion adults alive today, and almost four billion now have access to a smartphone—digital technologies have already connected virtually everyone.

The point to be emphasized is that this is just the beginning. Or, as venture capitalist and technology analyst, Benedict Evans puts it, we are at the 'end of the beginning' (the end of the 'access story,' in which digital technologies are made available to a significant percentage of the global population). We are now entering the beginning of the 'use story' in which these new digital technologies penetrate more and more areas

[6] For a general overview see, Chishti and Barberis (2016), King (2018), McMillan (2014), Sironi (2016).

of social and economic life and open more possibilities and opportunities.[7] Consider various near-future technological developments, such as more sophisticated forms of artificial intelligence, augmented and virtual reality, voice and mind interfacing, as well as quantum computing. It quickly becomes evident that the process of digitization is on-going, and new layers of technology will continue to transform every aspect of our world (economy, society, and culture).

And, as technology moves into less apparent markets, the scale and scope of that disruption will become even higher. We all now live in a state of a profound technological upheaval that will, amongst many things, transform what it means to be human. The scale of the economic, social, and cultural impact of these digital technologies justifies talk of a digital 'transformation' or 'revolution.' The effects of these changes are everywhere.

This is the context for the emergence and growth of fintech. Most obviously, new digital technologies have facilitated new actors (let's refer to them as start-ups) to enter the financial services sector, as they are better placed than incumbents to deliver new services on new digital platforms. As such, fintech has facilitated the emergence of start-ups and other non-financial companies that offer an alternative source of financial services. In particular, 'app-based' companies are emerging all over the world.[8] These start-ups challenge and disrupt incumbents, such as traditional banks, by supporting a wide range of financial services. These include marketplace lending platforms, equity crowdfunding platforms, insurance services, algorithm-driven 'Robo-advisors' offering smarter, more personalized financial advice, and blockchain-based cryptocurrencies and payment systems.[9] Crypto-assets have been particularly widespread in an Asian context, for example, as evidenced by the discussion in other chapters in this volume.

The second group of new actors is the large technology companies, which are similarly leveraging their expertise and data to move into the financial services sector. Tech companies (Chinese tech companies, in particular, provide a good illustration of this trend) show how quickly these large businesses can leverage their economic power and expand into new areas.[10] Think of ridesharing companies that become fintech companies that become insurance companies that become healthcare companies (Uber). Similar moves into financial services have been made by Amazon, Apple, Facebook, Google, Microsoft, Samsung, and Tencent, to give some high profile (and prominent) examples.[11]

However, the feature of fintech we would like to discuss here is the emergence of a friction-free user experience as a crucial—and distinctive—aspect of the contemporary fintech space. Overcoming user friction is a key element in this sector, and this

[7] Evans (2018).

[8] For an overview of such apps, see Pratskevich (2019).

[9] See, for example, Sironi (2016).

[10] For example, on Alibaba's move into financial services, see Zhou et al. (2015). Similar developments can be seen in Japan with the development of Line Pay.

[11] See Parker et al. (2016); Moazed and Johnson (2016).

reflects how the consumer and the consumer experience has taken on new importance in the context of the digital revolution, more generally.

To introduce the new significance of the consumer and the consumer experience, it is helpful to consider how digital technologies have impacted business in general, as well as financial service providers since digital technologies first had a significant impact in the 1960s. A distinction between first- and second-generation digital technologies can provide a useful framework for introducing our argument.

First-generation digital technologies that emerged and impacted business from the 1960s through to around 2000—most obviously mainframes (IBM) and later minicomputers, but also early personal computers—resulted in significant productivity gains for all businesses, including financial institutions. Such mainframes, minicomputers, and PCs were not connected via the internet. They did, however, facilitate a critical shift away from paper-based documentation and filing cabinets or—the previous high technology option—the microfiche, towards databases and hard drives. There is little doubt that these early digital technologies assisted incumbents in the more efficient implementation of traditional banking models and strategies.

However, this first-generation of digital technologies did not disrupt incumbent operations in any significant way, nor did they challenge the dominance of incumbents. On the contrary, by improving productivity and efficiency, these pioneering technologies ensured that incumbent financial service providers maintained and even enhanced their market power and influence. In short, first wave information technologies helped, rather than disrupted incumbents.

For sure, these technology-driven productivity gains benefited consumers in that products and services became more efficient, and possibly cheaper, as a result of technology. However, there wasn't a fundamental transformation in *what* was being offered to consumers of financial services. The impact and effects of this change in *how* banks, for example, organized and operated their back-office operations went mostly unnoticed by most consumers who—at best—paid a little less for what essentially amounted to the same product or service that had always been offered.

Nor did these new technologies necessarily benefit bank workers who were provided with new tools to work with but found themselves subject to new forms of workplace monitoring, surveillance and control, and, in many cases, under ever-greater pressure to be more efficient or productive.

On this type of account, the primary beneficiaries of first-generation information technologies were, therefore, the investor-shareholders of the incumbent businesses and financial institutions who found themselves in a stronger market position as a result of these technology-driven efficiency gains.

Post-2000 information technologies—specifically, the combination of powerful mobile devices, the internet, and cloud-based Big Data—that we have identified above as the underlying architecture of a digital age, have been different in their effects. This combination of technologies has fundamentally transformed the operating environment for incumbent banks and other financial service providers and, in many cases, undermined their market power. First-generation technologies made existing corporations more efficient. In contrast, more recent, second-generation digital technologies—by facilitating massive reductions in distribution and reproduction costs over long distances—have provided younger, disruptive competitors with the means to compete with and challenge the power of large providers, and—crucially—offer products and services that were previously not possible.

The fundamental change introduced by a combination of high levels of use of mobile devices and the internet, however, has been to make the direct distribution and retail of information, products, and services effectively free (in the case of digital goods—software or data). Or, at least, they have been made significantly cheaper (in the case of 'old-world' products that are now sold online), effectively negating the advantage that incumbent businesses who controlled distribution or retail previously enjoyed. The power of intermediaries—at least, those intermediaries who control the distribution chain—is reduced in a digital age when a direct-to-consumer model is made available by the proliferation of digital technologies.

For example, the rise of direct-to-consumer e-commerce involves a direct transaction between the manufacturer and consumer, and it provides the most obvious example of how control over distribution—and the power of intermediaries—is much less significant in a digital age. The global reach and relatively low cost of operating on the internet have made it viable for disruptive 'distributors'—like Amazon or Alibaba—to integrate 'forwards' with consumers on a massive scale. No longer do distributors compete based upon their control of the distribution network and their exclusive supplier relationships. Rather, the physical assets associated with control of the distribution chain can quickly become a burden and drain on resources. The demands on banks to maintain a network of local branch offices provides a useful analogy here. Instead, newcomer 'distributors' can focus on utilizing networked, digital technologies to deliver a unique experience to an enormous number of consumers and then leverage that market power to 'attract' the suppliers to them.

On this type of model, the most crucial factor in determining the success of any business is offering the best consumer experience that attracts the most users. The disruption of high street retailers by Amazon provides the most obvious example of this model, but fintech firms employ a similar strategy. By attracting large numbers of users, Amazon has been able to pull in more suppliers of goods, not through its control of distribution but its control of demand—vast numbers of consumers—that are drawn to the platform by the possibility of a smoother, more convenient customer experience. The point to be emphasized here is that the new technologies—in this case, the combination of mobile and the internet—have facilitated disruptive competition that challenges incumbents and their traditional business models. Digital technologies have disrupted all sectors of the economy, and every firm, no matter what industry it operates, is affected, in some way, by these changes.

In this way, digital technologies shift the focus to the consumer in a way that was not previously the case. This connects to a broader shift in which the most innovative entrepreneurs have recognized that technology is not an end but a means to an end. The goal of innovation is not better technology as such, but the delivery of a better user experience.

Steve Jobs, for example, recognized this shift very quickly and described it very well:

You've got to start with the customer experience and work backward to the technology. You can't start with the technology and try to figure out where I can sell it.[12]

Or:

Our DNA is as a consumer company—for that individual customer who's voting thumbs up or thumbs down. That's who we think about. And we think that our job is to take responsibility for the complete user experience. And if it's not up to par, it's our fault, plain and simple.[13]

The CEO of Europe's most valuable fintech firm, Klarna, Sebastian Siemiatkowski, has made a similar point, recognizing the power of this insight:

What is totally different from a traditional bank is that we are doing it in a customer-centric way. I don't think Steve Jobs built the iPhone to destroy Nokia but to make people's lives better. We are trying to do the same.[14]

The message seems clear. In a digital age, whoever 'owns' the customer experience wins. Understanding the ideal customer experience and integrating the consumer perspective and voice into the organization of a business has become central to innovation and business in a digital age. This realization gives disruptive start-ups a significant advantage over incumbents. Klarna provides an obvious example—their 'buy now, pay later' model has been hugely successful, particularly with a younger generation of Millennial consumers. It has created new competition for incumbent credit card companies.

But what precisely are Steve Jobs and Sebastian Siemiatkowski referring to when they talk about the customer experience in this way? In what follows, we suggest that the concept of a friction-free or frictionless consumer experience offers a helpful way of conceptualizing this issue and thinking about how to design and deliver such a frictionless experience has become a central preoccupation of any firm.

Amongst today's consumers, enormous value is placed on frictionless living and the importance of second-generation digital technologies—in particular, the combination of smartphones and the internet—is that they offer products and services that can better facilitate a frictionless experience or, at least, a significant reduction in friction.

By 'friction,' we refer to anything that holds a consumer up from the desire of wanting something to them getting it. Post-digital revolution, there is a new expectation and demand for a frictionless experience across all aspects of everyday life, and a much higher intolerance of friction has come to define what it means to be a consumer in a digital economy. Any experience of friction is likely to result in consumer migration to alternative products or services. Such intolerance of friction and the easy availability of 'better' alternatives has transformed everyday life. To

[12] Available at: https://www.imore.com/steve-jobs-you-have-start-customer-experience-and-work-backwards-technology. Accessed 31 March 2020.

[13] Available at: https://www.imore.com/steve-jobs-you-have-start-customer-experience-and-work-backwards-technology. Accessed 31 March 2020.

[14] Available at: https://www.ft.com/content/fb7a1cfc-84f7-11e8-96dd-fa565ec55929. Accessed 20 February 20, 2020.

be precise, digital technologies facilitate migration to the degree that was not previously possible, in the sense that information on rival products or services is widely available, and access to those alternative products or services is relatively easy.

A friction-free user experience has several elements or features. Most obviously, it is characterized by a feeling of effortlessness and flow. A friction-free experience is smooth, intuitive, and straightforward. Everything works harmoniously and without apparent effort by the user. Similarly, the activity moves forward or progresses smoothly, guided by an inner logic that is intuitively satisfying. At its best, all decisions arise spontaneously from the demands of the activity and don't necessarily require any deliberate reflection or conscious choice. A friction-free user experience isn't something that we consciously notice or control.

Conversely, friction can be thought of as anything that disrupts or disturbs that flow experience, and the experience of strain—of having to make an effort or even of simply being impeded or hindered from doing what you want—becomes a source of enormous irritation in the modern world. We are all familiar with a bad user interface (UI) that makes it harder to get things done or a limitation in the functionality of a product or service that prevents us from doing something that we would like it to do or—as we become more sophisticated or 'literate' in our knowledge and awareness of the possibilities that technologies can offer.

In this way, a frictionless experience is associated with a feeling of heightened control over one's actions and the world around us. The term 'control' can easily be misunderstood as a result of its association with domination. However, in this context, control is more akin to a state of comfort, security and relaxation as things move forward naturally, in a flow-state of 'control without controlling,' in which action and consciousness merge. Complete involvement of this kind creates a mental state in which there is little tolerance for distraction or irritation.

It might not be an overstatement to claim that in the modern world, frictionless living, particularly the frictionless consumer experience, is how we have come to define and understand freedom. Whereas an earlier modern conception of freedom focused on a privileged or protected space within which unperturbed choice was made possible, in a digital age, freedom is being re-imagined as a form of friction-free living.

Innovation in business today, including in the financial service sector, is closely linked to delivering this kind of frictionless user experience, and all companies must now reflect on how to provide this type of experience. What we want to suggest here is that delivering this kind of experience requires a different type of organization for any business and a new relationship with consumers compared to that of traditional businesses or financial service providers.

Consider the following examples of disruptive start-ups in Asia that aim to reduce friction and for whom such a reduction of friction is a defining feature of their business model. PolicyPal helps consumers to understand their insurance needs and provides them with financial planning solutions. It's supported by 500 Startups, PayPal, and angel investor Koh Boon Hwee. Smartcoin, a start-up that provides small-ticket personal loans to India's micro merchants, self-employed, and salaried individuals. Smartcoin runs a credit-underwriting algorithm that builds the risk profile of a prospective borrower and offer loan products that match. Hoolah taps into the same millennial desire for 'buy now, pay later' that made Klarna so successful, first in Europe and later in the US Or, teen-focused FamPay, which allows teenagers to get a card without having a bank account.[15] Examples of such consumer-centric products and financial services are everywhere in Asia. This is reflected in the fintech adoption rates, which are higher in China and India than anywhere else.[16]

In a financial services context, it is also essential that the provided services are secure and that users are well-protected. A particularly serious form of friction is created if one becomes a victim of fraud or some other security breach. This becomes an important issue for regulators and is discussed below in Sect. 4, in the context of secure customer authentication.

In short, in a digital age, the consumer experience becomes increasingly central to everything a business does, and the traditional border between the business and consumer breaks down as the consumer and company become mutually interdependent elements in a complex and dynamic ecosystem. Crucially, a firm needs consumer input to deliver a friction-free and secure experience, and institutionalizing mechanisms or strategies to achieve such an experience is vital in the design and delivery of that experience.

3 Implications for Incumbent Financial Service Providers

This new emphasis on user experience and the reconfiguration of the relationship between business and consumer creates a significant challenge to all incumbents, across all sectors of the economy. In a financial services context, banks have found themselves confronted with an unprecedented combination of new pressures as a result of this shift that all involve technology at some level. These new challenges include developing more customer-friendly services to attract more customers and deepen relationships with existing customers to retain them; rethinking distribution models and internal organization; responding to disruptive competition from challenger banks and new entrants to the market (both start-ups but also corporations from other sectors, most obviously the technology sector); rebuilding trust with all stakeholders, especially customers; and managing new regulatory, capital, and security risks.[17] The crucial point here is that all of these challenges require engagement with disruptive new digital technologies, either directly or indirectly. Technology both facilitates the delivery of better performance and is a crucial infrastructure for managing costs and risks. As such, digital technologies have now become the primary driver of change in banking.

How then can incumbents respond to this new challenge? Here, we briefly outline two related strategies.

---

[15] Available at: https://www.techinasia.com/category/fintech. Accessed 31 March 2020.

[16] Bloomberg Professional Services (2019).

[17] For an overview of these challenges, see Price Waterhouse Cooper (2014).

In other work, we have developed the argument that the most innovative companies in the world have responded to the unprecedented pressures and challenges of doing business in a digital age by reinventing themselves as decentralized ecosystems.[18] The main argument of our earlier work is that closed, hierarchical, modern company—which has dominated the global economy for the last two hundred plus years—is facing an existential threat. We are living through the beginning of the 'end of the corporation,' at least companies organized as closed, hierarchical systems that operate as proceduralized bureaucracies. New ways of organizing business have developed, and understanding the unique features of these business forms and thinking about how to design a regulatory environment to facilitate these new ways of operating a business have become crucial tasks for all businesses, as well as policymakers.

One effect of the emergence and global dissemination of digital technologies, therefore, is a transformation in how businesses structure themselves. We should not think in terms of traditional corporate structures anymore. Company boundaries have become more open. Traditional corporate organizations with their fixed roles, static procedures, closed departments, and hierarchical relationships between different groups of stakeholders are all changing as companies adapt to a new operating environment.

To make sense of this change in how firms organize themselves in a digital age, we have proposed the concept of the business 'ecosystem' as a description of this nascent organizational form.[19] In brief, such ecosystems combine the following features:

- Leveraging the unique characteristics of software technologies (e.g., low marginal costs) to deliver a powerful, frictionless experience to end-users.
- Adopting a flatter, fluid, and more inclusive style of organization built around networks of unbundled, high-performance, creative teams in which job roles and functions are evolving dynamically in response to the evolving business needs of the firm.
- Embracing a more open, transparent approach to communication and information management that relies on new computer-mediated communications, such as social media.
- Implementing a new style of digital leadership that focuses on creating an environment that facilitates creativity rather than an exclusive focus on supervising compliance or managing legal risk.
- Utilizing open collaboration with multiple external partners to feed the requirement of continually innovating—what we term partnering-for-innovation.

[18] Fenwick and Vermeulen (2015), Fenwick and Vermeulen (2019); Fenwick et al. (2019).

[19] The concept of an 'ecosystem' described here is based on the empirical study of the most successful technology firms today. As such, it represents an 'ideal type' or composite of how a business needs to organize its operations and governance in a digital age. References to specific companies in the following are not meant as blanket endorsements of those companies, but an acknowledgment that on the specific point cited that company has identified an interesting approach. In this respect, we hope to move beyond the 'all or nothing' attitude that currently characterizes discussion of the most successful tech-firms.

Together, these features distinguish an ecosystem from business organizations in a pre-digital world. In an age of hyper-competitive technology-driven markets, every company needs to consider reinventing itself as an ecosystem. The argument is that such ecosystems are better placed to design and deliver that kind of consumer experience necessary to succeed in a technology-driven economy. And, if a business does not reorganize itself in this way, younger and more agile competitors better attuned to the realities of the digital world will replace it.

The environmental pressures facing incumbent companies and financial institutions are similar, and solutions are connected to digital technologies, at least in some way. How, then, should financial service providers respond to the above-discussed challenges and utilize fintech to solve the legacy issues inherent to their history, size, and complexity? How might financial service incumbents transform into innovation ecosystems capable of flourishing in today's new economic and social environment?

This points to the second strategy available to incumbent financial service providers. In practice, the most comfortable option for incumbents—particularly for more conservative incumbents—may be the last one, i.e., open collaboration with external partners (i.e., start-ups) to develop and reinvigorate the capacity for innovation.

Of importance in this context, is what we would characterize as a new style of corporate venturing that has emerged over the last decade. Traditionally, the focus of corporate venturing was on corporate venture capital, i.e., incumbent investments in start-ups made by corporates to acquire a minority equity stake that would result in a financial benefit to the corporate buyer.

If we look at the most innovative companies in the world today, however, we can see that this strategy alone is not the only way of utilizing investments for large corporations looking to survive in a new operating environment where the pace of innovation is continuously accelerating and the demand for innovation has become incessant. Instead, the world's most innovative *companies* go beyond this traditional type of corporate venturing model. They realize that their future will be determined by developments in technology and that learning from the most innovative start-ups has become absolutely vital.

The crucial point here is that an incumbent corporation is open to the possibility of learning *from* an acquired start-up. The aim of a corporate venturing purchase is not 'assimilation' in the sense that a start-up is expected to lose its identity and be passively assimilated into a more substantial, fixed corporate identity. Rather, the aim of this more open style of partnering is a more fluid and dynamic relationship in which opportunities for mutual learning are emphasized. It is in this sense that we can talk (as was done in the Financial Times) of a large corporation borrowing the 'Start-up Genie's Magic.'[20] This contrasts with an earlier style of corporate venturing in which distance and assimilation were emphasized, or learning was conceptualized as primarily one-way (i.e., *from* corporate *to* start-up). In this way, we can see how corporate venturing—i.e., putting in place operational principles and practices that aim at creating an open, inclusive and fluid ecosystem—can help larger, established

[20] Newton (2015).

firms in meeting the complex (and unprecedented) business challenges of delivering the kind of new customer experience described above

These strategies can be beneficial in the case of financial institutions as they look to respond to the disruptive challenge of fintech. Banks, for instance, already seem to be engaged in some of the above strategies, and examples can be found everywhere.[21] For example, many banks have already established partnerships with fintech companies, such as J. P. Morgan Chase, partnering with OnDeck to offer fast approval and funding of small business loans. Another fintech company, Prime Revenue, provides supply chain finance through a cloud-enabled platform to banks, including Barclays. Finally, Spain's second-largest bank BVAA has actively engaged in fintech acquisition. They are a major shareholder in British start-up Atom Bank and have also acquired Holbi, a Finnish based fintech innovator, specializing in small business payments. Their strategy has been to open up their data to approved developer-partners.

Perhaps, as importantly, incumbent banks are increasingly investing in fintech start-ups, and many banks see fintech partnering as a crucial competency that they need to develop.[22] Other examples would include banks relying on external vendors for core banking and product systems, such as business process outsourcing or data analytics. Finally, a shift to more open IT models means they no longer have complete end-to-end control of data. In an Asian context, there are multiple examples of large financial institutions making similar acquisitions in the expectation of learning from and developing them.[23]

This trend has led some commentators to speak of a 'great new era of fintech partnerships' between incumbents and start-ups.[24] According to this line of thinking, banks need to become consumers of fintech because they do have the capacities to focus on delivering a new style of consumer experience by themselves. On the other hand, fintech start-ups are often focusing on an issue and solution. This creates a potential win-win in which larger banks benefit from the specific new product or service developed by a start-up.

Nevertheless, for such partnering-for-innovation to work effectively, incumbent banks need to re-evaluate existing practices. For instance, they need to strengthen their mechanisms for assessing their current internal capabilities, develop robust systems for evaluating potential partners, devise mutually acceptable financial arrangements, and ensure adequate testing capabilities for deploying new technologies (both, initially, on a small, experimental scale and later, when full-scaled implementation is planned, on a larger scale).

[21] For example, they seem to understand intuitively the power of co-working spaces; many smaller banks, for instance, have already turned their branches into co-working spaces in this way. See Macheel (2019).

[22] CBInsights (2018).

[23] Available at: https://www.techinasia.com/category/fintech. Accessed 31 March 2020.

[24] Tweddle (2018).

This is not always easy for incumbents, and there are many skeptical voices about the feasibility of such an approach.[25] The enormous cultural differences between incumbents and start-ups lead some to conclude that, as things stand, it is difficult for incumbent banks to follow the corporate venturing strategies outlined above. Banks are not ready to evolve into the kind of open ecosystems that characterize the world's most innovative companies. As Louise Beaumont put it:

Retaining relevance to increasingly savvy consumers whose attitudes and expectations have been shaped by the world's biggest tech brands is a huge undertaking for banks. Under GAFA's (Google, Apple, Facebook, Amazon) influence, people have come to expect services that function perfectly, are available on-demand, and are increasingly personalized. Banks can't simply 'fintech' their way out of the seismic shifts the industry is now feeling.[26]

Stated bluntly, the challenges of the external environment are too significant, the expectations of consumers are too high, and the banks do not—as things stand—have the internal capacities or resources to implement this new partnering-for-innovation and ecosystem style organization.

However, such skepticism seems to push against the tide of history. More partnering, rather than less, would seem to be inevitable, given the trend towards the 'unbundling' of banking. Of course, this raises challenges for incumbent banks that have become accustomed to working within their internal departments and settled procedures. Such partnering in an open ecosystem means giving up some control, but the benefits in terms of co-creation seem to justify this trade-off. Moreover, it is hard to see a better alternative, and preserving the status quo would appear to be in no one's interests.

4 Implications for Regulators and Financial Regulation

Traditional accounts of the role of, and justification for, regulation in financial services have focused on risk management. A crucial difference between financial service providers and other businesses is the regulatory environment in which they now operate. The goal of fintech, as described above, is to deliver a better consumer experience, while ensuring that the consumer is adequately protected. As such, it helps to begin with a clear distinction between the character of risk involved in a financial services context compared with other consumer situations. If I have a negative experience in the setting of online shopping, late delivery, for example, the consequences may be inconvenient to me. Still, they are not—in most cases and–serious. However, in the context of banking or other financial services, the risks are usually and potentially much more severe. The demand outlined above is for a better consumer experience but also a safe consumer experience. And, it is in the context

[25] See Beaumont (2018); Shevlin (2019).

[26] Beaumont (2018), Shevlin (2019).

of this risk profile, that regulation matters and that any discussion of improving the consumer experience needs to place regulation front and center.

Moreover, the level of regulation is much higher for banks, particularly post-2008. This difference complicates efforts to borrow some of the fintech 'genie's magic,' and a shift in approach by regulators may also be required, mainly if the goal is delivering the kind of consumer experience described in Sect. 2.

Two considerations have dominated post-2008, the regulatory environment for financial service providers. First, ensuring a higher degree of consumer protection, particularly for retail clients, investors, and depositors (i.e., the micro-prudential aspect of regulation) and second, ensuring financial stability by minimizing systemic risk (the macro-prudential aspect of regulation). The 2008 financial crisis exposed shortcomings across both dimensions, and these failures triggered a significant process of regulatory reform and the imposition of stricter regulatory requirements.

Moreover, a legacy of the 2008 crisis has been a shift in perceptions of innovation, at least on the side of regulators. Before 2008, innovations in financial products or services were generally perceived in somewhat positive terms, and this resulted in a 'light-touch' approach to the regulation of innovations in financial services. However, since the crisis came to be blamed, in large part, on such innovation (so-called 'financial weapons of mass destruction'), the regulatory trend shifted in the opposite direction. Innovation came to be seen in more negative terms by policymakers (not to mention the public), who were keen to avoid any repetition of the disruption and chaos of 2008-10.

The timing of the emergence of fintech has, therefore, proven enormously challenging for regulators.[27] Regulators have therefore been placed in the awkward position of having to balance the post-2008 regulatory objectives of consumer protection and managing systemic risk with the promotion of innovation. From the perspective of regulators, it is easy to conclude that fintech creates both micro- and macro-prudential risks or, at least, uncertainties.

However, as memories of the financial crisis fade, the relationship between banks and regulators has shifted to a new stage. As discussed above, most financial institutions already engage in the proactive management of regulatory risk through expanded compliance departments. Banks have better integrated the two post-crisis objectives of regulation into their daily operations, and, in consequence, the regulatory agenda has shifted. New regulatory approaches are now possible.

One evident and influential example of this shift is the post-2016 UK experience. Traditionally, five big banks—Barclays, HSBC, Lloyds, Santander and Royal Bank of Scotland—controlled over 80% of the retail current account market, offering near-identical products that remained mostly unchanged from thirty years ago. People would pick a bank and—barring some misfortune—stick with it for life. However, in August 2016, the UK Competition and Markets Authority issued a ruling ordering the nine biggest UK banks to allow licensed start-ups direct access to their data.[28] Account-holders need to consent, but if they do, then all data in current bank

[27] Zetzsche (2017).

[28] Available at: https://www.openbanking.org.uk/. Accessed 31 March 2020.

accounts—for example, utility bills, mortgage payments, etc.—is made available to fintech start-ups to deliver innovative new products and services.

To do this, Open Banking Limited, a non-profit set up to deliver 'Open Banking,' now builds APIs or Application Program Interfaces. These protocols can transfer data automatically from one piece of software to another.[29] What makes such APIs, so potentially game-changing is their open-ended character. They open-up something useful, in this case, current account data, and let the developers create new products that use that data in new ways. Examples of such an approach, in other contexts, include Uber or AirBnB. When you see your Uber moving around the nearby streets on your smartphone, you're seeing the Google Maps API. AirBnb, deploys the same API, just in a different context. A simple example, in a financial services context, would be an app that collected an individual's financial information together from several sources—several different bank accounts, for instance—and allowed that individual to manage their financial affairs from that single app. The ability to access data on multiple bank accounts might not seem immediately important. However, the thought behind Open Banking is to let transaction data out into the open in the expectation that start-ups will transform such date into innovative new products that disrupt incumbents, in ways that no one has yet thought of. Uber or AirBnB might seem obvious ideas now after the event, but the hope of the Open Banking movement is that innovative entrepreneur-founders will come up with similarly disruptive ideas in a financial services context.

After active lobbying by the UK, the European Union passed a set of financial services reforms in the Payment Services Directive (PSD2).[30] The aim was to develop the European single market in banking, by forcing banks to present their data in the form of APIs. Some EU directives give member states some flexibility in implementation, but the PSD2 does not. It adds new types of payment services and a greater opportunity for innovative online and mobile payments by creating new third-party access rules enabling non-bank organizations to provide payment initiation and account information services (known as XS2A or Access to Accounts).

Security is ensured under PSD2 by the introduction of Strong Customer Authentication (SCA), which requires that when customers access their payment accounts online, two of three mandatory authentication measures must be used, so-called two-factor authentication (or 2FA). These SCA measures are: Knowledge, something only the user knows (e.g., a password or a PIN); Possession, something only the user possesses (e.g., a token, code, or key); Inherence, something the user 'is' (e.g., a fingerprint, biometric, or voice.)

Asian countries have been monitoring this trend to open banking and the PSD2 closely. Japan's Banking Act, for example, was amended in June 2018 with the aim of promoting open banking. However, the consensus is that the new regulations are not clear on data portability, and implementation of open banking among Japanese

---

[29] See Camerinelli (2017).

[30] See generally Price Waterhouse Cooper (2016). For an account of the potential new risks, see Hacquedord et al. (2019).

companies remains voluntary. Nevertheless, around 130 chartered banks in Japan have plans to open-up APIs by mid-2020.[31]

For incumbent banks, such regulatory initiatives are often regarded with skepticism, if not fear. For example, it was reported that 41% of the Europeans banks failed to meet the PSD2 deadline in March 2019—the banks were supposed to provide a testing environment to the third-party providers but did not do so. The smarter banks have recognized the value of partnering with fintech firms in the way described in the previous section in order to minimize the business and regulatory risk of the new world of Open Banking.[32]

Another option—preferred by the fintech companies themselves—is for the government to give much higher weight to those actors that are driving technological innovation and its dissemination, namely the technology companies, in designing the regulatory framework. Stated slightly differently, the technology companies believe that to make the venturing strategy work, regulators need to become critical players in the open ecosystems described above. However, is this a sensible strategy? Or is it a case of putting the animals in charge of the zoo?

There is something to the idea that governments should outsource to companies the task of designing regulatory policies suitable for a digital age.[33] Disruption has become one of the main issues for any business. Markets are changing fast. New competitors enter the stage all the time. Business models must continuously evolve. As a result, companies take emerging technology very seriously to remain relevant. The effect of such pressures is that technology companies have greater access to information about the impact of technology. Companies are better equipped than states to take a leading role.

Moreover, new digital technologies empower the customers and employees of such companies in new ways. The voice of these stakeholders must be considered for such companies to survive. For instance, in many cases, employees no longer see themselves as cogs in a corporate machine, but as active stakeholders. In the context of the Gig Economy, for instance, such employees have become entrepreneurs themselves and will speak up or 'exit' when they do not support a company's policies or actions.[34] Advocates of this type of outsourcing see such stakeholders as an essential check on how technology companies behave and how they would approach the issue of designing a regulatory framework.

However, what is perhaps even more important is that the consumers of tech products and services have become much more critical, at least compared to an earlier industrial phase of capitalism. In technology-driven markets, consumers are not just consumers anymore. They have become an essential stakeholder in the ecosystem of the firm and its governance. This functions as a constraint on the behavior of larger firms. It is becoming more dangerous for them to abuse their market power, as such abuse will risk user migration to rivals and, in the medium-long term, damage to the

[31]Creehan and Tierno (2019).

[32]See Gupta (2019).

[33]Kaal and Vermeulen (2017); Malan (2018).

[34]See Kessler (2018).

brand and a decline in a firm's fortunes.[35] Such risks are particularly acute for firms that operate a platform as a crucial part of its business model (think Amazon, Airbnb, Facebook, or Uber) because platforms are dependent on the network effects created by having as many users as possible.[36]

Of course, there are risks. Even if technology companies have good intentions, they may have difficulties proposing effective regulatory schemes because their interests are not well-aligned inside the company. A recent example is Google's failed attempt to set up an ethics council to examine developments in artificial intelligence.[37]

So, what is the role of government in a digital age? If the entire delegation of policymaking and regulation to private companies would lead to the 'capturing' of policies and rules by established tech companies, what would be a better alternative? The government still has an essential role to play. However, a bureaucrat-led approach to policymaking has had its time. A new, more dynamic, and responsive approach must be implemented.

We would argue that one of the key elements in meeting this challenge is the co-creation and co-production of regulatory schemes. Here we do not refer to (rather traditional) consultation models in which the market is invited to respond to and provide input to policy and regulatory proposals. Regulatory sandboxes, if implemented in a bold and open way, in which a small number of actors are given permission test innovation in a tightly controlled environment, provide an obvious example of such an approach.[38]

As such, we must introduce ecosystem thinking into regulation, and companies, banks, start-ups, and governments must *all* work in partnership with the various stakeholders to ensure that vital interests are protected while facilitating innovation. There is already some evidence of such a shift. Regulators acknowledge their informational disadvantages and are participating in more events—training courses or hackathons. Moreover, regulators are building new collaborative relationships with actors in the private sector to understand and develop technologies. There is greater outsourcing of legal work and cooperation with public-private partnering to create new technologies, such as blockchain. Finally, the introduction of sandboxes and recognition of the importance of innovation suggests a growing awareness of the need for a different kind of approach.

Of course, national governments and other regulators must set 'smart' boundaries for the risk they are willing to take that are agreed with regulated entities. However, within these boundaries, they must allow and encourage freedom and innovation. This does not mean that within these boundaries, a 'Wild West' should be allowed. Instead, within carefully negotiated limits, it is all about building and maintaining trust amongst all participants via constant dialogue and openness. In this respect, trust must be earned from all the stakeholders that are involved and affected by new technology.

---

[35] Fenwick and Vermeulen (2019).

[36] Reddy (2018).

[37] Levin (2019).

[38] Fenwick et al. (2017).

As such, community-driven regulatory design is a version of policy experimentation. The crucial factor here is the changing context. In the context of the digital revolution and the new pressures it has created, there is a unique degree of openness and visibility both within society in general and within the emerging ecosystems. The check on regulatory capture is the new visibility that digital technologies have created and the dependency that open ecosystems have on remaining committed to the values of a free, open digital culture. If the check on power is visibility, transparency, and the demand for authenticity, then the key to ensuring these values are maintained are those infrastructures that facilitate speech, for example, social media. When any large institution exercises power, its actions expose the values of the powerful. The effect of the digital revolution is to create new visibility and check on such actions. This might seem a naïve view given the difficulties associated with social media; nevertheless, the possibilities of a more open digital culture should not be abandoned just yet.

The government is a crucial stakeholder and can establish the rules of the 'trust game,' and regulations that relate to transparency, disclosure, and open dialogue with the market. However, this means that everyone in the government needs to embrace 'going digital.' Regulators need to think more about the meaning of technologies, what they can do for us, and how they can help us to build a better future. Doing nothing or restricting innovation are worse options. This often means rejecting and replacing old, formalized ways of doing things, such as hierarchies, legacy processes, and settled procedures. Instead, 'going digital' will lead to looser connections and relationships, and more flexible forms of operation. As such, regulators must relearn what it means to interact, transact, and become visible in a digital environment. They must build their brand, and government officials must learn how to think more like entrepreneurs. Being creative and innovative in this way will ensure that 'going digital' creates more opportunities than it eliminates for everyone. And this includes incumbent financial institutions and the new fintech firms that are innovating in the sector.

References

Batiz-Lazo B (2015) A brief history of the ATM. https://www.theatlantic.com/technology/archive/2015/03/a-brief-history-of-the-atm/388547/. Accessed 31 March 2020

Beaumont L (2018) Banks can't partner themselves into digital relevancy. American Banker (26 June). https://www.americanbanker.com/opinion/banks-cant-partner-themselves-into-digital-relevancy. Accessed 31 March 2020

Bloomberg Professional Services (2019) Why Asia is leading the fintech revolution. Bloomberg News (27 January 2019). https://www.bloomberg.com/professional/blog/asia-leading-fintech-revolution/. Accessed 31 March 2020

Camerinelli E (2017) Open bank, APIs, and financial services ecosystems: The future of banking. https://www.softwareag.com/corporate/images/Aite_Group_Open_bank_api_and_financial_services_Research_Jul17_tcm389-167453.pdf. Accessed 31 March 2020

Campbell D, Meyer M, Xin Li S, Stack K (2015) Haier: zero distance to the customer (Harvard Business School Case Study 115-006). https://www.hbs.edu/faculty/Pages/item.aspx?num=49076. Accessed 31 March 2020

CBInsights (2019) Where top US banks are betting on fintech. CBInsights https://www.cbinsights.com/research/fintech-investments-top-us-banks/. Accessed 31 March 2020

Chishti S, Barberis J (2016) The fintech book: The financial technology handbook for investors, entrepreneurs and visionaries. Wiley, Chichester

Creehan S, Tierno P (2019) The slow introduction of open banking and APIs in Japan. https://www.frbsf.org/banking/asia-program/pacific-exchanges-podcast/open-banking-apis-japan/. Accessed 31 March 2020

Eroll D, Eroll J (2005) American genius: nineteenth century banks locks and time. Quantuck Lane Press, New York

Evans B (2018) The end of the beginning. https://www.ben-evans.com/benedictevans/2018/11/16/the-end-of-the-beginning. Accessed 31 March 2020

Fenwick M, Kaal WA, Vermeulen EPM (2017) Regulation tomorrow: what happens when technology is faster than the law. American University Business Law Review 6:561–594

Fenwick M, McCahery JA, Vermeulen EPM (2019) The end of 'corporate' governance: Hello 'platform' governance. European Business Organization Law Review 20:171–199

Fenwick M, Vermeulen, EPM (2019) A sustainable platform economy & the future of corporate governance (European Corporate Governance Institute—Law Working Paper 441). https://ssrn.com/abstract=3331508. Accessed 31 March 2020

Fenwick M, Vermeulen EPM (2019) The end of the corporation. 482 European Corporate Governance Institute—Law Working Paper. https://ssrn.com/abstract=3472601. Accessed 31 March 2020

Gupta N (2019) The PSD2 deadlines: Are the banks ready? https://medium.com/akeo-tech/the-September-14th-psd2-deadline-are-the-banks-ready-5c4c57e39ec5. Accessed 31 March 2020

Hacquedord F, McArdle R, Merces F, Sancho D (2019) Ready or not for PSD2: the risks of open banking. Trend Micro Research, London

Kaal WA, Vermeulen EPM (2017) How to regulate disruptive innovation: from facts to data. Jurimetrics J Law Sci Technol 57:169–209

Kessler K (2018) Gigged: the end of the job and the future of work. St. Martin's Press, New York

King B (2018) Bank 4.0: Banking everywhere, never at a bank. Wiley, Chichester

Levin S (2019) Google scraps AI ethics council after backlash: Back to the drawing board. The Guardian (5 April). https://www.theguardian.com/technology/2019/apr/04/google-ai-ethics-council-backlash. Accessed 31 March 2020

Macheel T (2019) Banks are turning branches into coworking spaces. Tearsheet https://tearsheet.co/modern-banking-experience/banks-are-turning-branches-into-coworking-spaces/. Accessed 31 March 2020

Malan D (2018) The law can't keep up with new tech. Here's how to close the gap. World Economic Forum. https://www.weforum.org/agenda/2018/06/law-too-slow-for-new-tech-how-keep-up/. Accessed 31 March 2020

Manning RD (2000) Credit card nation. Basic, New York

McMillan J (2014) The end of banking: Money, credit, and the digital revolution. Zero/One Economics, Zurich

Moazed A, Johnson NL (2016) Modern monopolies: What it takes to dominate the 21st century economy. St. Martin's Press, New York

Newton R (2015) How to borrow some of the start-up genie's magic. Financial Times (28 July). https://www.ft.com/content/6b5e4ba6-ffcc-11e4-bc30-00144feabdc0. Accessed 31 March 2020

Parker GH, Van Alstyne MW, Choudary SP (2016) Platform revolution: How networked markets are transforming the economy and how to make them work for you. Norton, New York

Pratskevich A (2019) Financial apps report. Liftoff. https://liftoff.io/blog/finance-apps-2019/. Accessed 31 March 2020

Price Waterhouse Coopers (2014) Retail banking 2020: Evolution or revolution. https://www.pwc.com/gx/en/banking-capital-markets/banking-2020/assets/pwc-retail-banking-2020-evolution-or-revolution.pdf. Accessed 31 March 2020

Price Waterhouse Cooper (2016) PSD2 in a nutshell. https://www.pwc.com/cz/en/bankovnictvi/assets/psd2-nutshell-n01-en.pdf. Accessed 31 March 2020

Reddy N (2018) How to harness the power of network effects. 2 January, Forbes. https://www.forbes.com/sites/forbescoachescouncil/2018/01/02/how-to-harness-the-power-of-network-effects/#2b41823462e8. Accessed 31 March 2020

Shevlin R (2019) Bank/Fintech partnerships will be a huge disappointment in 2019. Forbes (7 January). https://www.forbes.com/sites/ronshevlin/2019/01/07/ bankfintech-partnerships-will-be-a-huge-disappointment-in-2019/#3dc33dc837ba. Accessed 31 March 2020

Sironi A (2016) Fintech innovation: From robo-advisors to goal-based investing and gamification. Wiley, Chichester

Tweddle K (2018) Doomed? Fintech partnerships are vital. American Banker (10 July 2018). https://www.americanbanker.com/opinion/doomed-fintech-partnerships-are-vital. Accessed 31 March 2020

Wu T (2016) The attention merchants: The epic scramble to get inside our heads. Vintage, New York

Zetzsche DA (2017) Regulating a revolution: From regulatory sandboxes to smart regulation. Fordham Journal of Corporate and Financial Law 23:31–103

Zhou W, Arner DW, Buckley R (2015) Regulation of digital financial services in China: Last mover advantage? Tsinghua China Law Review 8:25–62

Index

M. Fenwick et al. (eds.), *Regulating FinTech in Asia*, Perspectives in Law, Business and Innovation, https://doi.org/10.1007/978-981-15-5819-1

The manufacturer's authorised representative in the EU is Springer
Nature Customer Service Centre GmbH, Europaplatz 3, 69115 Heidelberg,
Germany. If you have any concerns regarding our products, please
contact ProductSafety@springernature.com

Printed and bound by CPI Group (UK) Ltd, Croydon, CR0 4YY
30/09/2026
02225333-0006